Stratification and Inequality Series
The Center for the Study of Social Stratification and Inequality,
Tohoku University, Japan
Volume 8

Globalization, Minorities and Civil Society

Stratification and Inequality Series
The Center for the Study of Social Stratification and Inequality,
Tohoku University, Japan

Inequality amid Affluence: Social Stratification in Japan
Junsuke Hara and Kazuo Seiyama

Intentional Social Change: A Rational Choice Theory
Yoshimichi Sato

Constructing Civil Society in Japan: Voices of Environmental Movements
Koichi Hasegawa

Deciphering Stratification and Inequality: Japan and beyond
Yoshimichi Sato

Social Justice in Japan: Concepts, Theories and Paradigms
Ken-ichi Ohbuchi

Gender and Career in Japan
Atsuko Suzuki

Status and Stratification:
Cultural Forms in East and Southeast Asia
Mitsuhiko Shima

Globalization, Minorities and Civil Society: Perspectives from
Asian and Western Cities
Koichi Hasegawa and Naoki Yoshihara

Stratification and Inequality Series
The Center for the Study of Social Stratification and Inequality,
Tohoku University, Japan
Volume 8

Globalization, Minorities and Civil Society

Perspectives from Asian and Western Cities

Edited by
Koichi Hasegawa
and
Naoki Yoshihara

This English edition first published in 2008 by
Trans Pacific Press, PO Box 164, Balwyn North, Melbourne, Victoria 3104, Australia
Telephone: +61-3-9859-1112 Fax: +61-3-9859-4110
Email: tpp.mail@gmail.com
Web: http://www.transpacificpress.com

Copyright © Trans Pacific Press 2008

Designed and set by digital environs, Melbourne. http://www.digitalenvirons.com

Printed by BPA Print Group, Burwood, Victoria, Australia

Distributors

Australia and New Zealand
UNIREPS
University of New South Wales
Sydney, NSW 2052
Australia
Telephone: +61-2-9664-0999
Fax: +61-2-9664-5420
Email: info.press@unsw.edu.au
Web: http://www.unireps.com.au

USA and Canada
International Specialized Book Services (ISBS)
920 NE 58th Avenue, Suite 300
Portland, Oregon 97213-3786
USA
Telephone: (800) 944-6190
Fax: (503) 280-8832
Email: orders@isbs.com
Web: http://www.isbs.com

Asia and the Pacific
Kinokuniya Company Ltd.

Head office:
Shin-Mizonokuchi Bldg. 2F
5-7 Hisamoto 3-chome
Takatsu-ku, Kawasaki 213-8506
Japan
Telephone: +81-44-874-9642
Fax: +81-44-829-1025
Email: bkimp@kinokuniya.co.jp
Web: www.kinokuniya.co.jp

Asia-Pacific office:
Kinokuniya Book Stores of Singapore Pte., Ltd.
391B Orchard Road #13-06/07/08
Ngee Ann City Tower B
Singapore 238874
Telephone: +65-6276-5558
Fax: +65-6276-5570
Email: SSO@kinokuniya.co.jp

All rights reserved. No production of any part of this book may take place without the written permission of Trans Pacific Press.

ISBN 978-1-876843-79-3 (Hardback)
ISBN 978-1-876843-85-4 (Paperback)

Contents

Figures — vi
Maps — vi
Photos — vi
Tables — vii
Preface *Koichi Hasegawa and Naoki Yoshihara* — ix
List of Contributors — xv

Part I: Minorities and Social Change in Civil Society

1. Globalization, Minorities and Civil Society *Koichi Hasegawa* — 3
2. Citizenship Models in the Age of International Migration *Hideki Tarumoto* — 21
3. New Racism and 'Community Cohesion' in Britain *Satoshi Adachi* — 41
4. Ethnic Identities and Sharing of the Internment Memories in the Japanese American Redress Movement *Kumiko Tsuchida* — 58
5. Global Civil Society and Local Protest: Is an Alternative to 'Alter-globalization' Possible? *Nanako Inaba and Naoto Higuchi* — 76

Part II: Minorities in Asian Cities

6. Islam in Bali *Naoki Yoshihara* — 97
7. Unchanging Fortunes of Jakarta Informal Sector Workers *Raphaella Dewantari Dwianto* — 115
8. Street Homeless as an Urban Minority: A Case of Metro Manila *Hideo Aoki* — 154
9. The Reorganization of Ethnic Chinese Groups in Thailand, and the Background to this Reorganization *Kazuo Yoshihara* — 173
10. The Bangladeshi Community in London: Social Enterprises and the Transnational Development of Community Empowerment *Yaeko Nishiyama and Shiho Nishiyama* — 191

Notes — 212
References — 227
Index — 241

Figures

3.1	Modified version of Gaertner and Dovidio's model (2000: 75, Figure 5.1)	50
3.2	Modified version of Gaertner and Dovidio's model (2000: 85, Figure 5.2b)	51
10.1	Comparison of unemployment rate by ethnic group	195
10.2	Comparison of qualification by ethnic group	196
8.1	A typology of the new homeless in the world	221
8.2	Processes by which globalization forms the new homeless in Japan and the Philippines	225

Maps

6.1	Location of batik factories	103
7.1	Jakarta with Menteng Atas and Depok	133
10.1	Location of Spitalfields/Banglatown	194
10.2	Location of the city of Sylhet	201

Photos

6.1	Tents inhabited by KIPEM	104
6.2	Batik factory worksite	105
6.3	Shack-like housing inhabited by batik factory workers	106
7.1	Agus the apprentice	118
7.2	Parti the super-mom	119
7.3	Lestari the sales lady	120
7.4	Ketoprak hawker in Menteng Atas	133
7.5	Kerosene man in Menteng Atas	134
7.6	Hawkers in Depok elite residential area	142

Tables

2.1	Foreign or immigrant population in selected OECD countries	28
5.1	Castells's subject and identity types	86
6.1	Shifts in overseas tourist numbers (2001–05)	101
6.2	Changes in Bali's workforce by industry (1970–2004)	102
6.3	Population shift by religion (1996–2006)	107
7.1	The characteristics of the informal sector as represented in current literature	125
7.2	Percentage of revenue from informal sector in Asian countries	126
7.3	Percentage of workers in informal sector in Indonesia	126
7.4	People of productive age in informal and formal sector in Indonesia	127
7.5	Workers by employment type in Indonesia	128
7.6	Workers in informal sector by employment status	129
7.7	Formal and informal workers by educational attainment in 1998 and 2002	130
7.8	Labour market structure in Indonesia by urban/rural area and by sex in 2002	131
7.9	Menteng Atas *pedagang keliling* based on type of merchandise	134
7.10	Menteng Atas demographic features (a)	136
7.11	Menteng Atas demographic features (b)	138
7.12	Menteng Atas situation of *pedagang keliling*	140
7.13	Depok *pedagang keliling* based on type of merchandise	143
7.14	Depok demographic features (a)	144
7.15	Depok demographic features (b)	146
7.16	Depok situation of *pedagang keliling*	148
8.1	Families that were relocated and are planned to be relocated	165
8.2	Differences of squatter inhabitants and homeless people	167
10.1	Comparison of weekly wages of full-time workers	193
10.2	Development of the Forum's activities	204

Preface
Koichi Hasegawa and Naoki Yoshihara

There are so many books in bookstores carrying 'globalization' in their titles that it is not an exaggeration to say that there is a globalization boom. However, the number of books about globalization written from Asian perspectives is surprisingly small. Those written in English reveal European or United States perspectives, while those in Japanese reveal Japanese perspectives; we are afraid that each presents a rather one-sided view of globalization. The first feature of this book is that it discusses various impacts of globalization on minorities from several different sociological angles. The second feature is that it puts Asian perspectives at the forefront. Publishing the works of Japanese authors and one contributor from Indonesia in English is important in this regard.

Asian perspectives are presented throughout the book in the form of an emphasis on specific issues: first, Asian cities as fields, particularly in Part II; second, the issue of Islam and Islamization, particularly as discussed in Chapter 6; and third, the issue of Asian immigrants in European/United States societies, such as in the Japanese American redress movement discussed in Chapter 4 and the study of Bangladeshis in London, which is discussed in Chapter 10.

The advancement of globalization has given rise to the increase of Asian immigrants in European and United States cities and to the issue of citizenship, as well as globalization, of Asian cities accompanying urban restructuring. The multidimensional divide and issues configuration of ethnic minorities is becoming multifaceted, with a more layered and segmented structure in both Asian and European/United States cities. At the same time, it is becoming increasingly more difficult to hold to the conventional dichotomous perspective that tries to understand a minority in a contrastive relationship with a majority. Needless to say, these are the profound influences of post-colonial conditions.

In addition to the sociological examination of morphology/configuration of minority group issues based on field surveys of ethnic communities in Asian and European/United States cities, this volume also looks at anti-globalization movements and protests by locally based minority groups and presents a multifaceted view of social movements and social changes, including the transformation of civil society. We hope that this will give new impetus not only to the study of minorities but also to diverging globalization studies and civil society theories.

This book is the fruit of research efforts by the Division of Minorities and the Division of East Asia at the Center for the Study of Social Stratification and Inequality, Graduate School of Arts and Letters, Tohoku University. In the existing study of social stratification and inequality, their relationship with globalization and the positioning of ethnic minorities have been two relatively weak areas. The editors are quietly confident that this book may be able to play a breakthrough role in the study of social stratification and inequality by focusing on globalization and ethnic minorities in the Asian context.

Composition of this book

This book consists of Part I, *Minorities and Social Change in Civil Society*, and Part II, *Minorities in Asian Cities*. The five chapters in Part I are very much theoretical in nature. Hasegawa's discussion in Chapter 1 is intended to serve as an overview of globalization, minorities and civil society for the whole volume. Civil society acts as a useful mirror in identifying the properties of the Asian context. The issue of citizenship that ethnic minorities must face at the beginning of their new lives (Chapter 2), human rights redress for minorities and policy response (Chapters 3 and 4), and the achievements and possibilities of social movements (Chapters 4 and 5) are issues of extreme relevance to civil society.

The five chapters in Part II are empirical studies based on many years of fieldwork. Naoki Yoshihara's discussion in Chapter 6 and Dwianto's discussion in Chapter 7 are both about Indonesia. Aoki's discussion in Chapter 8 is a study in Manila, the Philippines, and Kazuo Yoshihara's discussion in Chapter 9 is a study in Thailand. Chapter 10 is a study of the Bangladeshis, not in an Asian city, but in London.

We outline the main points of each chapter below.

To serve as an overview of the whole volume, Chapter 1 organizes the implications of globalization into six categories and discusses both positive and negative impacts of globalization on the shift towards risk society, the formation of civil society and the minority issue. After identifying the fundamental difficulty of the minority issue represented by the Islamic 'head scarf' controversy in France and the risk of a growing gap between the periphery and the centre brought on by globalization, Hasegawa explains that what is needed for a breakthrough in the minority issue and the advancement of civil society is a governance-oriented consensus-building approach that emphasizes participation of multiple stakeholders at early stages and that opens dialogue among multiple stakeholders, including non-experts, to promote the taming of risks.

It has been assumed for a long time that citizenship is granted to members of the nation-state. This is the nation-state model of citizenship. With the rapid advancement of globalization, however, the issue of growing and diversifying international immigration, which erupted at the end of the twentieth century, has exposed the limits of the nation-state model of citizenship through various events. Is it possible to propose a new citizenship model to replace the nation-state? In Chapter 2 Tarumoto proposes, through the examination of specific incidents, a new citizenship model that recognizes the importance of 'residence' and avoids restrictions on freedom of the individual as much as possible, and discusses this issue as something that requires new publicness and new sociological imagination.

Tolerance towards ethnic minorities and recognition of their identities have been the keywords for Britain's ethnic minority policy and regarded as buffers against social tension for a long time. However, the policy of tolerance is facing serious challenges from a relentless increase in the black and minority ethnic population, and from a growing desire of second- and third-generation immigrants to participate in the mainstream society prompted by globalization during the 1990s. A succession of terrorist incidents by Islamic fundamentalist groups has also highlighted the issue of insecurity. Chapter 3 examines the nature of the philosophy of social solidarity that permits the politics of identity and insecurity, which is the focal point of today's minority issue in Britain.

The United States' policy of internment of Japanese Americans during the Second World War became an issue of civil rights violation for the victor country. The Japanese American redress movement was one of few social movements by people of Asian origin and a minority movement that was greatly influenced by the civil rights movement. This movement led to the passing of the *Civil Liberties Act of 1988* and an official apology, and US$20,000 compensation from the federal government to each person. The Japanese American redress movement consisted of three groups of people from different age groups and social strata, although they had a common, ultimate goal of achieving redress. Chapter 4 is a sociological analysis of the development process of the movement and these groups, focusing on their different *internment memories* (what it meant to them and how to carry on the memories, campaign strategies and basic principles).

Globalization has caused contemporary social movements to diverge in two directions: the emergence of transnational social movement organizations, which appear to embody the rise of global civil society, and the development of local movements that struggle with issues caused by globalization. Chapter 5 highlights the potential points of conflict between these two types of social movements, the difficulty inherent in 'globalization and social movements' as a research theme—the difficulty of pursuing solidarity amid a widening gap between global players and local resistance—and the difficulty of subject formation and identity building in anti-globalization movements against the background of a weakening civil society. Chapter 5 analyzes the arguments of the Touraine school, Castells and others.

The development of global tourism is prompting the rapid Islamization of Balinese society. Chapter 6 examines this trend at the local community level, focusing particularly on the state of the KIPEM—immigrant workers from Java. Bali's provincial government and local authorities have demonstrated their clear intention to control the influx of such workers. However, local communities have been acting discretely according to each community's interest, while totally agreeing with the measures taken by the provincial and local authorities. There has even been a move towards informal inclusion of the KIPEM. After the terrorist bombings on October 12, 2002, however, a movement—*ajeg Bali*—came to the fore and traditional locals blatantly insisted on the exclusion of the KIPEM. Muslims, who are a political, cultural and religious minority in Hindu Bali, are now in the midst of a chain reaction of inclusion and exclusion.

Chapter 7 first examines the definition of the minority group based on Schaefer's argument that a minority group is subordinate to a dominant group, has considerably less control and power over their own lives than members of the dominant group, and for whom opportunities for education, wealth, success and so on are disproportionately scarce. In view of this, people who are working in the informal sector of Jakarta are certainly a minority group. Jakarta city authorities have always regarded the people in the informal sector as the source of social problems and have tried to exclude them.

Chapter 7 focuses on the informal sector workers in these conditions and, in particular, street vendors. It sheds light on their daily survival strategies as it follows the cases of hawkers (street vendors) who are active in the *kampung* residential area and the elite residential area.

With the spreading of globalization, homeless people, who are distinct from squatters, have appeared on the streets of major cities, even in developing countries, since the 1990s (particularly the second half of the decade). The existence of homeless people, who belong to the lowest urban class, has not been established as a social problem and its true nature remains unclear. In view of this situation, Chapter 8 looks at the case of Manila to discuss problems relating to the definition of homeless, to examine the actual conditions of the homeless based on available information, to analyze the association between changes in the urban structure and the labour market that are caused by globalization, and to analyze the appearance of homeless people in terms of the factors that push or pull the poor to the street. This chapter constitutes a starting point for the study of homeless people in the cities of developing countries.

Chapter 9 centres on the process and the background of expanding networks of Thai Chinese between the 1960s and the 1980s. The Chaozhou dialect-speaking group was an overwhelming majority among the Thai Chinese during the period of rising nationalism in the era of Thailand's developmental dictatorship and economic growth. After the groups of same-Chinese surnames that originated from regions other than Chaozhou were established, as in the case of the Lin Clansmen General Association of Thailand, the Thai Chinese strengthened their influence over the national majority of Thailand. The Chaozhou majority group was successfully reorganized by less influential, or minority, groups of Chinese dialects through the ideology that people with the same Chinese surname should cooperate with each other since they share common ancestors.

The Bangladeshis, an ethnic minority group that lives in the poor neighbourhoods of London, are trying to solve their poverty issue by building a closer relationship between their home country and Britain. Chapter 10 focuses on the district of Sylhet in the state of Assam, where locals were employed in low-paid labour in tea plantations under the colonial policy of the British Empire and are still suffering from the after effects of this history. Sylhetis who relocated to East London in the suzerain state in order to escape poverty dealt with the poverty issue in their home country as they formed an ethnic community. The British government has been investing considerable resources in various attempts to resolve the problem of poverty in London's ethnic communities but has not found effective solutions. Rather, voluntary organizations such as development trusts have been achieving better outcomes by setting up projects to empower minority communities and individuals and commercializing such grassroots community revitalization projects. In other words, the Bangladeshis have found the key to a resolution of the minority issue through participation in projects by voluntary citizens' organizations. The achievements of these voluntary development trusts are showing signs of further development as partnership projects linking the transnational communities of London and Sylhet.

Acknowledgements

This is the eighth volume of the Center for the Study of Social Stratification and Inequality's series on Stratification and Inequality in Japan. Based at the Graduate School of Arts and Letters, Tohoku University, the Center for the Study of Social Stratification and Inequality (CSSI) runs a 21st Century Center of Excellence Program under the auspices of the Japanese Ministry of Education, Culture, Sports, Science, and Technology. We are very happy and honored to have a chance to publish this book through a CSSI grant. We gratefully acknowledge this financial support. We also would like to thank Airin Izumi and Hiroaki Ozaki for their excellent secretarial work at the CSSI. Three translators at Trans Pacific Press (TPP), Kikuko Onoda, Minako Sato and Danau Tanu worked extremely hard to provide lucid English texts under great time pressure, and TPP's two editors, Cathy Edmonds and Darrell Bennetts, polished the entire book to make it more systematic, more readable and clearer at different stages. The excellent production of this English edition is largely due to the care and encouragement of Professor Yoshio Sugimoto, School of Social Sciences, La Trobe University and Director of Trans Pacific Press. We thank him sincerely for his informed advice and patient support throughout the project.

Koichi Hasegawa and Naoki Yoshihara
December 2007

List of Contributors

Koichi Hasegawa
Professor, Department of Sociology, Graduate School of Arts and Letters, Tohoku University

Naoki Yoshihara
Professor, Department of Sociology, Graduate School of Arts and Letters, Tohoku University

Hideki Tarumoto
Associate Professor, Department of Sociology, Graduate School of Letters, Hokkaido University

Satoshi Adachi
Graduate Student, Department of Sociology, Graduate School of Arts and Letters, Tohoku University

Kumiko Tsuchida
Graduate Student, Department of Sociology, Graduate School of Arts and Letters, Tohoku University

Nanako Inaba
Associate Professor, Department of Humanities, Ibaraki University

Naoto Higuchi
Associate Professor, Department of Social Science, University of Tokushima

Raphaella D. Dwianto
Lecturer, Faculty of Business Administration, Atma Jaya Catholic University, Indonesia

Hideo Aoki
Director, Institute on Social Theory and Dynamics

Kazuo Yoshihara
Professor, Department of Asian Studies, Faculty of Letters, Keio University

Yaeko Nishiyama
Professor, College of Contemporary Society and Culture, Kinjo Gakuin University

Shiho Nishiyama
Associate Professor, Graduate School of Medicine and Engineering, Yamanashi University

Part I
Minorities and Social Change in Civil Society

1 Globalization, Minorities and Civil Society
Koichi Hasegawa

What is globalization?

Rapid globalization is drastically transforming both the status of minorities and the state of civil society. Of all the various effects of globalization, this volume focuses on its impact on minorities and civil society as the main theme. How will globalization affect issues concerning minorities? Will globalization intensify existing minority issues and make them increasingly complex? What kind of transformation will existing civil societies undergo under the pressures of globalization? Especially in the Asian context, will globalization accelerate the development of civil societies?

Globalization is the most significant trend in social change affecting the entire world since the 1980s. To begin with, then, what kind of social change does globalization represent?

Globalization carries various connotations. Let us sift through the common uses of 'globalization.'

First, it most obviously signifies an increase in economic activities across national borders. In particular, it refers to the increased movement of capital, information and labour. In short—economic globalization. Pioneering research on economic globalization is represented by Wallerstein's world system theory (Wallerstein 1983). According to Wallerstein, the scope of capitalistic economies has been expanding in stages since the sixteenth century. It can be said that economic globalization has today nearly reached its extreme limits.

Second, globalization more generally signifies an increase in various activities across national borders in the political, social and cultural realms, as well as increased interdependence, which goes hand in hand with it. The repercussions that accompany the movement of products, labour and information are not limited to the economic realm, but also carry political, social and cultural significance. In particular, as foreign cultures are introduced with the movement of labour and increased immigration, it generates problems caused by cultural friction. Examples include the treatment of civil rights, as detailed by Tarumoto in Chapter 2 and by Adachi in Chapter 3, and the French scarf ban issue, which is discussed later.

In 1957 the European Economic Community was launched after six countries (the Netherlands, Belgium, Luxembourg, West Germany, France and Italy) signed the Treaty of Rome. Following on from this, the European Union, consisting of twelve countries, was later established in 1993. This later expanded to include fifteen countries, and in 2004 it expanded to twenty-five countries, including former Eastern European countries such as Poland and the Czech Republic. At present, in 2007, there are twenty-seven member states. The European Union's expansion is a concrete illustration of how globalization crosses national borders. The number of immigrants increased since immigration policies became more accepting of immigrants after the Second World War. Not only that, the European Union, which allowed the open immigration of labour within its borders and is now referred to as the 'new immigration continent' (Thranhardt 1992), can perhaps be referred to as the 'labouratory' of globalization.

Third, globalization of the economic, political, social and cultural realm has, as it is often cited, been brought about by the increased compression in time and space through developments in the transportation network and the Internet. Today it is possible to communicate with someone on the other side of the planet in real time. The 'domino' collapse of the Soviet-style socialist regimes (from the late 1980s to the early 1990s) is proof that they were unable to weather the storm of globalization.

Fourth, globalization challenges the validity of existing concepts in which the nation-state is perceived as a whole society that is complete relative to other societies, and it signifies the increasing importance of perceiving the entire globe as one world or a whole society. A sense of 'Spaceship Earth,' which we first grasped when man landed on the moon in 1969, turned from being an abstract idea into reality for ordinary citizens. In China the word 'globalization' is expressed as 'quan qiu hua,' using three characters, which means 'shifting to the whole globe.' The connotation of the word has been cleverly expressed visually using ideographic Chinese characters. Beck is critical of how sociology has in the past used the nation-state as the presumed framework under the guise of 'methodological nationalism,' and argues that it is high time that the paradigm of sociology is shifted to one based on a cosmopolitan perspective (Beck and Willms 2004: 13–6; Beck 2005).

Fifth, globalization signifies a stronger link between the local and global levels through the increased interdependency occurring across national borders. Global influences now easily appear at the local level. No current society can exist independently from the world, as did Japan during its period of isolation in the Edo era. Even small communities located deep in the mountains are constantly being exposed to the pressures of global capital and information. For example, a local product from a particular area that previously held an established position within the domestic market may gradually lose its market due to an increase in cheap imported goods from China and the like. In this sense, it can be said that borders are being erased with the onslaught of globalization and 'there is no longer an *outside* on this planet' (Machimura 2007: 315). While it may differ in strength, every corner of the earth is currently being exposed to the strong pressures of globalization.

Global warming is another lucid example of how the effects of globalization can be felt at the local level. More importantly, the global warming issue is the result of individual activities that produced greenhouse gases at the local level, which then accumulated on a global scale over the long term and are now predicted to generate a destructive impact at the global level. In fact, the Chernobyl nuclear power plant accident in Russia, which occurred in April 1986, is a classic example of how a local accident resulted in radioactive contamination on a global scale, because radioactive materials finally reached Japan and other remote place on the opposite side of the globe.

Interesting, it can be said that in discussing globalization, most sociologists have focused on how it plays itself out at the local level.

Sixth, globalization is often treated as being equivalent to Americanization. Today, more and more people believe that obstacles in the form of national borders and states should be broken down. With the spread of the principles of free market competition, we also see the appearance of a world run by the principle of 'survival of the fittest' in the guise of *free trade*. Since the demise of the Soviet Union, which represented the only other superpower, the United States has become the sole superpower. Hence, *global standard* often means *American standard*. In particular, those who are critical of globalization argue that globalization is not about spreading a universal value, but is more about how local culture is being destroyed due to American standards being imposed on them. The *Slow Food movement*, which started in Italy to ban a McDonald's hamburger shop from expanding into

Rome, and then spread all over the world, is a classic example of an anti-globalization movement relating to food.

Needless to say, the change is not necessarily linear and each perspective stresses one side of the multi-reality of globalization. According to Held (Held *et al.* 1999), there are three perspectives to globalization: that of the *skeptics*, the *hyperglobalizers* and the *transformationalists*. The above description is closer to the perspective of the hyperglobalizers, who tend to focus on transforming impacts of globalization. The skeptics hold the view that the role of the state is still important, and in fact the state is playing an even greater role. Meanwhile, the transformationalists believe that globalization is taking a complicated zigzagged path, and they highlight the importance of a new role for the state and a reorganization of the state.

Another concept that has been in use in Japan for a long time and is related to globalization is *internationalization*. It is a concept that is relatively unique to Japan. Premised on the previously closed nature of Japanese society, it expresses the importance of increasing and promoting international exchange (it is closer in meaning to the second definition of globalization given above). In English, *internationalization* has a typical meaning of bringing something under international control, like bringing Antarctica under international control—a usage that differs from its common usage in Japan (Kajita 2001a: 1–3).

Globalization and risk—contemporary society as a global risk society

Let us first consider globalization and risk as a premise for examining the issues surrounding globalization and minorities, as well as those surrounding globalization and civil society. Among all the sociological studies conducted on globalization, Beck's global risk society theory offers the most interesting and stimulating discussion (Beck 1986, 1999).

With the advance of globalization, the latter half of the 1980s saw the word *risk* replace *growth* and *prosperity* as the keyword symbolizing modern society. *Risk Society*, written by the German sociologist Beck (1986), was a philosophical and speculative piece of work that was difficult to understand. It was not even presented in a systematic way. In spite of this, it became a bestseller. The English version carried a preface that stated that 60,000 copies of the German version alone were sold over the five years prior to 1991. This was an extraordinary record for this type of academic publication. It evoked a massive response, especially in Europe, because it was published, coincidentally, immediately after the 1986 Chernobyl nuclear power plant accident. The April 1986 Chernobyl accident occurred right after Beck had finished proofreading the book (Beck and Willms 2004: 116). Prior to Chernobyl, accidents were limited in their impact in terms of the number of victims claimed and how far the damages extended over space and time. In contrast, the number of deaths in the Chernobyl nuclear power plant accident could not be narrowed down without considering the impact it would have on future generations. Beck argues that Chernobyl presented a new type of accident in that it was impossible to calculate the impact of damages over space and time. It was an accident where neither the final impact nor the final responsibility could be defined in any concrete terms (Beck and Willms 2004: 115).

The synchronized terrorist attacks on 11 September 2001 on the New York World Trade Center and the Pentagon in Washington DC, both of which represented nerve centres of the United States, deeply impressed upon the world that we are indeed living in a risk society. The threat of terrorism lies in the invisibility and unpredictability of terrorists. They disappear and lie in wait among average citizens without anyone knowing when and how they will attack. It is this unpredictability that instills fear among people.

The environmental and social issues that we face today, such as radioactive pollution, dioxin, endocrine-disrupting chemicals, BSE (mad cow disease) and global warming, are characterized by their invisibility. None of these can be perceived through the five senses of the average citizen. With some issues even the experts differ greatly in their risk evaluation. For example, some view even minute traces of endocrine-disrupting chemicals as a paramount threat, while others play down the threat.

Living in fear of invisible risks marks the world we live in today. 'Risk society' is a term that describes precisely the psyche of the modern era. Compared to ambiguous adjectives that use the prefix *post*, such as postindustrial society and postmodernism, this term cleverly captures the current situation, especially the crisis we face today.

Beck argues that current society is seeing an increase in risks that are difficult to control and carry an invisible impact. This represents his main thesis. According to Beck, we are shifting from an industrial society (he calls it 'simple modernity' or 'first modernity') defined by struggles over the distribution of wealth, as in class conflict, or the distribution of abundance, to a risk society (called the 'second modernity') defined by struggles over risk distribution and risk avoidance. The core idea, which constitutes Beck's criticism of modernity, is clearly expressed in the subtitle for *Risk Society*, which is, 'Towards a New Modernity.' It is also expressed in the concept of the 'second modernity,' as well as the concept of 'reflexive modernization' (Beck, Giddens and Lash 1994). We live in a society terrified of exchanging abundance for risks or global risks. We have not simply been freed of the Cold War structure. Informatization and globalization produce more than just blessings. Under this banner we entered an age in which lurks invisible terrorism and the fear of an invisible enemy. The enemy is no longer limited to foreigners. They can be our neighbours or even a family member. Enemies are also lurking somewhere in the future. The increasing ferocity of nature as a result of global warming may also be the other enemy, as seen in the massive hurricane that hit New Orleans in August 2005.

The new risks are imperceptible and uncontrollable. The types of risks inherent in a severe nuclear accident, destruction of the ecosystem and global warming issues are risks that cannot possibly be guaranteed under the insurance system, which was originally designed to handle risks. As exemplified by the Chernobyl accident and the global warming issue, we live in a globalizing risk society today, or a 'world risk society' (Beck 1999). The risks have no regard for space, time or generation.

As the struggle over risk becomes more dominant, all sorts of realms, including corporate activities, scientific activities, law and the media, will become politicized. Everything will start to carry political significance and become 'subpoliticized' (Beck 1986). Risk is primarily a social construction. Objective knowledge concerning risks does not exist. The phenomenon of the *politicization of science* is an issue that has strongly dictated society since the twentieth century, or at least the latter half of the twentieth century, as seen in the debate over military technology, nuclear power and global warming, as well as bioethics and medical ethics.

Beck's second assertion is that risk awareness as outlined above corresponds to the individualization of people. Risks tend to become a private matter as they are assumed by the individual. Beck's concept of 'individualization' is unique to him.

Beck argues that we are, for the first time in history, living in an era when the unit of social reproduction is the individual. The next generation is not necessarily reared by a class or a family. Social categories are becoming increasingly ambiguous, fluid, multipolar and complex. The concept of the household, which is the basic unit of social science and supposed to be the most basic unit for various statistical surveys, such as the population census, is becoming ambiguous. Beck states that it is gradually becoming more and more difficult to define the household. Even when we call to mind the reality in Japan, the household is not necessarily as self-evidently defined as a unit in which people 'eat and live together' or have a 'shared family budget' as it used to be. Even marriage partners are not necessarily of the opposite sex. Many forms of marriages are now possible, and remaining unmarried is also an option.

Even the concept of *couples*, which forms the core of the household, can only be defined by a nebulously subjective feeling of *love* between the two people involved. The difficulty in defining the household or family makes us aware that the household and family are a type of fiction and a unit where anything is possible. Beck introduces a stimulating definition of couple, 'dirty laundry' (Kaufmann 2000), which is also the title of a work by the French sociologist Kaufmann (Beck and Willms 2004: 22). It comes from the idea that couples become a couple depending on whether or not they are able to wash their dirty laundry together. Being able to wash their dirty laundry together symbolizes, most of all, their respect for each other. A fresh sense of this definition can be felt when the love that has been described romantically over a long period of time can now irradiate, in turn, from the care shown towards what appears to be negative, such as dirty laundry or waste.

The breaking down of norms and social categories signifies two aspects of individualization. First, it implies that people can be based on nothing other than the essence of the individual. Second, it implies that the individual is gaining more and more choices and freedom. As the ambiguity of various social categories increases, we are left with none other than the individual to rely on as the final authority. It is, as Descartes says, 'I think therefore I am.' Neither the state, class, region, nor society can act as a bulwark.

Globalization and civil society—the danger of a weakening social capital

As outlined above, according to Beck's thesis, globalization occurs when there is a global transformation towards risk society, which, at the same time, brings about individualization. Now, then, how does globalization transform civil society?

First, in terms of the stream of sociological theory, Beck's thesis on individualization could be recognized as an argument stressing the dissolving and malfunctioning of an intermediate group between the state and the individual, together with Fromm, Riesman and Kornhauser. The weakening of civil society is an another example of a dissolving intermediate group. As such, the one who has to face the global risk society is the exposed naked and atomized individual void of any ties to a society to rely on.

The reason Putnam's social capital theory flourished corresponds to individualization. Putnam's book on current American society carries the symbolic title of *Bowling Alone*. The cover features someone bowling alone in a bowling lane (Putnam 2000). In the United States bowling is typically a group sport. The emphasis here is that even this sport is played alone. Based on various quantitative data from the 1990s, as well some from the late 1980s, he suggests that what he refers to as the 'social capital' is weakening in the United States, and that social networks are becoming increasingly brittle and people are becoming progressively isolated. It is with alarm that he makes this suggestion. The weakening of existing social capital such as family or relatives, community, clubs and a variety of voluntary associations reveals the weakening of civil society. Individualization has the danger of bringing about the 'segmentalization of society.'

Second, as the genealogy of social disorganization theory within sociology has stressed through the mass society theories of Durkheim, Fromm and Riesman, individualization, people's isolation and atomization are often linked to *intolerant* political opinion. It carries the danger of encouraging people to seek national heroes or fearing foreigners, as well as the risk of accelerating fundamentalist thoughts.

In fact, from the late 1990s and into the beginning of the twenty-first century, various European countries saw the rise of radical right-wing parties that called for the exclusion of immigrants. Parallel to this was the stagnation of social democratic parties as then-ruling parties. For example, even countries that took pride in a mature social democracy feared the spread of intolerant political opinion, as seen in the call for the exclusion of immigrants. Denmark saw a conservative government rise to power in November 2001, and the Netherlands saw a conservative centrist government come to power in May 2002. Even the conservative Christian right-wing forces supporting the Bush government in the United States may be a reflection of the weakening of social capital and the increasing isolation of people.

Third, some argue that globalization makes social integration an increasingly difficult task. This is due to the extensive contact it brings about between different cultures, and, in turn, gives rise to a myriad of new conflicts revolving around multicultural coexistence. I delve further into this matter later when discussing the French 'scarf affair.'

Fourth, globalization has the effect of intensifying activities of organizations whose existence is not premised on the state. Non-governmental organizations (NGOs) are examples of this. With the collapse of the Cold War structure, the late 1980s saw a widespread move towards a global re-evaluation of civil society, a renewed interest in NGOs and non-profit organizations (NPOs), and a reinstatement of public philosophy. The tone of the day was to overcome isolation and atomization, and to reconstruct new bonds by re-evaluating concepts such as solidarity, trust and kindness. Research that focused on making an effort to create a foundation of trust based on rational choice theory that is reliant on individualistic value rose in popularity (Yamagishi, Kikuchi and Kosugi 1999).

Beginning in the early 1990s, rising concerns in non-government circles gradually spread in Japan, leading to a call to grant corporate status to organizations involved in civil activities. After the 1995 Kobe earthquake, 1998 saw the enactment and enforcement of the NPO law. This originally came about after globalization introduced to Japan the activities and organizational realities of NGOs and NPOs in North America and Europe. It was through this that an understanding of the advantages and necessity of the mechanism behind granting corporate status gradually spread in Japan (Hasegawa, Shinohara and Broadbent 2007).

There has been a rapid rise in recent years in experimentation with *regional currencies* in various parts of Japan. This can be seen as a current attempt to revive the principle of *giving* and *exchanging*.

Fifth, most promising is the existing potential for a global civil society. The activities of various international NGOs working in the environment sector are believed to be precursors to a global civil society. Examples of these include WWF, Greenpeace, Friends of the Earth and other similar organizations concerned about various global environmental issues such as global warming. However, as described in Chapter 5 by Inaba and Higuchi, while civil society presents us with an appealing ideal, many practical issues remain on how it should be led and who should form the main constituency. Rose-tinted spectacles will not help us see the potential in the context of global civil society.

Globalization and minority issues—the double-barreled effect

What kind of impact will globalization have on minority issues? In this case the concept of *minority* exists vis-à-vis the dominant group or majority. It refers to a group of people who are in a disadvantaged position compared to the dominant group in terms of social and legal status, education, employment, income and political power. They are part of a socially inferior group due to the social category they fall under, such as race, religion, sex, sexual orientation, physical disability and age.

Globalization and the institutionalization of human rights relief

On the positive side, globalization has the potential of rectifying institutional discrimination of minorities as progress. It can be made in the institutionalization of aid provision to the weak and of human rights relief. For example, the Convention for the Protection of Human Rights and Fundamental Freedoms, and the European Union's Amsterdam Treaty (which was signed in 1997 and entered into force in 1999) have had the effect of converging the efforts of each European Union member state in the area of discrimination of immigrants and human rights issues in Europe (Miyajima 2006: 235).

The institutional advance of women's status in Japan can also be claimed as a positive outcome of globalization. Japan ratified the United Nations Convention on the Elimination of All Forms of Discrimination against Women (which was adopted in 1979 and entered into force in 1981) in 1985. In order to do this, Japan had to carry out certain domestic measures that were necessary to ratify it, including the revision of the Working Women's Welfare Law (1972) and the Equal Employment Opportunity Law between Men and Women (1985). The citizenship law was also revised in 1984 as part of the premise for ratification. It was revised from a law based on paternity (where a child was granted Japanese citizenship only if the father was Japanese) to one based on both paternal and maternal lineage (where a child was granted Japanese citizenship as long as either the father or mother was Japanese). Education guidelines were also revised in 1989, based on the principles of a curriculum for equal education outlined in the same treaty. In 1993 home economics became a compulsory course for both boys and girls in junior high school, and in 1994 home economics, which was previously only compulsory for girls, became compulsory for both boys and girls at the high school level. Although the 'Association for the Promotion of Co-educational Home Economics Course' was created in 1974 and civil movements calling for co-education of home economics had been active since then, there was great resistance from the Ministry of Education. It was the ratification of the Convention on the Elimination of All Forms of Discrimination against Women that provided the main impetus for realizing the co-educational stance.

The ratification of the International Covenants on Human Rights in 1979 and the Refugees Convention in 1981 led to the revision of Japanese domestic laws, which were not in line with the principles of equality between insiders and outsiders (Tanaka 1995; Kajita 2001b: 208).

Furthermore, the progress made in European Union integration has turned the nation-state into a relative concept and forged the way for decentralization in Europe. Those referred to as national minorities, such as in Scotland, Wales, and the Bretagne and Basque regions, have intensified their autonomism within the framework of the state and their movements, which lean towards regionalism. They are also bringing progress to diversification and multipolarization (Miyajima 2004: 18).

There is a growing trend towards granting denizens or permanent immigrants, who reside in the country for a long period of time as foreign citizens without adopting local citizenship, all civic rights except the right to vote. It is a move towards granting them the legal rights to freedom, including the freedom to live, move and work (Miyajima 2004: 67).

However, these are all mainly related to the legal system, and the move towards regionalism within the European Union was also a type of internal restructuring within Western Europe. Those who pose difficulties in the issue of coexistence are the Muslims and immigrants and refugees who are not from Western Europe.

Coexisting with Islam—the issues posed by the scarf affair

Contemporary issues and the complexity of minority issues in the face of globalization were typically exemplified in the controversy surrounding the establishment of the 'anti-hijab law' in 2004 in France. The law stipulated that children and students at public elementary schools, middle schools and lycées are banned from wearing any conspicuous religious insignia and other attires. Let us here introduce the issue based on Miyajima's critical comment about the law (Miyajima 2006: Ch. 7).

Three female Muslim immigrant students went to a public middle school in the outskirts of Paris in September 1989 wearing headscarves in accordance with Muslim teachings. When the principal banned them from attending classes while wearing the scarves, they resisted. This created a ripple effect, stirred up a controversy, and turned into a major incident.

Unlike the United States, Germany or Great Britain, France is a society that has strictly separated the church and the state. Equal rights as *citizens of the Republic*, irrespective of one's religious background, have acted as the major principle since the French Revolution. Basically, it is a country that has adopted *assimilationist policies* in order to ensure equal rights as citizens of the Republic for immigrants. The principles behind the separation of the church and the state and the *freedom of faith* exist to prevent politics, governance and public education from coming under the influence of any particular religion. This major principle of the separation of the church and the state acted as the underlying reason why the school principal banned the female students from attending classes while wearing their head scarves. Some also interpret the donning of the head scarf by women when travelling outside their homes as a symbolic manifestation of Islamic male dominance over women, and as an act of discrimination against women.

However, some argue that the act of wearing a scarf itself is an expression of individual freedom and an issue of religious freedom. They argue that it should not be seen as a propaganda tool of one particular religion. Furthermore, the original aim of the principle of the separation of the church and state was to remove the influential power of the 'organized church authority' of the majority, in other words that of the Catholic church. In contrast, Islam is a religion of a French minority. Muslim residents are considered a minority that makes up approximately 10% of France's population. Should not the principle of equality as a citizen of the Republic, irrespective of religious background, then be applicable to Muslim residents? To exclude those female students from public education due to the scarf issue has a high possibility of reproducing inequality and poverty because they can be deprived of the opportunity of education. On the other hand, those in support of such regulation perceive the hijab as a symbol of Muslim fundamentalism, which has come to the forefront on the international scene.

The scarf issue has thrown the question of whether or not it is possible for Muslim residents to coexist in a multicultural setting straight into our faces. It is an issue in which the principle of the separation of the church and the state at public schools and the protection of minority rights collided head on.

Environmental Justice, and issues of minorities and the periphery

Globalization could possibly aggravate city and regional rivalries, and finally lead to a concentration of waste material in regions that are left behind. As pointed out by the 'environmental justice' theory, which started with R. Bullard (Bullard 1994), dangerous facilities and waste material tend to be concentrated in socially peripheral areas, such as places inhabited by racial minorities, in the poorer segments of society, and in sparsely populated distant areas that fall outside the high-speed transportation network. At the global level they tend to concentrate in the peripheral areas of Third World countries.

Those who are positioned at the center of society have a higher income, and enjoy relatively better access to information and human resource networks. In other words, they enjoy more power to mobilize resources to resist environmental harms. Therefore they are highly independent and have a relatively easier time attracting alternative industries and developing their regions. They are hardly chosen as sites for dangerous facilities. In contrast, the more peripheral the area, the more likely it is to become a site for dangerous facilities. Furthermore, areas that have been polluted have a tendency to create new sources of pollution, one after another: environmental harms double and triple, and even bring about further environmental harms in multiple layers.

In 1996 Maki-machi (now a part of Niigata City after it was incorporated in October 2005) in Niigata Prefecture was the first site in Japan to successfully avoid becoming the site for a nuclear power station when residents expressed their opposition by voting against its establishment. The underlying reason was that while most other nuclear sites were found in sparsely populated areas, Maki-machi was located along the freeway and *shinkansen* (bullet train) lines. In recent years the population has increased, and part of the town is characterized by the way it is turning into a sleeper community for the neighbouring prefecture capital, Niigata City (Hasegawa 2004: Ch. 8). In contrast, Rokkasho Village in Aomori Prefecture has found itself as the area of the highest nuclear waste concentration in the world as a result of being a site for nuclear fuel cycle facilities. This village is located near the northern edge of Honshu Island and is plagued with snowstorms during the winter and often by cold-weather damage caused by *yamase* (a seasonal cold wind in summer) during the summer. As a result, development projects in the postwar era have failed one after another. It is a region that has always been afflicted by its peripheral nature in terms of history, geography and weather. Its choice as the site of nuclear fuel facilities, such as nuclear fuel reprocessing plants, was a result of last-ditch efforts brought about by the failure of the Mutsu-Ogawara development project.

The Mutsu-Ogawara development project site still has approximately 1,500 hectares of unused land. In store for the future are plans to construct a MOX fuel-processing plant. It is anticipated to concentrate other nuclear facilities, such as a second reprocessing plant, and hazard facilities related to industrial waste and recycling. Nuclear power plant sites carry the risk of a vicious circle described as follows: 'Depopulation → entices nuclear power plants → intensifies conflicts within the area → nuclear power plant starts to operate → ends the cycle of rising demand in construction work of nuclear and other related facilities → population decreases → local government relies financially on the nuclear power plant → construction of additional nuclear reactor → increases radioactive waste and stockpiling within the site → construction of interim storage facility for used fuel...'

Rokkasho Village in Aomori Prefecture and areas surrounding a nuclear power plant site demonstrate that the more peripheral an area, the more concentrated the environmental harm. As a result, the typical mechanism at work is that such areas attract further environmental harm.

It is a similar case with the issue of global warming. There are growing concerns about the risk of flooding in the Pacific islands and low latitude regions closer to the equator due to the rising sea level.

Globalization carries the risk of speeding up the pace at which wealth becomes concentrated in the hands of the winners, and splitting the winners and losers into polar opposites. It carries the risk of letting the structure of the 'global rich' and the 'local poor' (Bauman 2000) becoming entrenched. The losers who are unable to adapt to globalization are faced directly with the prospect of the 'expansion of poverty and restructuring that crosses national boundaries' (Kajita 2001a: 25). As a minority, they risk facing the miserable fate of social exclusion. The anti-global movements discussed by Inaba and Higuchi in Chapter 5 voice their objections based on this perspective.

How to measure coexistence—the possibility of governance and open discussions

What kind of paths will improvements to the minority issues take, then, in the face of various fundamental difficulties?

Governance and consensus building

In recent years the word *governance* has come to replace *government* in various contexts. Government, as represented by its three powers of legislation, administration and judicature, is a functional and institutional concept. It has always been premised on the existence of a hierarchy of powers and legal force backed by the institution (in short, the law).

In contrast, governance is based not necessarily on institutional backing, but is, rather, a concept that attaches a great deal of importance to the practical process of consensus building. In short, it emphasizes the importance of working together and collaborating with various major multi-stakeholders. It refers to the framework and form taken to manage the coordination of interests and consensus building. Apart from *global governance*, which is closely linked to globalization, the word is also used in many ways, such as *corporate governance* for the management of corporations, *local governance* for the management of the local government and *environmental governance* for the management of environmental issues.

Government suggests that citizen are *the governed* and their participation in politics has been limited mainly to voting as an electoral constituency. The top-down style represents the existing government-style political method.

In contrast, governance suggests that the citizen can actively take part in the consensus-building process as a constituent member of civil society. Specifically, the citizen can play the role of various interested parties as a local resident, as a member of a trade organization or as a member of all kinds of NGOs.

It is called governance when policies on specific issues are gradually formed and executed through the hearing and coordination of opinions among interested parties through non-institutional, as well as institutional, means. Institutional means include various commissions, public hearings and public commenting. Non-institutional means include unofficial panels and workshops that are also attended by government agents.

In the case of environmental issues, government-style regulation methods were effective for curbing industrial pollution. Examples of regulation methods include charging fines and levies for polluting enterprises that exceed emission standards, and issuing licenses. However, it proves difficult to ameliorate the global warming problem or resolve waste issues using only regulation methods in which governments one-sidedly issue orders from above. Guiding enterprises by providing financial incentives in the form of subsidies and tax cuts also has its limits. Cooperative behavior prescribed by the voluntary will and interest of enterprises and citizens is essential. It is important to provide opportunities for them to be involved in the policy making and consensus building processes from their initial stages.

However, leaving it completely to grassroots initiatives would create confusion and carries the risk of stagnating progress, as each step forward is canceled by a step backwards. It is vital to have a certain management style and method supported by collaboration and consensus.

Furthermore, it is inevitable that governance will create ambiguity as to who is shouldering responsibility. Some criticize governance in itself as a type of government method (Yoshihara 2002).

The international community offers a classic example of a social system that lacks a centralized government and is based on interdependency. Interdependency means that governance evolves and functions within this social system based on interest, coordination and consensus. Good examples of forms of governance can be found in the global governance representative of the United Nations, European Union and G8 (a summit for leading states). In recent years we have seen an increase in cases where NGOs are also heavily involved in global governance. In particular, the European Union leads the world in the area of governance.

The five basic principles of good governance can be found in the *White Paper on European Governance* (Commission of the European Communities, 2001). The five principles are (1) effectiveness, (2) reinforcement of democracy, (3) legitimacy, (4) better and more consistent policies, and (5) collaboration with civil society organizations. In the European Union the five principles are described as those that will strengthen the principles of subsidiarity and proportionality (the principle that states that European Union intervention may only be carried out to the extent that it is needed to achieve the objective, and the respect for state and individual freedom). The White Paper also states that the basis for today's legitimacy is found in the feedback, network and involvement at various levels of the policy formation and execution process. Furthermore, it stresses the importance of target-based tripartite agreements and contracts made at the three levels represented by national, regional and local players as demonstrations of multi-level governance. In particular, governance is discussed in relation to collaboration with civil society organizations.

The current style of governance is characterized precisely by the pluralistic and multi-tiered involvement and consensus forming of a diverse range of subjects. Governance can be explained as the politics of problem solving which emphasizes the importance of participation and consensus. From the point of view of citizens and minorities, governance can represent a practical route to reach the public, as well as an institutionalized route to voice opposition. From the point of view of the government, the main challenge is to create a forum for transparent and open governance based on the involvement of various stakeholders, including minorities.

Taming risks through open dialogue

The negative effects of risks these days and in this age of globalization are especially significant in relation to minority groups. As expounded by Klaus Eder (2000), before we do anything else, we need to 'tame' risks through open dialogue that are as extensive as possible and involve a range of multi-stakeholders, including non-experts. The governance method is one that expresses this general principle.

Specifically, the taming of risks via open dialogue is being put into practice, for example, in Germany, Denmark, the Netherlands and Sweden, through ventures in consensus meetings and the like.

Various attempts are being made across the world to restore civics in response to all that has become distant from civics. This is an attempt to resist the limitations to the rigidified three powers of judicature, administration and legislation, and the limitations to the bloated mass media, which is characterized by its increasing oligopolization and commercialization. Apart from consensus meetings, other experiments include the civilian jury system and civilian media (Shinohara 2004).

As emphasized by Habermas's discussion on rational discourse (Habermas 1984), the trust placed in consensus forming through communication and deliberation is precisely the hope of humankind for taming risks to create a sustainable society.

Needless to say, an open dialogue always carries with it an inherent danger of degenerating into a political pose or propaganda. It also carries a high risk of taming social movements, protest movements and NGOs instead. Also, as even the open dialogue becomes more and more institutionalized, they will carry a double-barreled danger of becoming inert and ritualized, as was the case when social movements became institutionalized. Furthermore, other challenges, such as whether or not minority groups have been provided with real opportunities to participate or with proper language support, also exist.

In this day and age, the spirit of the times should be characterized by a *wisdom* to endure unseen risks and to step up efforts to tenaciously engage in dialogue between experts and non-experts. The only way to clear a path for making progress in minority issues and strengthening civil society is to persist in making a step-by-step effort using this as a starting point.

2 Citizenship Models in the Age of International Migration
Hideki Tarumoto

Understanding the problem

What will ethnic minority research be required to investigate in the twenty-first century? As a clue for discussion, let us review several events involving international migration that occurred in advanced countries at the end of the twentieth century.

The first event is the attempted mass smuggling of Chinese immigrants into the United Kingdom. In June 2000 in the southeast British port city of Dover, fifty-eight Chinese stowaways were found dead on the platform of a large freezer truck (usually used for transporting vegetables) that had been landed by ferry. The immigrants had come from a coastal area of China and travelled by land via Moscow and Belgium before attempting an 'illegal' entry into the United Kingdom. People in the Western communities were shocked by the existence of international trafficking organizations and by the fact that as many as fifty-eight men and women were suffocated to death in a refrigeration container, which had been switched off (*Asahi Shimbun*, June 22, 2000, morning edition: 7).

The second event is the Elian Gonzalez incident in the United States. In November 1999 a ship loaded with Cuban stowaways attempted 'illegal' entry into the United States but was shipwrecked off Florida. Elian, a six-year-old boy, was the only victim to be saved by a fishing vessel. His mother, who was travelling with him, did not survive. Should the United States government give Elian a permit to enter and live in the United States as a refugee? As this incident coincided with the election of party candidates for the presidential election, it gave rise to a great controversy among the United States government/judicial authorities, ethnic Cuban residents in the United States and the general public. Eventually Elian was repatriated to Cuba in accordance with the decision by the United States Department of Justice that he should stay in Cuba with his father, who had divorced Elian's mother (*Asahi Shimbun*, April 8, 2000, morning edition: 8).

The third event is the mass voluntary appearance of 'illegal' foreign residents in Japan at the Tokyo Regional Immigration Bureau. In September 1999 foreigners from Iran, Bangladesh and Myanmar who had entered Japan during the period of the 'bubble' economy and had illegally stayed and worked in Japan appeared at the Bureau to apply for special residence permits. Ready to be deported, they reportedly appeared voluntarily to seek permits for such reasons as having family members who could live only in Japan, including school-age children, or feeling insecure about their lives as illegal residents. The Japanese Immigration Bureau under the Ministry of Justice gave residence permits to several families; the Bureau disclosed information on the cases where permits were given and the guidelines for giving permits, but denied the existence of any 'criteria' for giving permits (*Asahi Shimbun*, September 2, 1999, morning edition: 39; February 3, 2000, morning edition: 39; Komai, Watado and Yamawaki 2000; Watado, Suzuki and APSF 2007).

The fourth event is the Stephen Lawrence case in the United Kingdom. In April 1993 Stephen, an ethnic Caribbean male student, was killed in a knife attack by five white boys in Lewisham, London. The police arrested the suspects but dropped the case for lack of evidence. The racially biased handling of the case by the police, as well as the racist nature of the case itself, became an issue. An inquiry team was set up by Tony Blair's Labour Party administration. The team submitted a final report of the case to the House of Commons in February 1999. The report, which declared the police 'institutionally racist,' had a major impact on British society. Negative reactions to the case led to three nail bomb attacks in London. The bombing targets were the district of Brixton, populated by a large community of people of Caribbean origin and which had experienced a riot, the East End district, which has a large Bangladeshi community, and gay clubs in the Soho district (*Asahi Shimbun*, March 12, 1999, morning edition: 8).

The fifth event is the Austrian Freedom Party's participation in the country's coalition government. In February 2000 the Freedom Party of Austria established a coalition government with the conservative Austrian People's Party. The Freedom Party, a right-wing organization, had opposed European Union expansion and advocated anti-immigrant policies. In particular, the party president Jörg Haider had made statements advocating the Nazi reign. European Union countries did not wait for the launch of the coalition government before expressing to the Austrian government their concern about the proposed new government. After the launch, these countries imposed formal and informal sanctions on the Austrian government, including cutting off political contact and refusing to take commemorative pictures at international meetings. A political party that had repeated statements indicating anti-immigrant, anti-foreigner policies was now in power in one of the Western countries (*Asahi Shimbun*, February 2, 2000, morning edition: 2; February 4, 2000, morning edition: 8–9; February 6, 2000, morning edition: 6).

No one would deny that the problems posed by these events have not been settled in advanced Western communities during the period from the end of the twentieth century to the beginning of the twenty-first century and that they are among the issues of the highest priority. But what is at the core of these events?

This chapter first demonstrates that at the core of these events is the challenge to the nation-state. In other words, international migration, which rapidly became an issue at the end of the twentieth century, indicates the challenge to the national model of citizenship. Second, an argument is made that presenting a new citizenship model to replace the nation-state model is one of the most important tasks for ethnic minority research in the twenty-first century. Finally, limitations of the currently proposed models and a desirable direction for future research are presented as a preliminary discussion for presenting a new citizenship model.[1]

Challenge to the nation-state

Concept of citizenship and reference community

What is at the core of the events described above? Below, I present an argument that it is the challenge to the nation-state that is at the core of these events. This requires the introduction of the concept of citizenship. According to T. H. Marshall (1992), who formally introduced the issue of citizenship to sociology, the concept of citizenship can be defined as follows.

First, the intensional definition of citizenship is 'a status bestowed on those who are full members of a community:' each person who has this status is considered equal in terms of rights and obligations associated with the status (Marshall 1992: 18).

The extensional definition of citizenship can be interpreted as obligations and rights, including civil, political and social rights. Civil rights are intended to protect personal freedom and are protected by the judicial system, including ordinary courts. Political rights are intended to protect political freedom and are secured by individuals' participation in politics. Social rights are a broad concept and cover areas ranging from economic welfare and safety to the enjoyment of social heritage and culturally active lives.

Marshall studied British society up to the period immediately after the Second World War. His study pertained to factors inherent in the principles surrounding citizenship. He questioned whether there are any limits that cannot be, or are unlikely to be, overcome to achieve social equality, apart from the limits of economic cost, such as natural resources and productivity. Marshall argued that civil, political and social rights developed in the eighteenth, nineteenth and twentieth centuries (particularly in postwar periods), and became powerful enough to counter the social inequality known as class. His answer was that by the substantial improvement of citizenship as status, it became difficult to maintain economic inequality (Marshall 1992).

It is only too easy to criticize Marshall's concept of citizenship as too solid. Instead, let us appreciate the solidity of Marshall's concept and continue by focusing on the fact that one important term has not been defined.[2] The undefined term is 'community.' Depending on how this term is defined, different people would be entitled to citizenship. Marshall paid attention to the working class as being excluded from citizenship. Historically and socially, however, communities have often excluded women, the elderly, the disabled and so on. Under the circumstances during the period from the late twentieth century to the twenty-first century,[3] the relationship between immigrants/foreigners and the host community has become a significant issue, as described below. Let us conceptualize 'community,' which serves as a 'reference' for granting citizenship as 'reference community.'

Citizenship as membership in the nation-state

The above-described events are based on the premise that citizenship, which could be defined in many different ways, is based on the nation-state. In other words, the postwar global standard for citizenship defines 'nation-state' as the reference community for granting citizenship. As a result, citizenship has come to mean membership in the nation-state.

However, what is exactly meant by 'citizenship means membership in the nation-state?' According to William Rogers Brubaker, the nation-state represents not only the *fact* of political and social membership but also the *philosophy* and *ideal* of the nation-state (Brubaker 1989: 3). The philosophy and ideal, or 'what it should be,' is more important than the fact, or 'what it is.' This is because the philosophy and ideal enable people to define the framework of the nation-state and detect any deviation of membership from the framework. The philosophy and ideal can also supply legitimacy to system construction and practice.

What, then, are the principles underlying the philosophy and ideal of a nation-state? In the following discussion, I categorize these principles into social contract principles and emotive principles (Brubaker 1989: 3–4).[4] First, the social contract principles pertain to the rights and obligations between the state and individual persons. Specifically, a nation-state expects its members to comply with such principles as *egalitarian status*, *democratic participation*, *unique belongingness* and *consequential benefit*.

More specifically, each member must be equal in terms of rights and obligations. Second-rate citizens must not exist (egalitarian status). Each member must participate in national governance and, conversely, membership in the governance system must be open to the public. It is desirable that each and every resident of the community is a member of the governance system (democratic participation). In addition, each person should belong to only one state (unique belongingness). Finally, membership must be associated with benefits, such as welfare benefits (consequential benefit).

However, the nation-state is not based solely on 'pure' social contracts, or rights and obligations; its foundation includes other principles as well. These are emotive principles, which pertain to national belongingness. The emotive principles include *sacredness* and *congruence of polity and cultural body*.

Specifically, membership is associated with the concept of inviolability. Membership must not be changed easily. In an extreme example, members must be ready to sacrifice themselves for the state (sacredness). In addition, the political membership of a state should be based on cultural membership (congruence of polity and cultural body).

Thus, the nation-state as reference community is not formed in a kind of 'rational' manner based solely on social contract principles. It is based on a combination of these and emotive principles.

Emergence of deviated membership

The coexistence of the two types of principles—the social contract principles and the emotive principles—makes the nation-state, with its philosophy and ideal as reference community, firm but inflexible. Marshall, too, took it as self-evident that the nation-state is the reference community. In reality, however, communities have been faced with a new situation (Brubaker 1989: 4–5): the increase of memberships without the full sets of rights and obligations. Specific examples include foreign permanent residents who have been excluded from participation in elections for a long time and people with dual citizenship/nationality, who have rapidly increased in number. Unauthorized immigrants, who enter and stay in the host country illegally, are no longer uncommon. In some cases, immigrants—with their cultural backgrounds that are different from the host country's—demand the full set of rights, including political ones. On the other hand, the value of citizenship has deteriorated. Some even evaluate membership in terms of gain or loss, which indicates the desacralization of membership. In other words, advanced countries have an increasing number of people with deviations from the nation-state model.

This deviated membership played a role in the above-described events.

The attempted mass smuggling of Chinese immigrants and the Elian Gonzalez incident can be understood, from the host country's point of view, as attempted entry into and stay in the country by people outside the reference community who were motivated by the consideration of gain and loss.[5]

In the mass voluntary appearance of foreign 'illegal' residents in Japan, the demanders of citizenship had already entered and lived in the host country. If they had chosen not to appear and to make the demand, they would have continued to be regarded as outsiders by the reference community, despite their de facto residence in the host community.

The Stephen Lawrence case in the United Kingdom indicates the existence of people who do have citizenship but are susceptible to discrimination through prevention of the full exercise of their rights. Although these people are a formal part of the reference community, they are substantially regarded as outsiders of the community.

Finally, the Austrian Freedom Party's participation in the coalition government involves the possibility that measures to actively exclude immigrants and foreigners from the reference community may be taken by the formal government system. Immigrants and foreigners are susceptible to denial of their inclusion in the reference community.

Sociology has paid insufficient attention to these new realities. The framework of sociological research has been the nation-state, and this has been firmly self-evident. To break through this self-evidence and to deal with these phenomena occurring beyond the framework of the nation-state is the justification for the existence of transnational sociology and the principal task for ethnic minority research (Kajita [1992] 1996: 1–3). Therefore, these phenomena involving the challenge to the nation-state should inevitably be regarded as a central task for transnational sociology.

The next questions is why did the challenge to the nation-state occur, and why did the national model of citizenship have to be challenged?

Three factors involved in the challenge

Increase in, and diversification of, international migration

Let us follow the example of Marshall and examine potential answers to the question by focusing on factors inherent in the principles surrounding citizenship. One potential answer is the increase in, and diversification of, international migration.

Table 2.1 shows changes in the proportion of foreign residents in countries in the Organisation for Economic Co-operation and Development (OECD) from the 1980s to the 1990s. Most of the communities show increases in the proportion of foreign residents. This increasing trend is likely to be greater in reality because the figures in Table 2.1 do not include (i) immigrants who have become naturalized citizens of the host country, and (ii) immigrants from a colony or former colony, since they already have citizenship in the host country. It is therefore estimated that, in terms of foreign or immigrant population, the figures for France, the Netherlands and the United Kingdom, for example, are actually greater.

In addition, international immigrants have not only increased in number but have also diversified. An overview of the trends in international migration after the Second World War shows two distinct stages divided by the beginning of the 1970s. In the first stage, which ran until the beginning of the 1970s, labour migration was the

Table 2.1: Foreign or immigrant population in selected OECD countries[a]

	(% of total population)					Total foreign/ immigrant population in 1999
	1983	1989	1995	1997	1999	
Austria	3.9	5.1	9.0	9.1	9.2	748,200
Belgium	9.0	8.9	9.0	8.9	8.8	897,100
Denmark	2.0	2.9	4.2	4.7	4.9	259,400
Finland	0.3	0.4	1.3	1.6	1.7	87,700
France	n.a.	6.3[b]	n.a.	n.a.	5.6	3,263,200
Germany	7.4	7.7	8.8	9.0	8.9	7,343,600
Ireland	2.4	2.3	2.7	3.1	3.1	117,800
Italy	0.7	0.9	1.7	2.1	2.2	1,252,000
Japan	0.7	0.8	1.1	1.2	1.2	1,556,100
Luxemburg	26.3	27.9	33.4	34.9	36.0	159,400
Netherlands	3.8	4.3	5.0	4.3	4.1	651,500
Norway	2.3	3.3	3.7	3.6	4.0	178,700
Portugal	n.a.	1.0	1.7	1.8	1.9	190,900
Spain	0.5	0.6	1.2	1.6	2.0	801,300
Sweden	4.8	5.3	5.2	6.0	5.5	487,200
Switzerland	14.4	15.6	18.9	19.0	19.2	1,368,700
United Kingdom	3.1[c]	3.2	3.4	3.6	3.8	2,208,000

Notes:
a: These figures exclude immigrants who hold citizenship of the host country and immigrants who have been naturalized. Data for foreign populations are from population registers or registers of foreigners, except for France (census), Portugal (residence permit), and Ireland and the United Kingdom (labour force surveys).
b: Data for 1990.
c: Data for 1985.
n.a.: not available
Source: OECD SOPEMI (1995: 194, 1997: 218, 2001: 282).

main form of international migration. Most immigrants who crossed into other countries during this stage did so alone in order to work as unskilled labourers in the host countries.

The situation changed after the beginning of the 1970s (Castles and Miller 1993). In addition to labour immigrants who crossed national borders to look for work, there was an increase in the number of family reunion cases (in which foreign residents invite family members from their home countries to stay with them in the host countries) and the number of asylum seekers or refugees who sought political protection. Furthermore, highly skilled workers began to migrate to foreign countries.

This stage has also seen the diversification of both sending countries and host countries. In the first stage there were two major flows of immigrants: one to Europe and the other from Europe to the New World. In contrast, the second stage, which began in the mid-1970s, saw the diversification of both sending and host countries, with the emergence of a flow from Latin America to North America, a flow to the Middle East oil-producing countries from neighbouring countries, and a flow to Japan from other Asian countries.

This increase in the volume of immigrants, the diversification of the purposes of migration, and the diversification of sending and host countries during the second stage caused fundamental changes in the issues surrounding international migration. After the shift from the stage at which immigrants stay in the host country temporarily for work to the stage at which they settle in the host country permanently as residents, immigrants came to be required to fulfil various obligations and to need all kinds of rights. The geographic diversification of destinations also allowed them to pursue better lives in which they are vested with various rights. In other words, foreign or immigrant populations that were denied, or tended to be excluded from, membership in the nation-state increased and came to need all kinds of rights.

At this point a confrontation emerged between the nation-state and the increase and diversification of international migration.

The nation-state versus universal human rights

The increase in, and diversification of, international migration was not the only factor that triggered the challenge to the nation-state. Another significant factor was the emergence of a new concept relating to the definition of reference community—universal human rights. Comparative immigration policy studies, which compare and study the immigration policies of different countries, understand the challenge to the nation-state in terms of universal human rights.

Wayne A. Cornelius and his colleagues argue that national governments can no longer exercise strong control over immigrants. This is due to the emergence of 'rights-based politics,' as termed by them. According to these researchers, the pressure from various organizations and groups that demand protection of the rights of immigrants and foreigners based on human rights has made it hard for governments to flatly reject entry and residency applications submitted by immigrants (Cornelius *et al.* 2004).

Yasemin Soysal argues that although membership does tend to be granted exclusively by each nation-state as territory, this is not the only rule for granting membership. Membership is also systematized comprehensively based on universal human rights, independently of territory. Soysal says that as opposed to national citizenship based on nationhood, post-national membership whose legitimacy derives from personhood has emerged in Western European countries (Soysal 1994). At this point, a confrontation between exclusiveness versus inclusiveness of the nation-state has emerged.

According to Saskia Sassen, demands for guaranteeing non-members of a nation-state the equivalent of the human rights granted to formal members emerged in the process of comparison and discussion of measures towards immigrants by the United States and other advanced countries. The most typical example of this is the treatment of unregistered immigrants in the United States who have violated the law. 'Undocumented immigrants' illegally stay and work in the country, but the government cannot simply deport them because the United States' economy needs cheap labour. What is more important, though, is that 'appropriate' treatment based on human rights has come to be accepted as legitimate. According to Sassen's concept, a confrontation of the nation-state regime versus the international human rights regime is beginning to emerge (Sassen 1996).

According to the aforementioned researchers, the challenge to the nation-state has arisen from universal human rights. This means that a confrontation of the nation-state versus universal human rights has emerged.

The nation-state versus anxiety about social integration

I have thus far discussed the increase in, and diversification of, international migration and the rise of universal human rights as factors that have triggered the challenge to the nation-state. On one hand, these factors confront the nation-state in that they 'threaten' the nation-state. On the other hand, there is a factor that attempts to defend and protect the nation-state from the challenge to it. This factor may be called *anxiety about social integration*.

Every advanced country has anxiety about social integration. However, let me use immigrants in Britain as a clue for discussion, since most of these immigrants have already been granted citizenship and this emphasizes the characteristics of the factor in question. Most of these immigrants who entered Britain after the Second World War were from Caribbean islands, India, Pakistan, Bangladesh and other former British colonies. As they were members of the former British Empire, British citizenship was promised to them. During the period from the 1950s to the early 1970s a large number of immigrants were permitted to enter Britain. Britain's reference community was the 'Empire' (Tarumoto 1997).

By the mid-1960s the British community was aware of two issues. One involved complaints from the white majority, which now had to compete with immigrants in the labour markets and other markets. The other involved complaints from immigrants, who were excluded from various opportunities. The majority's reaction to these issues resulted in the immigration stock policy.[6] The policy intended to integrate immigrants who had already entered and lived in Britain into the British community. The intention of this policy was represented particularly in the policy on public education. First, the policy established English as a Second Language education program. The program was intended for the education of residents who had problems with English. Second, the 'policy of dispersal' was adopted. This policy intended to require immigrant children to go to suburban schools by bus in order to prevent inner-city schools from having too many immigrant children. These policies aimed at social integration by means of cultural assimilation and coexistence based on a cultural hypothesis. This cultural hypothesis states that the immigrant issues have arisen from the *oddness* of immigrants' cultures and from personal 'discrimination' by white citizens based on their unreasonable prejudices and intolerances. It follows that the achievement of integration would require correction of people's cultures, prejudices and intolerances, not correction of the social structure or systems. The hypothesis expected that if immigrants coexisted with the majority and possessed 'British culture,' the problem would be solved. In other words, the British community attempted to become a nation-state with the 'congruence of polity and cultural body' (Tarumoto 2000: 7–8).

However, anxiety about social integration was not eliminated; instead it developed into fear of so-called 'race riots.' After several riots during the twentieth century, the dawn of the twenty-first century saw three cities in northern England experience riots as early as 2001. After these riots British public opinion on the nation-state went through two extreme phases (Tarumoto 2002).

In the first phase public opinion held that the nation-state would not be able to maintain social integration. Amid the criticism that the immigration stock policy was not functioning well, the goal of the policy—that social integration will be achieved by achieving congruence of polity and cultural body— came to be regarded as impractical. After the enactment of the *Race Relations Act 1976* the nation-state as the reference community on which the cultural hypothesis had been based was shelved. Instead it was argued that the immigrant policy should focus on those people with more 'special needs.' Specifically, by improving vocational training programs for ethnic Caribbean youths, for instance, supporters of this opinion intended to prevent 'social time bombs' from exploding. This made the British reference community vague and prevented the immigration stock policy from becoming fully effective.

So, as a rebound from the first phase of public opinion, in the second phase another opinion emerged from the public. It held that social integration might be the only way to protect the nation-state. To the majority, repeated race riots looked like a sign of the breakdown of social integration. Their logic was, 'The only way to prevent riots would be to build the community only with people sharing the same culture. In other words, we must reconstruct and maintain the nation-state in order to prevent riots.' To the majority, the nation-state and social integration began to appear equivalent. A typical example illustrating this is the rise of extreme right-wing political forces. For instance, the British National Party (BNP) clearly expressed antagonism against immigrants under the slogan of 'fighting anti-white racism' (BNP n.d.). In September 1993 BNP's Derek Beacon won the by-election of Millwall Council. BNP's candidate won again in the local election in 2001 in the northern English town of Burnley, which had experienced a riot.

Even in Britain, where no far right-wing forces or opinions had emerged in the political mainstream, anti-immigrant forces have begun to secure a firm position in the official political system, as is the case with other Western European communities (Tarumoto 2000: 8–10). As described above, even United Kingdom immigrants who have supposedly been granted citizenship are exposed to the bursting anxiety about social integration and the majority's confusion of the nation-state and social integration in value. This can be described as the emergence of a confrontation of the nation-state versus anxiety about social integration. This movement has been accelerated by the July 2005 London bomb attacks by Islamic extremists and subsequent attempted bomb attacks and discoveries of bomb plots.[7]

Proposed citizenship models

Relaxation of the emotive principles

How should we propose a new citizenship model that would replace the nation-state, amid the above-described confrontations surrounding the challenge to the nation-state? This is one of the most important tasks for transnational sociology and ethnic minority research in the twenty-first century. Several alternative models and their combinations have been proposed since the end of the twentieth century, but none has become conclusive.

First, in order to avoid a drastic change from the nation-state model, the emotive principles of the nation-state model could be relaxed. In other words, the idea is to relax the principles of sacredness and the congruence of polity and cultural body.

The first attempt to do so is represented by *the multicultural model*. This model defines nation as the political community defined by the constitution and laws and regulations and regards all newcomers as new members as long as they respect the existing political order. It also accepts cultural differences and the formation of ethnic communities. The multicultural model is said to have taken hold in Australia, Canada and Sweden, and to have been introduced in the Netherlands, the United States and the United Kingdom (Castles and Miller 1993). This model can be adopted in order to maintain the nation-state model by moderating its assimilation-oriented aspects. However, in terms of theory, the multicultural model will change the nation-state model practically by modifying the congruence of polity and cultural body. The acceptance of multiple cultures may cover the multiple cultures maintained by immigrant and foreign populations that legally live in the host country, but would not fully cover the cultures maintained by new immigrants who may come in the trend of the increase in, and diversification of, international migration. In addition, as seen in the British example, this model has failed to propose an effective potential solution to anxiety about social integration.

The second attempt is represented by *the naturalization model*. This model attempts to include immigrants and foreigners in the nation by significantly relaxing the requirements for naturalization. For instance, Germany's revisions of its Foreigner Act in 1991 and 1993 reduced the discretionary power of the government on decision-making in the naturalization procedures and granted foreigners the right to apply for naturalization, subject to certain conditions (Feldblum 1998: 247–9). After January 2000 all foreigners were granted citizenship if either of their parents had been born in Germany. In addition, all foreigners staying in Germany for at least eight years were granted the right to apply for naturalization (Kuboyama 2003: 139). These measures indicate relaxation of the traditional requirement of blood relationship for granting citizenship.

Unless combined with the acceptance of dual citizenship (described below), the naturalization model seems to intend to maintain the nation-state model with as little change as possible and even to reinforce it. However, as is the case with the multicultural model, the naturalization model conflicts with the congruence of polity and cultural body. This is because immigrants and foreigners may become part of the nation without fully learning the culture of the host country. If, for example, the requirement for filing an application for naturalization is significantly relaxed to five years of residence in the host country, it seems to have no implication for sacredness, or the inviolability of membership. This may even lead to a waver by the national government of the authority to determine who should be permitted naturalization (Hammar 1990). Furthermore, some immigrants and foreigners are likely to refuse to become part of the nation. Many of them feel that abandoning citizenship (that is, nationality) of their native countries would result in a loss of identity and many other costs.

Relaxation of the social contract principles

Relaxing not only the emotive principles but also the social contract principles, including egalitarian status, democratic participation, unique belongingness and consequential benefit, results in models that are further from the nation-state model.

The first is *the dual nationality model*. Immigrants and foreigners who feel reluctant to become naturalized in the host country may find it acceptable to do so if they are allowed to maintain nationality of their native countries. The 1997 European Convention on Nationality set out a policy to accept dual nationality (Okuda and Tateda 2000). Sweden enacted a new civil rights Act in 2001 under which immigrants who naturalize are no longer obligated to waive nationality of their native countries (Dingu-Kyrklund 2001: 53–5). Mexico revised its constitution in 1997 to allow Mexican-born foreign citizens and family members who have naturalized in a foreign country to restore their

Mexican nationality (Koido 2002: 188). One concern of the German and Turkish governments is whether the German government will allow the two million Turkish residents in Germany to have dual nationality. In 1981 the Portuguese government relaxed its restrictions on dual nationality of Portuguese citizens living overseas (Feldblum 1998: 237).

The dual nationality model does not only conflict with sacredness and congruence of polity and cultural body as components of the emotive principles; the acceptance of belongingness to more than one country conflicts with unique belongingness as one of the social contract principles. In addition, this model involves the concern that the increase in, and diversification of, international migration may be accelerated by further increasing the number of immigrants who seek nationality in host countries for instrumental purposes.

The second model is *the voting-right model*, which intends to grant political rights to immigrants and foreign residents who do not have citizenship in the host country. There can be two types of the voting-right model.

The first type grants voting rights at the local level only. In Japan, for instance, in January 2000 the Liberal Party and the New Kōmeitō Party, which had formed a coalition government with the Liberal Democratic Party, submitted a Bill for local voting by foreigners. This model was proposed as early as the 1960s in Sweden. Sweden granted the right to vote in local elections and national referendums to foreigners who had held legal resident status for three years. In 1976 the country held the first election in which voters included immigrants (Hammar 1990: 131–77, 155–65). This local voting-right model pays attention to the aspect as residents of immigrants and foreigners and seems to be highly feasible at the policy level. Needless to say, however, the model not only requires modification to the emotive principles, including sacredness and congruence of polity and cultural body, but also conflicts with the unique belongingness of the social contract principles. On the other hand, it is in accordance with the principle of democratic participation, which represents the openness of membership. However, even if foreigners are granted voting rights at the local level only and not at the national level, the majority's anxiety about social integration would not be eliminated easily. Another problem is that voter turnout among foreigners is lower than expected, as has been the case in Sweden (Hammar 1990: 155–65).

The second type of the voting-right model grants immigrants and foreigners voting rights at both local and national levels. Tomas

Hammar argues that the national voting-right model would be difficult to realize but should be introduced as an alternative to the naturalization model, unless the latter model is adopted (Hammar 1990: 198–200). The national voting-right model would perfectly realize democratic participation on which the local voting-right model is based. This would result in a strong violation of the emotive principles and may increase the majority's anxiety about social integration and the concern that the community may be taken over by foreigners. Even the Swedish political parties, which had been liberal enough to grant immigrants and foreigners local voting rights, were negative about granting national voting rights (Kondō 1996: 74).

The last model is *the human rights model*. This model grants civil rights to immigrants and foreigners based on the fact that they are humans. The difference between this model and the voting-right model is that it grants all kinds of rights, including the right of entry and residence. For example, it could be said that the European Union is aiming at the human rights model by its internal liberalization. Post-national membership proposed by Soysal (1994) is, if its implication is taken faithfully, very close to the human rights model. The human rights model would completely destroy the nation-state. In terms of the social contract principles, first, egalitarian status could not exist in a community that had no limitation on its membership. The biggest problem would involve who in the world would guarantee various civil rights or, in other words, who would satisfy the consequential benefit as one of the social contract principles. In the movement towards European Union integration, currently the nation-state is the only entity that would directly guarantee various civil rights. If the human rights model was adopted completely, there would be no 'citizens' who would support the new 'state' that would emerge.

Necessity of sociological imagination for minority research

Pursuit of new legitimacy: Birth/blood relationship versus residence

Amid the above-described difficulties, what will a final new citizenship model for the twenty-first century be like? It is difficult to predict its final form just after the turn of the century. If we focus on the issues of principles, how should ethnic minority research explore these issues? Based on the above discussion, let us make a preliminary discussion to explore a new citizenship model.

Selecting a citizenship model is a matter of defining the boundaries of the reference community on which citizenship is based and granted. A model that can secure the legitimacy of the reference community will replace the nation-state model. The nation-state model is based on the social contract principles and the emotive principles. More specifically, the nation-state model defines the scope covered by the social contract principles using the emotive principles.

However, there are no ultimate means to secure sacredness and congruence of polity and cultural body, which constitute the emotive principles in the nation-state model. In other words, ultimately no one can tell for sure if people regard citizenship as sacred or share the same culture. To solve this problem, the nation-state uses birth and blood relationships as indicators in granting citizenship (that is, nationality). The model assumes that the principles of sacredness and congruence of polity and cultural body are satisfied if the person was born in the nation-state or if the person's parent or parents are citizens of the nation-state.

In this case, naturalization is handled as an exceptional case. Specifically, the nation-state model assumes that a foreigner's acquisition of citizenship (that is, nationality) in the host country by naturalization should be allowed if and only if the foreigner has learned the culture of the host community and regards citizenship in the community as sacred. Dual nationality is also handled as an exceptional case, unless the citizen with dual nationality frequently changes his/her residence between the two countries.

Discussion on the currently proposed models has revealed that, as alternatives to blood relationship and birth, 'residence' and 'being humans' have been proposed as a new potential basis of the legitimacy of a reference community.

As has already been mentioned, 'being humans' as a potential basis of legitimacy carries with it a fairly difficult problem—the human rights model completely destroys the state system. On the other hand, residence has already been used tacitly as a basis of legitimacy in actual policies. In particular, the naturalization model, the dual nationality model and the voting-right model would not hold without adopting residence as a principle.

The problem depends on whether residence can provide the majority and immigrants and foreigners with an emotive principle that would be proportionate to all the rights and obligations granted to citizens. It is desirable that a new citizenship model would have the effect of supplying identity to immigrants and foreigners and of eliminating the majority's anxiety about social integration. It is also desirable that the reference community to be established by the new model would be approved by both the majority and immigrants and foreigners.

In search of a new imagination

Under the above-described circumstances surrounding the issues, what contributions can transnational sociology and ethnic minority research make?

'Residence,' as used in this context, is not the same as 'domicile,' which is determined by legal requirements. In other words, residence is not a legal fact. It is a sociological fact meaning 'to live' in the sense that people are daily and jointly engaged in activities in a certain place. It means that a person is actually 'based in the place.' Will residence produce some sort of communality? And will this communality provide a basis of the legitimacy of publicness? This questioning and reasoning is where sociological imagination is at its best and has been used in many fields of study, including urban sociology and regional sociology.[8] The same type of questioning and reasoning has been used in the discussion on new citizenship models. Many researchers studying immigrants and foreigners have also found residence a promising source of legitimacy (Watado, Suzuki and APSF 2007).

However, under the conventional sociological imagination, residence seems insufficient to provide legitimacy of the reference community. The relationship among people implied by residence is a local one that is similar to a face-to-face relationship. In contrast, the relationship on which citizenship models is focused is found in an 'imaginary community,' which is almost at the national level, far beyond the level of face-to-face relationship. How can a relationship beyond the level of face-to-face relationship be derived from a face-to-face relationship? Does residence have enough authority to be presented as a basis for granting citizenship to denizens (permanent residents), as proposed by Hammar (1990)? The legitimacy of the reference community for granting citizenship cannot be derived directly from residence at the local level.

The conventional sociological imagination described above is insufficient to complete a theory to derive the legitimacy of the reference community from residence. Transnational sociology needs a new sociological imagination.

In the background of the discussion on the new citizenship models we can catch glimpses of simple but important facts. Since its creation, sociology has assumed that the development of modernization will result in isolation of individuals and has discussed resulting negative effects. In order to eliminate these negative effects, individuals must construct a 'community.' However, the construction of a community requires individuals to give up their freedom to a certain extent. As implied by the emotive principles in the nation-state model, a reference community cannot be established without imposing some restrictions on individual freedom. The problem is how to balance freedom and restrictions.

Free individuals are not homogenous. Whether intended or not, or desirable or not, free individuals are inevitably divided by political, economic, social and cultural boundaries. In the national model of citizenship, the reference community has been defined in accordance with these boundaries. Can these individuals, who are divided by all the boundaries, be included in the reference community based on residence? Or, alternatively, how can residence as a sociological fact nullify the boundaries and provide a basis for creating a community of people? If the boundaries are defined too strictly, the community would be an 'ascribed group' that allows no immigration from outside. Conversely, if the definition is too flexible, the community would be a 'functional group' and would no longer be able to fulfil its obligations or maintain solidarity. The community for the twenty-first century should stand at some point between the two types of group.

The task for ethnic minority research of presenting a new citizenship model is part of the broader issue that has been focused on by the sociological imagination. How can new publicness be generated by imposing as little restrictions as possible on the freedom of individuals at large? We must be sensitive to the existence and functions of the boundaries among individuals when we work on tasks focused on the inclusion of immigrants and foreigners. Transnational sociology requires the contents of the imagination to observe social phenomena in the context of these boundaries, particularly the nation-state; in other words, to discuss the legitimacy of the reference community from the viewpoint of finding the balance point between individual freedom and restrictions imposed on individuals who are divided by the boundaries, and to look for the balance point from the viewpoint of constructing a logic that will win people's sympathies beyond the boundaries. This is the transnational sociological imagination necessary to discuss ethnic minority issues.[9]

Author's note

This article is a revised version of my previous work published in 2001 in *Shakaigaku hyōron* (Japanese sociological review), 51 (4). The research for this article was aided by the Matsushita International Foundation in fiscal year 1999; and the Grant-in-Aid for Scientific Research from the Japan Society for the Promotion of Science from fiscal years 2005 through 2007.

3 New Racism and 'Community Cohesion' in Britain

Satoshi Adachi

Background and issue

The issue of identity entered the political arena during the 1970s when the welfare state was falling out of favour as an ideal and making way for multiculturalism. 'Tolerance' became the keyword at the time. Tolerance for the growing population of ethnic minorities in the developed countries, particularly in urban areas, and recognition of their identities were considered to serve as buffers for social tensions. However, tolerance in old multiculturalism assumed a relatively small population of ethnic minorities and a certain distance between their communities and mainstream society. Accordingly, a constantly growing population of black and minority ethnic groups and an increasing desire among second and third generation immigrants to participate in mainstream society pushed tolerance to its limits during the 1990s. The swaying of identity by cultural contact and cultural erosion, which had been concealed until then, has become clearly visible. A succession of terrorist incidents by Islamic fundamentalist groups, including the September 11 terrorist attacks on the United States in 2001 and the July 7 London bombings in 2005, has added an ontological dimension called 'insecurity' to the identity issue (Goodhart 2006).[1]

Politics of identity and insecurity is advocated by the National Front movement and 'the hate industry' (Kundnani 2003) through the media. While this is positioned as an extension of the old binary opposition between 'politics of redistribution' and 'politics of recognition,' it acutely reveals their limitations. The politics of recognition increases a sense of insecurity among communities by emphasizing their heterogeneity rather than promoting equality among them. The politics of equality prohibits overt discrimination against ethnic minorities and provides a premise on which equality among citizens can be constructed, but it cannot eliminate latent discrimination. Similarly, eclectic politics aiming for real equality among heterogeneous people cannot secure sufficient financial and moral support for such policy without resolving the issue of identity, which is supposed to be the common basis for its realization. This has given rise to the politics of insecurity and identity and caused an impasse in the formation of society that guarantees diversity and cohesion.

A breeding ground for the politics of identity and insecurity is 'new racism' (Barker 1981). New racism is a form of racism that effectively excludes minorities by emphasizing cultural differences rather than a racial or genetic hierarchy. It does not take a blatant form of racial discrimination but leads people to avoid contact with different ethnic groups and to withdraw from one another, thus breeding insecurity based on mutual ignorance. This feeling of insecurity has led to the emergence of far-right political parties such as the British National Party and the National Front.

One consequence of new racism was the series of riots that occurred in northern England in the summer of 2001. Violence against racists and the police by hundreds of youths from ethnic minority communities left major scars on British society. In response to this situation, the British government has put forward a comprehensive racial relations policy called 'Community Cohesion'. It aims to generate dialogue, tolerance and solidarity between the majority and the minority based on shared nationality and citizenship.

No comprehensive study of community cohesion has been produced as yet, but several analytical or evaluative studies and arguments do exist. They argue and evaluate community cohesion from the viewpoints of, for example, binary opposition between responsibilities and rights or tolerance and cohesion (Yuval-Davis 2002), Foucault's governmentality concerning social capital and active citizenship (Marinetto 2003; Mcghee 2003), or the causes of the 2001 riots (Hussain and Bagguley 2005; Malik 2002). This study occupies a place in such discourse.

In addition to the above, this study also conducts analysis from a new viewpoint by focusing on new racism, by referring to the 'common in-group identity model' as a theoretical model for the resolution of new racism, and by analyzing and evaluating Britain's racial relations issue and community cohesion as a countermeasure. It then illustrates social inclusiveness of 'Britishness' as a representation emphasized by community cohesion, and proposes a possibility of a new philosophy of solidarity to overcome the politics of insecurity and identity.

New racism

The scourge of Nazism and the efforts of the United Nations and UNESCO made public expressions of science-based and biology-based racism difficult after the Second World War. However, a form of racism armed with new rhetoric has emerged since the 1960s. This is the phenomenon called 'new racism' (Barker 1981).

New racism focuses its attention on cultural differences rather than biological differences and relies on incompatibility of different cultures and negativity towards cultural mixing. This new phenomenon is attracting wide attention in the fields of political science, sociology and psychology.

The term 'new racism' simply means that it is a contrastive concept against old racism (which was based on biological racial hierarchy), and it has many connotations. It has been variously described and characterized as, for example, 'symbolic racism' (Sears 1988), 'modern racism' (McConahay 1986), 'aversive racism' (Gaertner and Dovidio 1986) and 'smiling racism' (Wilkins 1984). Accordingly, different fields or approaches emphasize different aspects of it. However, it is possible to point out the following general characteristics:

1. new racism is based on cultural differences, not on biological grounds
2. new racism takes subtle, rather than overt, forms of discrimination
3. in new racism the perpetrator of discrimination is not aware of his/her discriminatory action
4. new racism opposes affirmative action based on ethnic differences and regards such action as reverse discrimination.

The first characteristic, the emphasis on cultural differences, is the core logic of new racism. The theoretical mainstay of old racism was biology. In contrast, new racism relies on culture (or cultural differences). It asserts that there is no racial hierarchy of a white majority and a non-white minority but that their cultures are different and incompatible. It also argues for the preservation of the original culture of majority and the exclusion of minorities by using the discourse of nationality. Etienne Balibar calls it 'racism without race' based on this characteristic (Balibar 1991).

The second characteristic, subtle forms of discrimination, is a prominent characteristic of new racism. Old racism took blatant forms of discrimination such as hate speeches. However, the civil rights movement and anti-racial discrimination laws developed during the 1960s imposed restrictions on discriminatory acts in public and private situations. Yet subtle forms of discrimination remained. For example, Samuel L. Gaertner and John F. Dovidio distinguish between anti-minority discrimination and pro-majority discrimination and call the latter 'aversive racism' (Gaertner and Dovidio 1986). It effectively excludes and discriminates against minorities by assuming a more favorable attitude towards a majority rather than being blatantly discriminatory against a minority. This type of discrimination takes indirect or subtle forms.

The third characteristic, lack of awareness, is both the consequence and the cause of the second characteristic. Those who are committed to liberty and equality deny that they are racists. However, latent attitude tests and various empirical studies in psychology have found various discriminatory attitudes, which are not recognized by the perpetrators themselves. These tests and studies have revealed that racial discrimination takes 'pro-majority' forms through differential treatment, not blatant 'anti-minority' treatment. This type of discriminatory attitude is widely shared by well-meaning, white liberals with an egalitarian tendency who believe they are unprejudiced (Gaertner and Dovidio 2000: 13–31).

The fourth characteristic, the claim of reverse discrimination, suggests that new racism is employed in a political reaction to anti-racism. While the third characteristic of new racism involves a difficulty to recognize discrimination, it culminates in a difficulty to rectify discrimination. Labeling someone with an egalitarian view or who avoids contact with minorities out of latent insecurity or uncertainties as a 'racist' can elicit an angry response. This point can easily lead to the neoconservative 'anti-anti-racism' political campaign, which I discuss in detail in the next section (Ansell 1997; Barker 1981).

Following the above overview of new racism, I discuss how new racism is manifesting itself and what problems it is causing in Britain.

New racism in Britain

The term 'race' was derived from 'ratio,' which originally meant 'chronological sequence' (Memmi [1982] 1994–1996: 177). The term was used to mean a super-temporal link between ancestors and descendants for the first time in John Foxe's *Book of Martyrs* published in 1570. It had a religious connotation meaning the descendants of

Abraham (Banton 1988: 16). It quickly came into wide use as European countries maintained their territorial expansion policies from the late fifteenth century onwards. From the eighteenth century the scientific revolution and the disenchantment of the world produced a biological explanation of racial differences. Combined with the spreading and deepening of imperialism, the biological explanation was linked to a racist interpretation.

After the Second World War the protection of ethnic minority rights was legislated in many countries following the creation of a worldwide human rights system by UNESCO and the United Nations. Britain passed the Race Relations Act in 1965, the year in which the United Nations adopted the International Convention on the Elimination of All Forms of Racial Discrimination, prohibiting discrimination on the bases of race or colour at hotels, restaurants and several government agencies. The 1968 amendment extended the racial discrimination ban to housing and employment and set up the Community Relations Commission for the purpose of improving race relations. The 1976 amendment established the Commission for Racial Equality, which was given the power to counteract discrimination and took more comprehensive and practical measures to eliminate discrimination. Another amendment in 2000 saw the banning of racism at almost all government agencies, including the police, which had been exempt until then.[2] The power of the Commission for Racial Equality was increased and over 43,000 organizations were required not only to eliminate prohibitive or passive discrimination but also to take active measures to achieve good relations and equality of opportunity among different ethnic groups (British Home Office 2004: 3.6).[3]

Nevertheless, racial conflicts continued to occur during this period. There were race-related riots in Brixton and Southall in 1981, Handsworth and Brixton in 1985, and in northern England in 2001.

Why do racial conflicts persist despite the ban on racial discrimination or the implementation of measures for better racial relations? I would like to examine new racism in Britain in order to answer this question.

Powellism

New racism was publicly expressed in Britain by Enoch Powell, a Conservative Party politician during the 1960s. Britain began to accept immigrant workers from the new Commonwealth regions (i.e. the British Commonwealth countries except Canada, Australia and

New Zealand) in order to resolve the labour shortage after the war. The *British Nationality Act 1948* gave Commonwealth citizens from Asia and the West Indies the right to live and work in mainland Britain. Consequently, the population of non-white immigrants increased, which created tensions between the immigrants and the white people as early as the 1950s. The conflict became more apparent during the 1960s. Powell went into the center of the political scene in such circumstances.

Powell came into the spotlight when he made the 'Rivers of Blood' speech in Birmingham in 1968. The speech, which rejected the immigrant intake and proposed the repatriation of immigrants, was meant to be a direct criticism of the *Racial Relations Act 1968*. It contained some of the characteristics of new racism.

In the speech Powell talked about the case of one elderly white woman in West Midland. She had lost her husband and sons in the war. She renovated her home, which was her only asset, and operated a boarding house to make a living. Immigrants moved into the area, turning the once quiet neighbourhood into bedlam. Her boarders left and she became the only white resident in the area. She no longer felt safe and no longer had an income. She went to her local authority to ask for a reduction in her rates. A council officer accused her of racial prejudice and told her to let her room to black people for an income. She was labeled as a 'racialist' and abused by her black neighbours.

After telling this anecdote, Powell asked his audience: 'When the new [1968] Racial Relations Bill is passed, this woman is convinced she will go to prison. And is she so wrong?' He claimed that the racial relations improvement measures represented by the Racial Relations Act were discriminatory against his fellow white citizens.

However, Powell did not portray black people as inferior in his speech. Nor did he use blatantly discriminatory language about them. He simply stirred up fear and insecurity about black people gaining a majority status, and said that their cultures were incompatible with the lifestyle of the white British people and would destroy their purity (National Front 2007).

Such an argument is called 'anti-anti-racism.' It is the view that anti-racism in itself is racism against white people. Its advocates stir up a feeling of insecurity in the majority population and exploit liberal values such as liberty and equality to criticize preferential treatment of non-white minorities and racial relations measures as racism (Ansell 1997: 181–90).

While Powell was removed from the shadow cabinet of the Conservative Party on the day after his speech, the central idea of the speech was inherited as part of neoconservatism ideology, which was adopted by Margaret Thatcher and held sway throughout the 1980s and 1990s.

Institutional racism

The Macpherson Report (Macpherson 1999) revealed that new racism, which had been linked to the political discourse of Powellism and neoconservatism, had in fact penetrated British society deeply.

The Macpherson Report was the result of an inquiry into the incident in which Stephen Lawrence, a youth of Caribbean descent, was murdered by a group of white people while waiting for a bus in Eltham, London, on the night of April 22, 1993. Specifically, it addressed the issue of police conduct in the Lawrence murder investigation. For example, it was initially assumed for no apparent reason that Lawrence was a gang member. Some of the statements (such as that the killing was racially motivated) made by Duwayne Brooks, a Caribbean friend who waited for a bus with Lawrence and who was the only eyewitness, were ignored. Immediately after the incident, Brooks was treated only as an eyewitness and was not given appropriate care as a crime victim, either by the police or at the hospital. And five juvenile suspects escaped prosecution in the end.

The Macpherson Report used the notion of institutional racism to describe this type of racism, which is deeply rooted in general society, particularly in professional organizations such as government agencies. Institutional racism means '[t]he collective failure of an organization to provide an appropriate and professional service to people because of their colour, culture, or ethnic origin' and '[i]t can be seen or detected in processes, attitudes and behaviors which amount to discrimination through *unwitting* prejudice, ignorance, thoughtlessness and racist stereotyping which disadvantage minority ethnic people' (Macpherson 1999: 6.34; italics added).

This notion had already been introduced in the Scarman Report (Scarman 1981), which investigated the cause of the 1981 race riots in Brixton, London. Although Lord Scarman, the author of the report, was aware of '*unwitting* discrimination' within the police and various government agencies, he did not admit that it was institutional (Scarman 1981: 9.1). Ironically, this was the reason why the report was accepted by many organizations and communities (Neal 2003). At the same time, it led to the ambiguity of multicultural policy, which was earnestly introduced at the local authority level from the 1980s, and the inadequacy of support from members of the central government and agencies. One such example was Training in Racism Awareness (TRA) conducted during the 1980s.

TRA was initially conducted under the name of 'racism awareness training' (Institute for Employment Studies 2002: 19–20). It responded to the demands of so-called 'political correctness.' TRA was fraught with problems from the start. For example, the City of Bradford, where a 2001 riot occurred, announced the 'policy statement on race relations' in 1981 in response to the Brixton riots and started to veer round to multiculturalism. It implemented TRA as part of the multicultural policy. While the principle object of training was racism awareness, white trainers were opposed to this objective and considered that the focus and description of the program should be 'cultural awareness,' which was more neutral. Consequently, no proper supportive relationship was formed between black trainers and white trainers. The program did not receive sufficient support or funding and many of the trainers lacked necessary knowledge and experience. It created a strained atmosphere at the city hall and turned discrimination into more latent forms (Singh 2002: 120–1). This provided a breeding ground for the 2001 riots.

The above example demonstrates that simply putting prohibitive measures for racial discrimination in place does not lead to the resolution of institutional racism. On the contrary, it risks being exploited for neoconservative political campaigns. A politically correct approach in relation to multiculturalism induces the politics of reverse discrimination, or 'anti-anti-racism,' as an adverse reaction.

In-group identity model

This discussion so far has seen that new racism has penetrated deeply into society and it is peculiarly difficult to resolve. How can the issue of new racism be resolved?

According to social psychologist and philosopher, Albert Memmi, *'After all, racism is one of the most equally distributed attitudes in the world.* In other words, it is a *social fact'* (Memmi [1982] 1994–1996: 127). This way of thinking is widely shared by psychologists in particular. Studies of self and social categorization theories, which have seen a rapid development since the Second World War, illustrate the inevitability of the human cognitive construct to carry out 'us/them' segmentalization. However, it does not necessarily mean that multicultural coexistence and cooperation are impossible.

Based on the result of their 1986 study *Prejudice, Discrimination, and Racism* in which they presented 'aversive racism,' Gaertner and Dovidio proposed the 'common in-group identity model' (Gaertner and Dovidio 2000). The common in-group identity model is a hypothesis that 'the causal relation between the conditions of contact and reduced intergroup bias is mediated by changes in members' perceptions of the aggregate from two groups to one more inclusive group' (Gaertner *et al.* 1996: 273).

To illustrate this, they reinterpreted Allport's contact hypothesis (1954) in terms of the in-group identity model. The contact hypothesis states that the conditions of contact between different groups—equal status, cooperative mutual dependency, opportunity for members to get to know one another personally, egalitarian norms and so on—influence intergroup prejudice. They added member's awareness of one's own and other's identity as a parameter—whether being a member of a common group, a different subgroup within a common group or a different group, or an individual—in order to explain the mechanism of the contact hypothesis and demonstrated that positive contact condition generated an awareness of being members of a common group and reduced prejudice against other groups.

For example, they expressed the contact condition as an independent variable, the form of the individual's self-awareness as a parameter and the assessment of an out-group as an outcome, and illustrated their relationship in a regression analysis. As shown in Figure 3.1, positive intergroup contact (equal relations, complementary roles, personal contact and so on) reduces the awareness of being two groups (–0.74) and conversely increases the awareness of being 'one group' (0.69). The representation and awareness of being one group also resulted in positive mutual assessment of each group (0.47). The important point is that intergroup contact conditions and out-group assessment are associated in Allport's hypothesis (0.62), but the direct association is weakened when the representational mediator is controlled (0.09).

Another more interesting finding in a series of experiments and surveys is 'dual identity.' Dual identity means the coexistence of the awareness of being a member of a more inclusive group and the awareness of being a member of a subgroup within it, which is found also to reduce intergroup bias. Studies of ethnic group relations and bias at American high schools found that optimal contact conditions

Figure 3.1: Modified version of Gaertner and Dovidio's model (2000: 75, Figure 5.1)

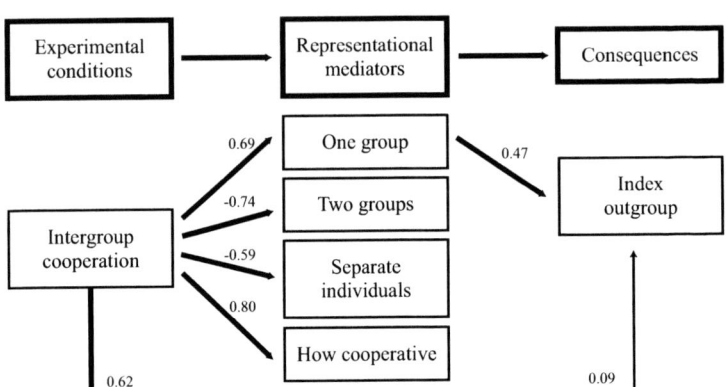

promoted the awareness of being in the same group or different subgroups in the same group (i.e. on the same team) (0.40, 0.46) and such awareness reduced intergroup bias (–0.08, –0.09, p<0.05) among students of different ethnicities (Figure 3.2). This result supports the hypothesis about the importance of in-group identity for intergroup bias (Gaertner and Dovidio 2000).

The study indicates that the extension of an in-group circle inhibits negative intergroup bias and conflicts while retaining the in-group/outgroup distinction. In view of this finding, I examine the current racial relations policy in Britain through an analysis of the Cantle Report, *Community Cohesion* (Cantle 2001), in the next section.

'Community cohesion' policy

The Cantle Report

Starting in Oldham, a succession of race-motivated riots erupted in various parts of northern England in the summer of 2001. Over 500 Asian youths joined the riots and clashed with more than 100 police officers. The riots climaxed in the Bradford riots in which nearly 1,000 people were involved, 270 rioters were arrested, 300 police were injured and the amount of damage totaled £25 million (Allen 2003). The riots that took place in Oldham, Burnley and Bradford were the worst in twenty years. Most of the rioters were Asian youths who were not only excluded from mainstream society but also in

Figure 3.2: Modified version of Gaertner and Dovidio's model (2000: 85, Figure 5.2a)

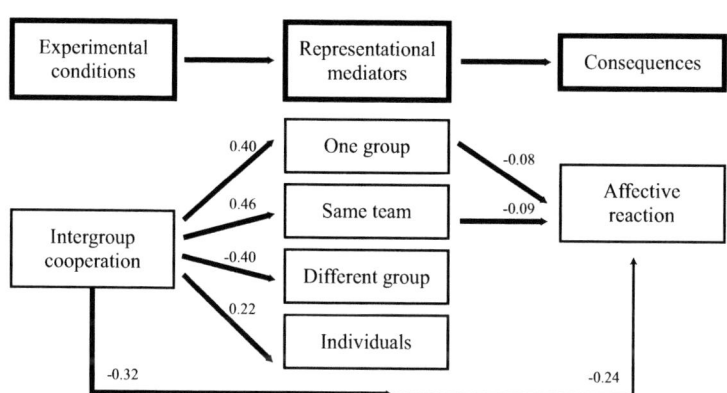

vulnerable positions in their communities. The riots caused by these young people contained an entrenched problem of 'the violence of the violated' (Kundnani 2001).

The Home Office took this trouble seriously and in 2001 commissioned an inquiry led by Ted Cantle, the then chief executive officer of Nottingham City Council. The Cantle Report, *Community Cohesion* (Cantle 2001), was submitted in the same year. This report has since become a model for race relations policy and its title, 'community cohesion,' has become a general term for race relations policy.

The landmark policy clearly formulated the desirable state of race relations in terms of 'community cohesion.' The idea of community cohesion was defined by the following conditions:

3. There is *a* common vision and *a* sense of belonging for all communities;
4. The diversity of people's different backgrounds and circumstances is appreciated and positively valued;
5. Those from different backgrounds have similar life opportunities;
6. Strong and positive relationships are being developed between people from different backgrounds and circumstances in the workplace, in schools and within neighbourhoods
   (Local Government Association 2002: 6, italics added).

This formula is based on the Cantle Report, which features the following points.

First, it states 'parallel lives' as one of the causes of the 2001 riots (Cantle 2001: 2.1). In Britain multicultural policy was explored mainly at regional education institutions and government organizations from the late 1970s onwards. While empowerment of ethnic groups allowed minorities to have positive identities and confidence, it resulted in segregation under the rule of the conservative government.

For instance, the 'opt-out' system and the guaranteed right of parents to choose schools under the *Education Reform Act 1988* had important implications for community segregation during the 1980s and 1990s. Under the opt-out system, public schools were entitled to opt out of local education authority control and become government grant-maintained schools. This was part of Thatcherism policy to curtail the powers of multicultural education-oriented local authorities and to centralize the system. It promoted segregation because not only could conservative white-dominated schools with an aversion to multiculturalism opt out, non-white-dominated schools were also able to opt out, prompting bilateral segregation (Sakuma 1998: 499–519).

The Cantle Report points to a negative cycle in which lack of mutual contact between ethnic groups engenders intergroup 'prejudice and fear,' which in turn create mutual 'no-go areas' (Cantle 2001: 2.16). The lack of mutual contact generates intergroup inequality and fuels the urge in disadvantaged youths in particular to resort to violence. The Cantle Report regards this as the root cause of the racial relations problem and emphasizes the importance of intergroup communication in exploring a new form of solidarity in multicultural society.

The report states that, while 'a greater knowledge of, contact between, and respect for, the various cultures' (Cantle 2001: 2.12) is needed for that purpose, 'a greater sense of citizenship, based on (*a few*) common principles' (Cantle 2001: 2.13; italics added) must form its foundation. This is the second feature of the report. Citizenship refers to the rights and responsibilities of a British citizen. The report places a special emphasis on the responsibility aspect. 'Whilst respect for different cultures is vital, it will also be essential to agree some common elements of "nationhood"' (Cantle 2001: 5.1.7). These common elements are democratic law, language and major national institutions. In particular, the common language is a pre-condition of citizenship. It enables dialogue between a white majority and non-white minorities and functions as an essential medium for shared values and purposes. Also, commitment to national symbols such as the Royal Family and the Union Jack represents a sense of belonging to the same community.

Third, however, these inclusive values should not be regarded as an attempt to undermine cultures peculiar to ethnic groups. This is rather a 'two-way process' (British Home Office 2004: 1.6), which aims for 'the promotion of cross cultural contact between different communities at all levels' (Cantle 2001: 2.17). It promotes exchanges and mixing between all groups, including churches, schools, regions and sporting organizations, transcending ethnicities and creeds. It calls on members of both the existing community and immigrant communities to change their boundaries.

The Parekh Report

In order to understand the characteristics and significance of the Cantle Report more deeply, it is useful to compare it to the Parekh Report, *The Future of Multi-Ethnic Britain* (Parekh [2000] 2002), which was published one year earlier in 2000. It was compiled by a commission set up by the Runnymede Trust and chaired by Bhikhu Parekh, a British left-wing political philosopher. Both reports were born out of Britain's deteriorating race relations and offered visions of a good society based on cohesion (trust), equality (justice) and difference (tolerance) among its citizens. However, they placed emphasis on somewhat different points.

The Parekh Report sees the crux of the race relations problem as 'racial discrimination by a majority against a minority.' Accordingly, while it takes into consideration a balance between cohesion (trust), equality (justice) and difference (tolerance) (Parekh [2000] 2002: 4.2), its main theme is the issue of diversity and equality, and cohesion is given a secondary position, although its importance is acknowledged. Based on different weightings of the three elements that are considered to be ideal, Parekh proposes five possible models:
1. 'procedural' model to play the role of a referee
2. 'nationalist' model to seek assimilation
3. 'liberal' model based on a distinction between non-cultural public domain and cultural private domain
4. 'plural' model based on recognition of cultures
5. 'separatist' model as a federal system.

The Parekh Report adopts a mixture of the liberal model and the plural model, or the liberal model with its deficiencies compensated by the plural model. In other words, it proposes that Britain should develop an awareness as 'a community of diverse communities' to recognize various cultures publicly and at the same time to guarantee the maximum rights of individuals as 'a community of citizens' (Parekh [2000] 2002: 4.2–19).

The issue of cohesion transcending communities and individuals arises here, but it is only based on the recognition of diversity and difference. The report cites two factors for broad social cohesion: 'common values' and 'symbols and ceremonies.' The common values can be separated into two categories. One is 'procedural values,' which maintain the pre-conditions of democratic dialogue such as tolerance and mutual respect. The other is 'substantive values,' which include personal freedom and humanity-wide equality and support the pursuit of a better life. These values are embodied by international human rights standards. Symbols and ceremonies are visible representations to connect immigrants and their communities to a broader society. However, what is suggested by the report as a practical example of such representations is a welcoming ceremony for immigrants, which is devoid of British cultural elements. In the vision of the Parekh Report, cohesion is perceived to be something that should be achieved through the recognition of equality and diversity (Parekh [2000] 2002: 4.29–36).

In contrast, the Cantle Report attributes the cause of worsening race relations to 'community segregation.' It points out that multicultural policies since the 1980s have undermined the concept of 'society' containing various ethnic groups and led to the deterioration of race relations. It cites a shared feeling of 'belonging to a common society' among various groups as *the first step* towards the resolution of this problem. In other words, community cohesion is considered to be the very thing that makes possible the recognition of diversity in multi-cultural society and equality among communities. Its ideal society entails 'diversity within unity' (Cantle 2005: 81).

The difference of social vision between 'a community of communities' and 'diversity within unity' is based on a difference in the recognition of the race relations problem. The former is based on the view that old racism is still a serious problem and the containment of it is fundamental for the development of a just society. Consequently, 'long-term action to tackle it [street racism] depends to an extent on greater social justice' (Parekh [2000] 2002: 5.3). The elimination of racism and the establishment of equal relations among ethnic groups based on citizenship *as a right* are the primary goals. By contrast, the latter stresses that absence of a shared sense of belonging among communities is the problem. Over the post-Race Relations Act period, blatant anti-minority discrimination may have decreased. However, inter-racial inequality and conflict are being reproduced by the people and institutions who avoid contact with minorities and by members of minority groups themselves who promote self-segregation in order to avoid alienation from mainstream society. In order to overcome this situation, the restoration of shared goals and sense of belonging based on citizenship *as a responsibility* is required.

Such different social awareness and visions are neither right nor wrong because, as many commentators have pointed out, new racism has not completely replaced old racism.[4] However, when we recognize new racism as an issue, we can appreciate a certain degree of significance of community cohesion policy as the 'diversity within unity' model. It is a new attempt to establish a sense of common identity and assumptions in order to overcome the intergroup negative cycle (lack of contact > prejudice > fear > conflict > lack of contact...), to create intergroup and interpersonal cohesion beyond community boundaries, and, as a result, to preserve multicultural society and make the best use of its dynamic energy.

Possibility of Britishness as a representation

I have discussed the significance of creating an inclusive category in order to eliminate (new) racism and the importance of the citizenship-based shared vision and goals against Britain's new racism. In this section, I examine the possibility of a socially inclusive function of a category called 'Britishness' to represent such vision and goals.

The importance of representation for the development of a community was formulated by Emile Durkheim in the context of sociology. He considered that an aesthetic form of representation of the god we worshipped was in fact a symbol of our society itself. Worshipping social representations signifies one's commitment to social morals or moral society (Durkheim 1912: 294–5). Therefore, having common representations has a crucial meaning for people in order to interact with one another peacefully.

In modern society, one of the meaningful representations to unite a broad spectrum of people is national identity. However, the issue of revitalization of nationalism or national identity has been the subject of past debates and its oppressive aspect has often been stressed. Representation marks a distinction between us and them, which is a criterion for exclusion as well as for solidarity. In that case, is the vision of 'diversity within unity' under Britain's race relations policy achievable without exclusivity in the form of conceptual representation of Britishness, or 'to be British' (British Home Office 2004: 2.1–2.10), as proposed by the government?

In answering this question, it is useful to refer to a survey study on the recognition of the concept of Britishness among people with different ethnicities conducted by ETHNOS, a team of British ethnic minority research experts, in 2005. The object of this study was to discover the role played by the concept of Britishness in the process of integration of immigrants. It used focus groups, word association and sentence completion to discover how Britishness was perceived by ninety-six people from different ethnicities, age groups and regions who resided in England, Scotland and Wales.

Looking at the conclusion first, the study revealed that the concept of Britishness did not exclude other identities and that people of ethnic minorities were positively committed to Britishness.

Interestingly, in England white people perceive themselves as English as well as British, whereas non-white people strongly perceive themselves as British but not English. In other words, the representation of Englishness has a strong element of whiteness, but Britishness is not considered to have such colour bias. Similarly, people living in England embrace both the concept of Britishness and religious identities such as Catholic or Sikh. Only Muslims gave distinct priority to their religious identity over Britishness, but they were not mutually exclusive (ETHNOS 2005: 39). The representation of Britishness has the diversity and inclusiveness for people of diverse backgrounds to be able to commit to and identify with it.[5]

What one has be careful about is that a simplistic test of allegiance for the country may stir a sense of injustice in ethnic minorities. Most of them manage to accommodate both Britishness and other identities. However, a discourse by politicians to set national identity against other identities and force people to choose one or the other will diminish their willingness to integrate. 'You really feel like an outsider when they ask you to almost choose [between Islam and Britain]. Why should I choose? Nobody asks you to choose between being a Church of England and a British' (ETHNOS 2005: 40): this comment of a man of Asian descent suggests that whether or not Britishness as a representation can be revitalized depends on the context, and a very careful approach needs to be employed to promote ethnic minorities to integrate. Any test to measure one's allegiance to Britain, such as the cricket test proposed by Conservative Party politician Norman Tebbit, poses the risk of reducing diversity in society and even damaging a sense of unity as a nation. Common values and their representations must be *concrete* enough to generate a sense of unity as a nation. At the same time, they must be *abstract* enough to facilitate agreement among people with different backgrounds.

Conclusion: In search of a new philosophy for solidarity

As I mentioned at the beginning, the politics of identity and insecurity against the backdrop of globalization are about to cause social division by community segregation. The politics of recognition of identity leads to indifference at best and conflict at worst among communities. The post-September 11 politics of insecurity is encouraging chauvinism of the far-right. In these circumstances, faint hopes that multiculturalism would be brought on by full-scale globalization following the end of the Cold War were mercilessly crushed. The old style of multiculturalism was declared dead (Kundnani 2002; Malik 2002).

However, it does not necessarily mean that we have to abandon our attempt to form society with diversity. What we need now is a new philosophy for solidarity that can bring tolerance and cohesion together. This chapter has its focus on the community cohesion policy, which emphasizes a common identity called Britishness as the shared foundation of a multicultural society. In a similar vein, liberal nationalism theory has been drawing attention since the 1990s as a political philosophy that is homological to this attempt. I shall attempt a detailed discussion another time but, in short, liberal nationalism is 'the view to recognize the diversity and uniqueness of various ethnicities while defining nationality as the important basis for liberal social relations and supporting freedom, equality and solidarity by the abstract identity of nation and citizenship based on it' (for example, Kymlicka 2001; Miller 1995; Poole 1999; Tamir 1993). Community cohesion analyzed in this study has the same origin as liberal nationalism and can be considered as one of the examples.

It has been only six years since the start of the community cohesion policy. Many issues and criticisms have arisen during this period.[6] However, the focus on new race relations policy in Britain, which has experienced assimilation policy (postwar to 1980) and multiculturalism (1980s and 1990s) in the past, will provide either positive or negative reference points in our consideration of political philosophy for the twenty-first century and new social policy models.

4 Ethnic Identities and the Sharing of Internment Memories in the Japanese American Redress Movement

Kumiko Tsuchida

Locating the issue of the Japanese American redress movement

Among the issues surrounding postwar reparations, little is known either internationally or in Japan about the significance of the redress movement in the United States through which Japanese American victims of internment demanded an apology and compensation from the federal government. The Japanese American redress movement represents an additional perspective to the Second World War and is another illustration of how a war can affect the average person.

The Japanese American redress movement[1] refers to the movement that was started in the 1970s by Japanese Americans demanding an apology and compensation for the damages they suffered under the internment policy enforced during the Second World War.[2] Under the Constitution of the United States, the term 'redress' refers to the demand for the indemnification of damages, or rectification or elimination of a wrongdoing grounded on a citizen's right to petition against the government. As a result of the redress movement, the *Civil Liberties Act of 1988* was established.[3] Under this Act, those who were recognized as victims obtained an official apology and monetary compensation of $20,000 per person.

Since the Second World War, various movements have been arising throughout the world and demanding redress for damages suffered through past injustices. Some of these have succeeded in obtaining an apology, or both an apology and compensation.

Compensation granted to particular groups that suffered damages can largely be classified into two types. The first is postwar reparations. Most notable of these is probably the compensation made by the German government and businesses to those who were victims of the Nazi regime. The second type is apologies and compensations made for injustices and policies carried out against particular races or ethnic groups. It includes, for example, apologies and compensation made towards indigenous groups whose cultures and livelihoods were destroyed through assimilation policies carried out by the dominating group. The number of apologies and compensations made for past injustices increased—and the activities of movements led by victim groups making related demands intensified—during the 1990s (Yamamoto 1999). In reference to the repeated apologies made by governments, businesses and sometimes religious organizations of various countries, the legal scholar Yamamoto uses the term 'apology crazy' (Yamamoto 1999: 3).[4] In fact, the Japanese American redress movement was not merely a movement demanding postwar reparations; it was also significant as a movement led by a minority group to realize its rights. It had a strong impact on movements led by other ethnic minority groups within the United States in demand of their rights.[5]

Takezawa (1994) brings to our attention the fact that, when viewed from the perspective of ethnicity theory, the Japanese American redress movement represented the process of (re)gaining the ethnic pride that was bruised as a result of the internment policy. After all, not only did the wartime internment policy cause financial losses, it also brought about the dissolution of ethnic pride among those of Japanese ancestry residing in the United States. This tangible and intangible loss was first made public during the 1981 public hearings held by the Commission on Wartime Relocation and Internment of Civilians (CWRIC), the presidential study commission on the internment policy. Moreover, as Maki, Kitano and Berthold (1999) point out (based on their comprehensive analysis of the movement), the study commission, through its investigative activities, became a strong authority on the legislative process of compensation Bills. The study commission report, based on public hearings and investigative activities, later gave legitimacy to the movement's demands and formed the basis for establishing laws regarding compensation.

The public hearings saw Japanese Americans who denounced the internment policy as unjust and demanded redress, as well as those who supported the internment policy, take a stand in the witness box. However, it became apparent during this time that there were differences in opinion in terms of how to interpret the internment and redress movement, even among the Japanese American organizations that promoted the movement. The focus of the public hearings in relation to this point thus turned to the memories of the internment and to how the internment policy should be defined. In other words, the public hearings became a forum where those holding different perspectives argued over the memories of the internment policy in their attempt to define the appropriateness of the internment policy and legitimacy of the redress movement.[6]

So far, the focus of existing research on the redress movement has been limited to analyzing either the legislative process of compensation Bills (Hatamiya 1993) or the movement's political process (Maki, Kitano and Berthold 1999). The significance that the participants of the movement attached to the internment and the movement, however, was left outside the scope of study. Meanwhile, the historian A. Y. Murray made a comparative study of the three Japanese American organizations that propelled the movement forward, and focused on the differences in the significance that those groups attached to the internment and the movement (Murray 1995). Yet she did not touch on the implications posed by the movement's complexity.

This chapter takes existing research (especially Murray's research) into account while focusing on the plurality and complexity of the different memories of the internment policy held by each of those involved, and reassesses the role played by the 1981 public hearings in relation to the movement. Through this, the chapter then examines the underlying importance of the legal system in relation to movements promoted by minority groups demanding their rights. In doing so, it focuses on analyzing the National Coalition for Redress/Reparations (NCRR), one of the organizations involved in the redress movement. This is because NCRR's activities played an important role in uncovering the plurality and complexity involved in defining the significance of the internment policy and the movement. Also, since its early stages, the principles behind NCRR's activities have always carried the potential of seeing the movement as something more than a demand for rights specifically for the Japanese Americans.

First, an overview of the formative period of the Japanese American redress movement is provided in order to clarify the point at issue for the subsequent analysis. This is followed by an elucidation of the differences and correlation between the organizations involved in the redress movement, and focuses on the presidential study commission on the interment policy. Taking this into consideration, the chapter then examines the significance of the diversity of memories of the internment policy and the movement that became apparent over the course of the 1981 public hearings. Finally, the above analysis is be used as the basis for assessing the role played by the public hearings and its importance in relation to the movement.

Development of the redress movement and the 1981 public hearings

Dissolution of the ethnic community through the internment

The attack on Pearl Harbor in 1941 presented a direct motive for the forced relocation of Japanese Americans, which was carried out under the 1942 Executive Order 9066.[7] The order was justified as a 'military necessity.' After being freed from the relocation centres, the Japanese Americans vigorously pushed forward to rebuild their lives, and, as a result, succeeded in achieving a certain degree of improvement in their social standing.[8] However, it must be noted that as they were being freed, the War Relocation Authority urged the Japanese Americans not to interact exclusively within the Japanese American community as they did prior to the war, but to 'become integrated into the larger communities' (CWRIC 1997: 206). In other words, they were urged to actively assimilate into the wider American society. Thus, the dispersion of Japanese Americans was promoted and resulted in the dilution of their ethnic cohesion in the postwar era.

Moreover, internment served to engrain the direct victims (mainly first and second generations) with a sense of guilt and shame for being Japanese American. After the war, a majority of these victims hardly spoke of their experiences and tended to bury even their memories of the internment in their attempts to avoid passing on their negative views of their ethnicity to the next generation (Kitayama 1993). Many of the first- and second-generation Japanese Americans aged or even died without ever speaking out about the internment. Consequently, many memories on the internment were not shared between the generations who were victims of it and the postwar generations (Tsuchida 2006).[9]

Demands for redress and the Japanese American community

How, then, did the demands for redress develop, and how was it posed to the Japanese American community when there existed a disconnection between the generations in their understanding of the internment policy? According to Murray (1995), the civil rights movement and the Vietnam anti-war movement, as well as the so-called 'ethnic revival,' had an impact on historians, who then presented research questioning the reality and justification of the internment policy. This helped the younger second generation and the third generation to gain an understanding of the internment policy and formed the social basis for making the memories of the internment policy publicly known.

The demand for redress was first raised within the Japanese American community during the 1970 national convention of the Japanese American Citizens League (JACL).[10] During this convention JACL passed a resolution calling for a redress, and the resolution was confirmed at the following conventions. However, the movement failed to take off because many Japanese Americans were either critical of, or indifferent towards, the demands for a redress (Maki, Kitano and Berthold 1999: 64–8). These attitudes were prevalent for two reasons. First, the Japanese American community was split between those who were for and those who were against demanding compensation. Second, they anticipated opposition towards the demands from the wider American society.[11]

Due to this backdrop, the issue for the various individuals and organizations that wanted to promote the movement was how to involve the first and second generations who were direct victims of the internment policy, as well as the general Japanese American community, which included the later generations. Faced with the reality that the different generations within the community did not even share a common understanding of the internment policy, even the issue of who would lead the movement became a problem. In order to overcome this issue, it was necessary to first present the points to be claimed in the demands for redress to the Japanese American community and the wider community, as well as to let the movement take root within the Japanese American community. This would form the basis of mustering support from both inside and outside the Japanese American community.

Study commission and public hearings

In 1981 public hearings were held by CWRIC, the presidential study commission, which was established in 1980. It was then that the demands for redress were raised as an issue across the Japanese American community, as well as the wider community.[12] The establishment of the study commission was based on the proposals made by Japanese American members of Congress to the JACL redress committee. The strategy was to make the existence of the internment policy widely known within the broader American society, and thus minimize the anticipated opposition towards the demands for redress. Initially, JACL had planned to propose the Bill directly and seek redress legislation, but it accepted the plan to establish a study commission. Instead, it decided to urge Congress to establish the commission. Thus, the Bill for creating a study commission was passed in 1980, and public hearings were then held in ten cities across the United States in 1981.

The public hearings ran for twenty days and involved over 750 witnesses. The witnesses consisted of direct victims of the internment policy and government officials involved in executing the policy. In addition, various non-Japanese American organizations and politicians supporting the demands for redress, as well as supporters of the internment policy who opposed the demands for redress, testified in accordance with their perspectives. It can be said that the public hearings created a forum that presented an intricate blend of diverse interpretations of the internment and the movement by the supporters and opponents of redress, direct victims, and the younger generations who were not victims.

In light of the above discussion, the public hearings were seen as having the potential to fill the gap between the different generations of the Japanese American community in their understanding of the internment policy, and to help form a constituency for the movement by uncovering the reality of the internment.[13] Also, the public hearings were expected to function as a forum for encouraging the wider American society to question the justification behind the internment policy, and make the redress campaign publicly known. How, then, did the three leading organizations involved in the movement perceive the public hearings, and what kind of approach did they follow? Furthermore, how did the various organizations relate the internment during the public hearings, and what significance did they attach to the movement? These issues are analyzed in further detail in the following sections.

Redress movement organizations and the presidential study commission

As JACL shifted its activities from the legislation of the redress Bill to the establishment of the study commission, new redress movement organizations were launched within the Japanese American community. The first to be started in 1979 was the National Council for Japanese American Redress (NCJAR). In 1980 this was followed by the launch of NCRR.[14] This section analyzes the differences and relations between these three organizations by focusing on their responses to the 1981 public hearings.

JACL

As the largest of the three organizations, let us first examine JACL's approach to the movement. JACL was established in 1929 by second-generation Japanese Americans. Many of the founding members were highly educated and were professionals such as doctors and lawyers. The founding members considered JACL to be an organization created by *American citizens* who were interested in the welfare and political and social improvement of Americans with Japanese ancestry.[15]

As the only organization representing the Japanese American community, JACL took a cooperative stance towards the internment policy during the war. Specifically, the JACL leadership agreed to cooperate with the eviction and incarceration orders, to provide support to Japanese Americans to relocate to internment facilities, to maintain communication with government agencies, and to conduct public relations activities to demonstrate Japanese American loyalty towards the United States. JACL's underlying motive was that it believed that if the Japanese Americans could demonstrate their loyalty towards American society and the federal government, the government would surely respond by treating them sympathetically and in goodwill. JACL also agreed to allow the government to segregate those identified as subversive at designated internment camps. The policies adopted by JACL at the time were in line with its intent to prevent Japanese Americans who were already becoming targets of anti-Japanese sentiment (prevalent within the wider American society) from being put in an even more difficult situation (Maki, Kitano and Berthold 1999: 34). Notwithstanding, many within the Japanese American community remained distrustful of these decisions, causing JACL to be a target of criticism even after the war ended.

Nevertheless, as previously discussed, it was JACL that first campaigned for redress. By 1980 JACL had 113 chapters across the United States, with approximately 25,000 members, and was the largest organization within the Japanese American community (Murray 2001). Deep-rooted criticisms were still being made against it from within a section of the Japanese American community. Yet, in the midst of this, JACL succeeded in bringing about the formation of CWRIC because it had placed lobbyists in Washington DC and had forged connections with political elites from Congress and other places by the time the movement was being formed. That said, opinion was divided within JACL regarding the redress movement—namely, on whether it was appropriate to seek compensation in addition to an apology. The organization tended to split in two between proponents and opponents of this matter (Murray 1995).

JACL's proposed formation of a study commission (CWRIC) seems to have been an attempt to minimize both the difference in opinion on compensation demands within JACL and criticism from the wider American society against the demand. From JACL's point of view, the formation of the study commission was a 'carefully planned strategy' aimed at wheeling the redress movement down the road of success (Murray 1995: 148). J. Tsujimura, JACL's chairman at the time, emphasized that the investigative activities carried out by the study commission would benefit not only Japanese Americans but all Americans. He saw it as an investigation of government competence in dealing with a nation-wide emergency situation.[16]

NCJAR

NCJAR remained consistent from its inception in its continuing criticism of JACL. NCJAR was created in 1979, mainly by second-generation Japanese Americans in Chicago, as a means to promote a redress movement that was different from that of JACL. Most of the central members consisted of white-collar Japanese Americans. NCJAR published a newsletter in order to raise funds for its activities, and its readership rose to 1,500 people. However, it did not succeed in establishing any chapters (Murray 1995: 165).

NCJAR was a strong proponent of the redress movement, and was forging a collaborative relationship with JACL members who voiced their opposition towards the study commission at JACL's Seattle office. NCJAR's first activity was 'to test the legislative branch of government' (Hohri 1984: 50). In other words, it did not want to simply wait for a report to be made by the study commission, but wanted to directly propose a Bill to Congress demanding redress. NCJAR introduced a Bill demanding redress with the cooperation of Washington's Congressman Michael Lowry. The Lowry Bill was reviewed by the subcommittee, together with the study commission formation Bill. The Lowry Bill was scrapped, and only the study commission Bill was laid before the plenary session. After CWRIC public hearings, NCJAR filed a class action lawsuit against the federal government demanding compensation.[17]

After NCJAR abandoned the legislative approach with the scrapping of the Lowry Bill, it could no longer ignore the investigative activities of CWRIC. Nevertheless, NCJAR criticized the study commission Bill promoted by JACL as nothing more than 'a more publicly palatable alternative, [which was] to be opposed to efforts at a direct challenge to [the] nation for restitution under the Constitution' (Hohri 1984: 45).[18] William Hohri, a second-generation Japanese American who was a former internee himself, harshly criticized JACL's study commission approach as a 1970s repeat of the compromising stance taken by JACL in 1942 (Hohri 1984: 45).

With this in mind, Hohri feared that the public hearings may hurt the Japanese American community, as 'such a procedure would impose further humiliation—publicly forcing us to relive a cruel degradation [i.e. internment].'[19] NCJAR felt that the educational purpose of making the internment policy publicly known and the issuance of an official apology were not good enough to justify the investigative activities of the study commission. Not only that, but it was seen as 'an affront to our dignity as [US] citizens.'[20] NCJAR felt that the priced paid by the Japanese Americans during the war was unfair, and was reparable only if the perpetrator, that is the government, paid monetary compensation.

NCRR

Most of the central members of NCRR were relatively young second- and third-generation Japanese Americans. Many of them could hardly remember the internment, as they were either very young when they were incarcerated, or were born after the war. Although many of the central figures were relatively highly educated, it generally consisted of Japanese Americans from a variety of social backgrounds. NCRR is an amalgamation of twenty-one organizations,[21] which had approximately 1,000 members in the early part of the 1980s, and grew to 8,000 members by the end of the decade.

The central figures of NCRR either participated in the civil rights movement, the student movement and the Vietnam anti-war movement of the 1960s and 1970s, or grew up during this era. It was a generation that received the full impact of these movements. Among the members were many who had been actively involved in the intensifying Asian American movement during the time of the so-called 'ethnic revival.'

NCRR, like NCJAR, opposed JACL's campaign policy. Yet, while JACL and NCJAR openly confronted each other on the basis of ideological differences, NCRR endeavored to play the coordinating role between organizations involved in the movement (Kitayama 1993: 49–50). NCRR's members questioned JACL's top-down approach and authoritarian organizational structure; this was their main concern, rather than their distrust towards JACL that evolved out of the war.

When NCRR was initially established, its members were also critical of the formation of the study commission. Their underlying reason was that the formation of a study commission meant that the redress campaign would be stretched over a long period of time. Meanwhile, the first- and second-generation Japanese Americans who were the actual victims and target of redress would probably die before they saw the end of the campaign. Consequently, some of the members criticized the study commission's activities as a waste of time. They argued that the injustice of the internment policy was plainly self-evident, and objected to letting the victims take on the burden of proof. However, a debate over NCRR's position on the study commission, including the public hearings, did take place within the organization. The outcome saw NCRR shift its position. It decided to utilize the public hearings in line with its conclusion that the hearings were 'a focus of activity [to demand redress] in Japanese [American] communities;' moreover, it was seen as 'an important vehicle' in publicly announcing the redress demands claimed by NCRR (1980: 5).

NCRR strategized to have the voice of Japanese Americans recorded in American history.[22] NCRR posited the public hearings as 'a very important means of educating the public about the concentration camp and the impact it made on the Japanese American community.'[23] Furthermore, rather than a place to assert the sense of loyalty felt by Japanese Americans, NCRR saw the public hearings as a place for non-elite or 'common/ordinary Japanese Americans' who had been victims to speak out, in their own words, on their experiences of the internment and the impact it had on them. It was a place for them to demand redress in the form they sought.[24]

With JACL in mind, NCRR opposed having only one section of the Japanese American community speak on the internment policy and redress demand. In its campaign, NCRR held to the principles of promoting participation by non-elite Japanese Americans in the redress movement and public hearings. As such, to NCRR it appeared as if JACL showed less interest in its approach to the public hearings involving non-elite Japanese Americans.[25] JACL seemed to emphasize the importance of internment policy investigation and analysis conducted by experts, and testimonies made by JACL executive leaders and those in influence. NCRR members were of the opinion that history is more powerful when told in the words of those who actually experienced it, rather than basing it on explanations provided by experts (Murray 1995: 217). Non-elite Japanese Americans were precisely the ones who had been placed in the internment camps, and who had suffered not only material damages, but also psychological and cultural damages.

Accordingly, NCRR laid particular emphasis on taking a grassroots approach. One of the principles that dictated NCRR's activities was to use a grassroots approach to allow members of the Japanese American community to participate in the movement regardless of their social standing and educational background. Indeed, NCRR's activities did put many non-elite Japanese Americans on the witness stand. According to a representative of NCRR at the time, the grassroots activities were significant in relation to the redress movement in the following way:

> They are the most important people to tell the stories...it's more important for people who went through the experience [to] share what it is. And that's what NCRR was trying to do, to organize people, to empower the people, to share the [camp] stories, to get them [to] be active in the campaign...That makes you a part of the redress campaign...[what is] important [is] that NCRR organizes grassroots, because they are the voice of community.[26]

As discussed above, all three organizations posited the public hearings in different ways. All three organizations agreed that the internment policy violated the United States Constitution. However, all three organizations approached the movement in different ways. Let us now examine the significance that the three organizations attached to the internment and the movement. The following section again uses testimonies given at the public hearings to analyze this point.

Plurality and complexity of internment memories as seen in the 1981 public hearings

JACL

As previously mentioned, JACL has always leaned towards highlighting the sense of loyalty and patriotism that Japanese Americans have towards the United States. This has been the emphasis not only in relation to the public hearings, but ever since the war, as well as in the redress movement as a whole (Murray 1995). This is especially evident in the testimony given by Mike Masaoka, who worked as a prominent JACL member and a lobbyist for a long period of time following the Second World War.

> Most importantly, for the sake of al[l] Americans and free people elsewhere, as well as our children and our children's children, we want the record to show that under the most extreme demands of our government, we demonstrated a courage, a loyalty and…a faith…[27]

Here, the internment policy is seen in the following light: the compliance and the sacrifice that the Japanese Americans showed towards the internment orders served as testimony to their loyalty to the United States during the war. Japanese American loyalty and patriotism was further underscored by the great achievements and sacrifices made by the 442nd Regiment Combat Team formed by Japanese Americans during the war.[28] Furthermore, the sense of tragedy behind the internment experience was used to form an image of the Japanese Americans as a group worthy to receive compensation from the federal government. Once the Japanese Americans were posited in this light as *worthy Americans*, the internment policy was depicted as a violation of the Constitution in that it was executed without the due process guaranteed by the United States Constitution. It was argued that the Japanese Americans had 'no hearings, not even by hearing boards let alone the courts.'[29] In the eyes of JACL, the redress movement was none other than a campaign to highlight the fact that Japanese Americans were indeed Americans who should be protected by the United States Constitution.

NCJAR

How did NCJAR, which was critical of CWRIC and its public hearings, posit the redress movement? While JACL posited Japanese American compliance with the internment policy as a testimony of loyalty, NCJAR drove home the point that the federal government failed to protect Japanese Americans despite the fact that they were American citizens. William Hohri, an NCJAR representative, took to the witness stand during the Washington DC public hearings in

1981. Before anything else, he criticized JACL's approach, which emphasized Japanese American loyalty by citing the heroism of Japanese American soldiers as follows:

> it is not appropriate to make continued reference to their [i.e. Japanese American combat team] bravery as though it were necessary for our being accepted as full citizens. We are all citizens by reason of birth and by law, not by the blood sacrificed by our brothers on the battlefield.[30]

From this we can glean the following points. Japanese Americans in the United States are *American citizens* to be protected by the United States Constitution regardless of their ancestry.[31] The execution of such an unjustifiable policy on such a group, and the failure, thus far, of the federal government in making reparations for the losses suffered under the policy, represented a rift within American democracy. Another point that needs to be clarified is that NCJAR argued that Japanese Americans were also pillars of American democracy precisely because they were American citizens. With this in mind, Hohri posited the redress movement as follows:

> We believe that a small group...can act to repair a breach in our democratic society, despite the best efforts by our government to intimidate and silence us. Our movement has become part of our legacy to America, our contribution to American democracy (Hohri 1984: 225).

NCRR

NCRR also agreed with JACL and NCJAR on the point that the internment policy violated the Constitution in that it targeted a specific group of people in its execution without any justifiable reason. However, NCRR perceived the losses from the internment policy in a different light to the other two organizations.

As an organization that sprouted from a community support organization in the 1970s, NCRR found that the scars from the internment that remained unhealed were at the root of the issues faced by the community at the time, such as poverty, welfare for the elderly and youth drug abuse. Additionally, the redevelopment plan of Little Tokyo in Los Angeles, which became a point of dispute in the 1970s, was what actually propelled NCRR's predecessor to involve itself in the redress movement. When the redevelopment plan was being executed, the low-income population was once again forced to evacuate. Members of the community support organization drew a comparison between this and the forced evacuation in 1942 (Kitayama 1993: 40; Murray 1995: 211). In other words, evicting a population in accordance with the redevelopment plan was, as in the forced evacuation of 1942, an act of community destruction by the government/public administration. In their eyes, it was grounded on racism, prioritization of financial interests and contempt for minority rights (Kitayama 1993: 47).

Based on the above, during the public hearings NCRR underscored the cultural and psychological damages suffered by the Japanese American community as a result of the internment policy. In NCRR's view, the impact of the internment policy could not be measured merely by the financial losses that were incurred. The internment policy intensified the sense of guilt and inferiority held by Japanese Americans regarding their ethnicity. The casualties it claimed did not stop at those who were actually incarcerated, but extended to Japanese Americans of subsequent generations. In addition, the internment destroyed the Japanese American community: it caused the community to lose its ethnic identity and to feel shame and guilt for being Japanese American, and disrupted the process of cultural succession. NCRR found that a redress was essential as a means to set the Japanese Americans free from these issues.

Additionally, due to their understanding of the damages caused by the internment as described above, NCRR members even opposed the tone of argument that attempted to posit the internment as an 'event in the past.' This sentiment can be clearly felt in the following testimony given by an NCRR member.

> Many of us go to work every single day—gardeners, produce workers, clericals, small business people. We are building our lives after the war [that we had lost during the war].[32]

According to NCRR, demanding a redress from the federal government was primarily a legitimate right of anyone who suffered under an unjust policy carried out by the federal government.[33] For NCRR, participation in the public hearings did not mean going 'into the hearings with bowed heads, "presenting pleas to the [study] Commission"' (NCRR 1981: 2). NCRR argued that any compensation paid by the government was by no means a 'gift or welfare:' instead, it was because the Japanese Americans suffered unjustifiable damages deserving of such compensation money (NCRR 1981).

Since the beginning of its involvement, NCRR defined the redress movement in both a narrow and broad sense (Tsuchida 2006). In the narrow sense of the word, redress signified holding the federal government responsible for the unjust nature of the internment policy, and for redressing the damages suffered, not only by the direct victims of the internment policy, but also by the Japanese American community as a whole. Moreover, the members of NCRR were of the opinion that this could not be achieved only by a handful of influential people, but that to succeed it required the participation of people of diverse backgrounds in the movement. With this principle guiding their activities, NCRR members called for as many Japanese Americans to participate in the public hearings as possible, and thus led many into the halls where the public hearings were held.

The broad meaning of redress that NCRR aimed for was 'supporting others who have or are suffering from unjust actions taken by the U. S. government' (NCRR 1980: 1).[34] NCRR saw redress as 'a part of a broader motion in which other nationalities are also involved in seeking justice.'[35] It was not something that should end once the Japanese Americans received an official apology and monetary compensation. Instead, it was something to be pursued in solidarity with other ethnic minority groups who suffered under unjust policies.

CWRIC's report and recommendations

In what way did the CWRIC's report and recommendations incorporate the diverse memories of forced relocation that were given as testimonies during the public hearings as discussed above? Let us now briefly examine this final point. In 1983 CWRIC issued a study report entitled *Personal Justice Denied*. First of all, it pointed out that the internment policy was not justifiable, even in the light of military necessity.[36] The report indicated that the internment policy was a 'grave personal injustice' carried out by the federal government against Japanese Americans without any due process (CWRIC 1994: 459). CWRIC also condemned the fact that the internment policy was not forged by only one group of government-related personnel, but that the policy determination was more or less supported and approved by the whole political spectrum. What is more, it did not arouse any continued or active opposition within American society (CWRIC 1994: 460). The internment policy was concluded as an illegitimate policy carried out by the government against American citizens and permanent residents who should have been protected under the Constitution. It was a violation of the Constitution. On these grounds CWRIC recommended Congress to issue an official apology and pay compensation in the amount of $20,000 to each survivor of the internment policy (CWRIC 1997: 462–4).

The report and recommendations reflected the views shared by the three organizations in its positioning of the internment policy. However, it did not go beyond this to incorporate the expansive redress sought by NCRR. That said, the report and recommendations formed the basis for demanding redress in the movement as it further evolved from this point. It is important to highlight, at this time, the following point: the debate that questioned the unconstitutional and illegitimate nature of the internment policy was not merely limited to a remonstration made by the Japanese American community—it evolved into a debate shared by the federal government and American society.

Conclusion

Finally, with the above discussion in mind, let us identify the significance of the 1981 public hearings within the redress movement from the perspective of giving meaning to the memories of internment and the movement.

Disclosing and publicizing the issue

First, the public hearings held by CWRIC functioned as a forum for disclosing the issues underlying the redress movement. It was made plain in the hearings that during the policy determination and execution process, the internment policy was carried out against Japanese Americans without any due legal process. Namely, the public hearings highlighted the illegitimacy, or unconstitutional nature, of the internment policy. This gave legitimacy to the redress demand made by the Japanese Americans. That is, if an American citizen suffers loss under a government policy in violation of the Constitution, then it is the citizen's natural right as an American to demand reparation. It follows that the government is required by the Constitution to make reparations.

Making evident the fact that the injustice and illegitimacy of the interment policy and the legitimacy of the redress demands were based on the Constitution carried with it a broader significance. The issue was posited as one that needed to be grappled by American society as a whole. In this sense, it became a highly public issue within American society. Consequently, not only did the public hearings disclose the issue of the internment policy and redress demand, it also functioned as a forum for publicizing these issues. Furthermore, the role played by the United States Constitution must also be highlighted. The United States Constitution acted as a basis for questioning the legitimacy of the internment policy and as a basis for policy formation and its execution. In turn, it also acted as a basis for raising redress demands.

Blending and sharing of memories

Second, the public hearings created so-called 'shared memories.' The reality of the internment policies was revealed through the public hearings to the broader American society, which until then had remained ignorant of it. The fact that the report prepared by CWRIC confirmed the matter meant that the history of the Japanese American internment was added to the United States history of the Pacific War. In other words, it required a rewriting of American history. It signified the 'reconstruction of memories' between the Japanese community, which represented the minority group, and mainstream American society, which represented the majority.[37] However, it did not suggest a sense of assimilation in which the history of the Japanese American community was to be incorporated into the history of the majority. Instead, it suggested a transformation of the relationship between the two parties in their memories of the war.

On another front, the public hearings brought about the 'reconstruction of memory' for the Japanese American community between the different generations and social strata. It thus provided an opportunity for the movement to take root within the community. Nevertheless, the testimonies given at the public hearings presented memories of the internment, which were plural and complex in nature. On this basis, the 'reconstruction of memories' within the Japanese American community can be understood as none other than a blending of memories with diverse narratives. In other words, this 'blending of memories' allowed the different orientations within the Japanese American community to come together temporarily to push the movement forwards without actually unifying them. This formed the basis for the movement to mobilize the direct victims and those who were not direct victims. NCRR's activities were particularly instrumental in this area.

Reconstruction of ethnic identity

The public hearings were significant in a third way in relation to the reconstruction of ethnic pride for Japanese Americans. As the injustice of the internment policy was made evident through the public hearings, it served to restore the ethnic pride of Japanese Americans and recognized their ethnic identity. In this, we need to draw our attention to the fact that the public hearings created an opportunity for Japanese Americans to assert themselves as 'American citizens' of Japanese ethnicity. This point was also confirmed in the report. Namely, that the internment policy targeted American citizens and permanent residents who represented a group that was protected under the Constitution of the United States. In this instance, the federal Constitution functioned as the basis for identity formation as an American citizen. It also functioned as a nodal point for the two dimensions of identity formation and institutional formation to meet within the redress movement. Specifically, the Constitution, first, formed the basis of identity formation as an *American citizen*, and, second, functioned as a basis for law-making and the legal system in relation to the appropriateness of the internment policy, which was carried out against these American citizens.

As seen above, the study commission, which was officially formed in accordance with the system, and its 1981 public hearings meant that the debate on the internment and redress demands expanded beyond the Japanese American community to include the broader American society. This acted to transform relations between the two parties. Meanwhile, we need to also draw our attention to the fact that Japanese Americans were forced to reassert themselves as Americans based on the Constitution. It is believed that these points offer important clues for analyzing the social conditions affecting ethnic minorities in the United States, particularly the minority movements and the state of the legal system.

Acknowledgments

This paper is based on a study conducted by the writer in 2004. I would like to use this opportunity to express my deep gratitude to all the members of NCRR who offered their assistance.

5 Global Civil Society and Local Protest: Is an Alternative to 'Alter-globalization' Possible?

Nanako Inaba and Naoto Higuchi

Introduction

It has been almost a decade since the large-scale anti-World Trade Organization (WTO) demonstration that occurred during the WTO Seattle Ministerial Conference in 1999. Since then, such demonstrations have become the norm, as anti-globalization marches are staged wherever a major intergovernmental meeting is held. Opportunities for international exchange between various social movements such as the World Social Forum (WSF) have markedly increased. 'Globalization and social movements' has become a major research theme and a wide range of studies—from individual case studies to quantitative analyses—have been conducted about the conditions of relevant movements (e.g. della Porta and Tarrow 2004; Imig and Tarrow 2001; Keck and Sikkink 1998). In terms of theory, concepts in sociology and international politics such as 'political opportunity structure,' 'transnational diffusion' and 'boomerang effect' are applied in the development of frameworks that can be used for analysis.[1]

The main purpose of this chapter is to discuss the divergence of social movements in two directions. Such divergence was brought about by globalization in the light of these advances in research. One direction is the appearance of transnational social movement organizations (TSMOs), which embody the sudden rise of global civil society (GCS). The appearance of TSMOs has prompted lobbying activities on global issues. These movements are attracting interest in the fields of political process approaches to social movement study and international relations study and are regarded as the driving force for alter-globalization to counteract neoliberal globalism. In fact, the number of transnational non-government organizations (NGOs) increased rapidly during the 1990s after the end of the Cold

War. According to Smith (1997), the number of international NGOs increased from 183 in the early 1970s to 631 in the early 1990s.

The other direction in which globalization is pushing social movements is in the development of local movements whose activities are not as spectacular as the activities of TSMOs, but, nevertheless, that are grappling with problems caused by globalization. These movements have the same anti-globalism stance as TSMOs but they are not the subject envisaged by the argument on the alter-globalization movement. Globalization involves the exclusion of subjects (usually including local movements) that are locked inside localized spaces in the first place. Although they both are movements against neoliberal globalization, TSMOs with cross-border activities and social movements rooted in localized spaces must have different enemies and goals. This chapter focuses on these points of potential disagreement between them and attempts to highlight difficulties inherent in the 'globalization and social movements' theme— difficulties in trying to achieve solidarity as the gap between global players and local resistance increases.

Different agents in different theories

TSMOs as agents for global civil society

In discussing globalization and social movements, GCS is a key concept for one side. GCS is defined as a 'slice of associational life that exists above the individual and below the state, but also across national boundaries' (Wapner 1996: 4). It is said to attempt to challenge the nation-state system 'from below' and to reconstruct international politics from the side of civil society.[2] The theory of GCS that analyzes social movements on this premise is closely linked to the rising tide of criticism that questions the premise of international relations theories led by the realist. At the same time, GCS is even expected to act as 'vanguards' of social change in the situation where the state's ability to respond to global issues is questioned (Beier and Crosby 1998: 270–2).

Yet, many have questioned how well GCS functions. In the absence of a global state, GCS theory does not necessarily assume a strict corresponding relation between the state and civil society (O'Brien et al. 2000: 13). Protection of the individual's rights may be the source of legitimacy of GCS but we must rely on state sovereignty to guarantee the rights for the time being. This creates a paradoxical situation in which GCS is founded on state sovereignty (Baker 2002). Also, there are hardly any channels for civil society actors to participate in the international political system even though the sovereign state system is on the verge of a crisis. On the other hand, GCS has served as an infrastructure for the establishment of international norms such as the concept of human rights and the change of policies in various countries (Risse, Ropp and Sikkink 1999). However, the influence of GCS is measured by the extent to which its international norms are accepted by each actor. Although international NGOs have been given consultative status at the United Nations since the 1990s, they only play a ceremonial role in presenting the chairperson with the NGO declaration of the NGO forum, as the voice of civil societies, prior to the plenary session of the General Assembly.

Nevertheless, GCS, with non-governmental actors as the main subjects, is worthy of note because it urges conventional international politics to reconsider their state-centred paradigm (Lipschutz 1992: 390–1). GCS is not a monolithic concept at the academic level and has more than one basis for the argument. In terms of doctrinal history, it is deeply related to liberalism, constructionism and Marxism (especially Gramsci's theory of hegemony) in international politics (MacDonald 1994). The liberalist approach assumes separation of the state and civil society and allows some scope for analysis of the role of non-state actors. The constructionist approach has a connection with civil society theory on the point that it criticizes the realist who claims that 'power is the norm' and analyzes norm setting in international politics. The Marxist approach regards civil society as an ambiguous arena of confrontation between intervention by the state and reform of the system by resistance, and recognizes the possibility that civil society can counteract the formation of a world order by states.

There is more than one theoretical ground for GCS theory, as above, but there is little difference of opinion as far as its arenas and specific driving forces are concerned. In short, the arenas range from multinational decision-making processes, such as the United Nations and other international institutions, to non-institutional politics, such as international boycotts against corporations in a broad sense. It is considered that TSMOs (and their networks) are the driving forces (Boli and Thomas 1997; Sikkink and Smith 2002; Smith 1997).

Lack of social movements in the Touraine school

By contrast, new social movement theory does not attach importance to TSMOs as much as GCS theory does. The new social movement theory here refers broadly to the approach that has as its central question the relationship between the transformation of modernity and social movements, and it is not limited to the argument put forward by European scholars such as Touraine, Habermas, Offe and Melucci during the 1980s. New social movement theory flourished during the 1980s but in reality such social movements defined by Touraine have since stagnated.

Among the new social movement theorists, it was the Touraine school that analyzed these changing realities while maintaining its own theoretical framework. Social movements in the 1970s primarily centred around protest against state intervention in the life-world. Since the 1980s the criticism of 'dependent participation' that was initially put forward by Touraine receded into the background due to the emergence of the more pressing issue of social exclusion caused by racial discrimination and poverty. In addition, the politics of identity concerning ethnic minorities began to surface, and narrow-minded nationalism became conspicuous in ethnic conflicts such as the Yugoslav civil war and in the emergence of the extreme right. Accordingly, the Touraine school turned its attention towards the fact that modernity, which was supposed to create independent individuals, ended up returning to communal society. In *Fragmented Society? Discussion on Multiculturalism* (Wieviorka 1997) and *Can We Live Together? Equality and Difference* (Touraine 1997), the Touraine school asked whether the assertion of cultural identity could form social movements without fragmenting civil society. According to Wieviorka, who is regarded as Touraine's successor, TSMOs do not have any 'novelty' under the present conditions from such perspectives. He considers that TSMOs are most likely to become institutionalized. Other anti-globalization movements risk being absorbed into an extreme-left ideology or retreating into closed identity groups with no universal appeal (Wieviorka 2003: 45–9).

With regard to TSMOs, since international NGOs were practically incorporated into the United Nations upon receiving consultative status (even though they have not been institutionalized in a strict sense), they are said to have lost the dynamism to protest (Wieviorka 2003: 47). The lifeline for international NGOs that have expert teams that can rival international institutions and governments is to propose projects or arguments to rival those of international institutions. However, in return for their participation as NGOs with consultative status, they conduct their activities only in the same arena as the international institutions that are supposed to be the target of their criticisms and they end up being incorporated into the activities of governing bodies at either the national or supranational level. They lose dynamism in their opposition, their protest aspect, grassroots mobilization and radicalism and, as a result, the projects and arguments of TSMOs tend to become constrained in their ability to raise conflicts (Wieviorka 2003: 47). Under the present conditions, no TSMOs have been able to demonstrate the level of ability to raise conflicts expected by new social movement theory.

So, let us look at the argument of the Touraine school to see which actors are considered by new social movement theory to be subjects in the globalization age. Touraine (1969) once stated that conflicts of post-industrial society would emanate from the center of society, and research on anti-nuclear movements reflected such expectations. However, the Touraine school turned its attention towards 'non-formation' of subjects after the 1980s. It has continued to search for an alternative potential historicity based on the perception that not only labour movements but also new social movements are no longer historical actors.

According to the Touraine school, it is marginalized actors of society who are regarded as potential subjects to replace new social movements. As Dubet and Lapeyronnie (1992) point out, production relations are no longer the main constituting principle of social relations today. Touraine shares this understanding and describes this change as a shift from 'vertical society' to 'horizontal society.' The worker–employer relationship in industrial society and the technocrat–dependent class relationship in post-industrial society represent 'vertical' control relationships. On the other hand, in 'horizontal society' it is a question of being 'in or out' of a certain society, not 'up or down' within a society (Touraine 1991).[3] Because the question of 'in or out' is expected to become a cause of new social conflicts, the actors who are pushed 'out' of a society are regarded as potential agents of historicity.

Wieviorka has been studying racism, populism and juvenile 'delinquency' as specific examples. The question here is how the identity of the excluded can form a social movement. In other words, by analyzing the meaning and intention of action in the forms of racial discrimination or 'delinquency,' it is possible to identify social and political relations constituted by such actors (Wieviorka 1992; 1993: 19; 2003: 20–1). Similarly, the question of whether ethnicity and national identity can also be regarded as social movements with historicity provides a focal point (Touraine 1994: 213–5).

Wieviorka (1993) makes the positive assessment that the excluded create new subjects when they turn their attention to culture, experience and subjective meaning. However, such subjects are cut off from society as a whole and have no point of view about the historicity of their own action. Consequently, the action of the excluded and the action of supporters of racism or populism have the potential to become social movements, but they cannot realize the potential and end up in a 'social anti-movement.'

Wieviorka also approaches the social movement for 'alternative globalization,' which has become active in France since the 1990s, from the viewpoint of historicity of action. In categorizing multiple characteristics inherent to anti-globalization movements, he proposes three stages of movements (Wieviorka 2003: 28–30). At the first stage, a movement proposes a counter project or even a utopia, and actors have the capacity to negotiate with the opponent based on their identity. At the second stage, the movement is defensive and popular; it only confronts its opponent when its existence is threatened or when it tries to avoid its destruction. The third stage is the social anti-movement. Totalitarian states, sects and terrorist groups are the typical examples that cause conflicts to break down without articulating their own viewpoint on historicity through conflicts. There is no counter project or opponent here. Wieviorka considers that anti-globalization movements are presently at the second stage and exhibit a social anti-movement character in the worst cases (Wieviorka 2003: 33).

Dubet, another successor to Touraine, had not yet abandoned the task of identifying historical actors prior to 1990 (Dubet 1987, 1991). However, since he conducted an analysis of youths at the bottom of society in *La galère* in 1987, he has stopped looking for 'prophets' among actors (Corcuff 1995: 102). Since the 1990s Dubet has kept a distance from the idea of historical actors and worked on the evaluation of marginalized subjects whose emergence was noticed by Wieviorka.

As above, no subject can carry historicity in the Touraine school's view. Modern systems have created subjects that are adapted to society and, at the same time, because of the systems' universality, have created historical actors who put forward universal claims rather than simple adaptation (Dubet 2002). However, systems such as family, school and church no longer function the way they did in the classical model and what is happening now is the coexistence of disintegrated subjects (Dubet and Martuccelli 1998).

Therefore, according to Touraine, although modernization theory predicted a shift from closed communes to diversifying and rationalizing societies, the present condition is moving in the opposite direction. What we are witnessing at the twilight of modern society is global networking of production, consumption and communication on the one hand and a return to communes on the other hand (Touraine 1997: 14). Based on Touraine's understanding of the present condition, there is no actor who is capable of establishing historicity. The return to communes is considered to be a social anti-movement. However, there is someone who attaches a positive meaning to social movements brought on by globalization. It is Castells, who actively theorizes the split between global networking and communes and finds the potential to become subjects in the latter.

Excluded groups as agents for anti-globalization

Castells (1989: 2) analyzes the globalization process of structural adjustment in socio-technological organizations and capitalism by using the term 'informational mode of development.' In the informational mode of development, 'the source of productivity lies in the quality of knowledge' and 'what is specific to the informational mode of development is that here knowledge intervenes upon knowledge itself in order to generate higher productivity' (Castells 1989: 10). This expression is not substantially different from the post-industrial society theory of Touraine and Bell, and Castells' information society theory follows Touraine's post-industrial society theory to a considerable extent, as he himself acknowledges.

However, Castells has made an analysis of globalization possible by introducing the spatial concept that Touraine's sociology lacks. He introduces a binomial model composed of 'space of flows' and 'space of places.' The space of flows is a space in which information is produced and circulated beyond the constraints of geographical spaces and states thanks to the information technology revolution. On the other hand, the space of places is a living space of (a majority of) people constrained by geographical spaces (Castells 1996: 412).

In the space of flows, 'exchanges...do not depend on the characteristics of any specific locale for the fulfillment of their fundamental goals' and the 'new professional-managerial class colonizes exclusive spatial segments that connect with one another across the city, the country, and the world' (Castells 1989: 348). Meanwhile, the meaning of place is being lost and the existing political system is unable to control the space of flows and loses its power. The birth of this space of flows is the greatest feature brought on by the informational mode of development, which creates a network society connected via the space of flows. Unlike a programmed society, a network society assumes an expansion in the global space.

Further, Castells analyzes the relationship between globalization and social movements as a factor that explains the formation of a space of flows accompanying globalization. He declares that his research subject is not confined to social movements of the global north and looks at the global-scale impact of globalization on social movements (Castells 1996: 24–5). In contrast, Touraine school researchers have become unable to discuss social movements themselves, although they persist with the framework of social movements. How did Touraine and Castells diverge from each other during and after the 1980s?

The information technology revolution has transformed the physical infrastructure of society, increased the level of mutual dependency between economies and strengthened the power of capital based on increased flexibility of management. The 'net' is a global network for instrumental accumulation and control, and it is the 'space of flows' that supports its logic in the aspect of infrastructure. What is important here is sharing of 'time,' not 'place,' and a space is liberated from a place by the electronic network.

On the other hand, actions and politics surrounding primary identities such as religion, ethnicity, region and nation emerged in various parts of the world during the 1990s. While spaces develop after being liberated from places, some groups that insist on the inherent nature of places are putting up resistance. Modern societies are composed of the 'net' and the 'self' at opposite ends (Castells 1996: 1–3). The conflict between the net and the self becomes a factor that gives rise to social movements and prompts social changes.

Why do the progress of globalization and the identity-based resistance occur simultaneously (Castells 1996: 22–3)? Why do identities become the grounds for resistance? Castells explains the generation of resistance on the basis of the two logics of the space of flows (Castells 1996: 23–5).

First, information and networks strengthen people's ability to organize and integrate but they undermine the Western idea of independent subject at the same time. Information technology forces the naked self to face the net by directly connecting the abstract system and the self. As a result, the self loses its connection to its surroundings and becomes isolated. The reconstruction of identities that can be shared with others is a countermeasure against the isolation and therefore seeks new connections.

The second logic is more important. The elite who control the space of flows become more cosmopolitan, while the masses have to become a local existence. The space of power and wealth expands to every corner of the world but the lives and experiences of the masses remain rooted in a particular place, culture and history (Castells 1996: 415–6). Those who are excluded from the space of flows try to protect themselves by excluding those who exclude them. In other words, the excluded become detached from universality, which is global and instrumental. In this case, the basis for the construction of meaning cannot be something that is global. Instead, it is the space of places and the associated identities that provide the basis. While the cosmopolitan elite embody universality, the local masses resort to specificity in ethnicity, religion and nation. The third possibility for social movements against globalization ('retreat into an identity group') described by Wieviorka (2003) refers to this tendency.

The importance of identity has been emphasized in new social movement theory and it is not a novelty. However, in a core argument of new social movement theory, Castells proposes an expression that is different from the conventional argument. If the characteristics of new social movements are opposition to state intervention in civil society and an attempt to revive civil society, Castells's schema is missing the middle term, which is civil society.

In fact, Castells (1997: 11) states that 'subjects, if and when constructed, are not built any longer on the basis of civil societies, that are in the process of disintegration, but as prolongation of communal resistance.' Thus, civil society that constituted the central parameter in new social movement theory began to lose its meaning amid the advancement of globalization. The picture of 'communal groups confronting the space of flows' has become the overall motif (Castells 1997: Ch. 1) in which communal groups[4] (which are more 'microscopic' than civil societies) and the space of flows (which are more 'macroscopic' than states) face each other directly. In this sense, what ties the selves together is no longer civil societies of heterogeneous others but more homogeneous and fragmented primary groups.

Touraine considers that civil society is 'a field which forms actors who wish to be recognized as "subjects",' and communitarianism ends up in 'ethnic cleansing' because individuals are not formed as 'subjects.' According to Touraine, 'subjects' cannot recognize others as 'subjects' in intercultural communication unless they break out of their communities (Touraine 1997: 209). Because of the absence of civil societies that are the fields for the formation of subjects, there have been incidents of radical communitarianism excluding others by violence. Therefore, in counteracting the order imposed by the global economy and communitarianism, the re-emergence of civil societies for the formation of subjects is anticipated (Touraine 1997: 361).

Both Castells and Touraine assume the weakening of civil societies, and this type of expression with a missing middle term is not uncommon in discourses relating to globalization. Giddens (1991), who is a leading theorist on globalization, also considers that the 'self' and the 'global space' have a point of direct contact. However, these theorists, including Giddens, Beck and Melucci, and Castells have different views on one important point. The former consider that subjects are individuals who are individualized in late modern (or second modern/complex) societies and choose their own lifestyles reflexively between the 'self' and the 'society.' According to Castells, this type of identity construction has become difficult amid the rise of the network society. Since most individuals are living in a space of places, cut off from the space of flows, 'reflexive life-planning becomes impossible, except for the elite inhabiting the timeless space of flows of global networks and their ancillary locales' (Castells 1997: 11).[5]

Further, as the space of flows increases its control over network societies, the function of states and civil societies decreases. This is different from new social movement theory that locates a resistance base in civil societies. Therefore, subjects for social change in Castells's view must be communes with identities, not individuals or civil societies.

Now, what potential do identity groups have as subjects for social change? Castells divides them into three levels: legitimizing identity, resistance identity and project identity (see Table 5.1). In network societies, civil societies move towards contraction and disintegration because they are rooted in particular societies and cultures and have no connection with global network powers. And a search for meaning is conducted within communal groups, not in civil societies with heterogeneous others. In other words, the reconstruction of resistance

Table 5.1: Castells's subject and identity types

Identity type	Actor type	Characteristics	Examples
Legitimizing identity	Civil society	Introduced by dominant institutions in society for labour expansion and rationalization of their dominance	Church, union, political party.
Resistance identity	Commune or community	Generated by devalued and stigmatized actors; build trenches of resistance and survival based on principles that are different from those of dominant institutions.	Religious fundamentalism.
Project identity	Subject	Generated when new identities are created by social actors who attempt to redefine their position in society and transform the overall social structure.	Environmental movements, feminist movements.

identity based on communal principles provides the meaning of resistance. Even project identity positioned at the highest level may be generated as an extension of communal resistance (Castells 1997: 11).

This analysis leads to something that is different from GCS theory regarding subjects for social change; communes nurture resistance identity, which provides the foundation for the formation of project identity. As networks dissolve time and space, identities provide resistance based on places and historical memories. In the situation where civil societies and nation-states are facing structural crises, subjects based on project identity become the source of social changes in network societies (Castells 1997: 66–7).

Between communal groups and TSMOs: hierarchical or horizontal?

Reducing vernacular issues into global problems

According to the above arguments, two broad types of subjects have emerged in relation to social movements concerning globalization. What Castells has found is the absence of subjects in civil societies and the rise of alternative subjects based on communes. By contrast, international relations theories have been empirically analyzing the emergence of GCS driven by TSMOs. They are not necessarily mutually exclusive and, in reality, have been cooperating with each other in advancing transnational social movements.

Transnational social movement networks have been enormously effective in addressing problems that are difficult for a single country to solve. The movement against dams on the Narmada River in India would not have succeeded if it was left to a locally based opposition campaign by communal groups (Khagram 2002). The problem is that such outcomes are not simple success stories of beautiful solidarity. Most of the organizations that engage in protest activities beyond national borders are TSMOs from the global north. Communal groups in the global south (or excluded groups in the north) are chosen by them only as their partners. To TSMOs, a particular theme individually addressed by communal groups is only one of many issues they are concerned about, and they selectively form a temporary network with particular communal groups that seem meaningful. To communal groups, external support is of vital importance. Due to this power relation between them, global social movements are created in forms that are acceptable to TSMOs in the global north.

Here are some examples. A movement opposing dam construction in southern Brazil began as a movement for the protection of farmers' rights, as suggested by the name 'Regional Committee of Those Displaced by Dams.' The organization reframed its campaign into an environmental issue in order to secure support from overseas, which changed the nature of the issue (Rothman and Oliver 2002). In the case of the Ogoni people's protest against oil drilling by Shell in Nigeria, they initially put it to NGOs in the global north as a domestic minority issue but they failed to gain support. When they reframed it as an environmental issue, they finally saw the formation of an international support network (Bob 2005). Women's movements in India tend to concentrate on activities that conform to their donors' policies or activities, rather than the grassroots needs, so that they can receive assistance from foundations and international organizations in the global north. For example, donors who acknowledge poverty as the cause of human trafficking but do not permit prostitution may support measures such as rehabilitation and protection, which do not help to improve the economic independence of the victims (Subramaniam, Gupte and Mitra 2003).

In the formation process of 'global social movements,' vernacular issues of the global south are recast in forms preferred by the global north. The resistance identity of communal groups is driven to isolation if it is incompatible with the norms of GCS. It is perhaps possible to consider that GCS is created by absorbing complex and diverse issues into the domain of TSMO activity and repainting them in more desirable colors.

TSMOs and communal groups are, to start with, polar opposites in their motives to mount social movements. Communal groups are born out of a lopsided relationship between the space of flows and the space of places. They are excluded from the space of flows and put up resistance by excluding the excluder. In short, it is a protest against alienation *from* the space of flows.

Meanwhile, the leaders of TSMOs are the highly perceptive new middle class and choose to protest because they are sensitive to contradictions in the systems. This tendency is found not only in the global north but also in the global south, where an overwhelming majority of leaders are from the new middle class. They are by no means inferior to the small number of elites in the space of flows in their information production capacity, which determines their hierarchical positions in the network society. However, they choose to protest because they are sensitive to alienation *to* the space of flows, which helps preserve the world that does not respect their own roots or the rights of others.

Which part of the idea of alter-globalization conceived by the haves and the have-nots is sharable and which part is incompatible? Let us consider this question based on criticisms of the WSF made by some have-nots' movements in France.

World Social Forum and its critics: voices of the voiceless

The WSF can be called the embodiment of the activities of TSMOs that grew post-Seattle. In opposition to the Davos Conference of the world's political and economic leaders gathering in an exclusive Swiss resort town, the WSF was established in 2001 with the slogan that it would take place in the global south. Since then, the forum has been held in Porto Alegre, Mumbai, Caracas, Karachi, Bamako and Nairobi and has attracted over 100,000 participants. Its catchphrase is 'another world,' not a market economist society.

In 2003 a rival network called NoVox (the voiceless) was founded to coincide with the third WSF in Porto Alegre. It was organized by social movement groups against social exclusion that were formed in France during the 1990s, such as DAL (Droit au Logement, or right to housing) and AC! (Agir ensemble contre le Chômage, or act together against unemployment).[6] Since then, it has participated in every WSF as a network representing have-nots' movements for housing rights, farmers' rights, undocumented migrants and the unemployed. The network has spread to France, Belgium, Brazil, India, Portugal, Italy, Kenya, Mali, Togo, Benin and Japan to date.

The key French have-nots' movements have become active since the 1990s, with their main tactic being the occupation of public spaces. The homeless movement involves squatting in vacant buildings held by government agencies for speculative purposes in order to oppose commercialization of housing (due to deregulation of the property market and speculation) and to demand provision of housing as a public service. The movement by the unemployed involves occupation of jobs—working at empty service counters of post offices without permission—to protest against decreasing job security due to downsizing. The illegal occupation of public transport without paying demands free use of the public transport system by the unemployed, claiming that the poor are even deprived of means of transportation. The 'popular university' was founded in protest against the monopoly of the privileged few over 'knowledge' production and distribution. These movements have been carried out for the purpose of exposing, through the have-nots' acts of occupation, the reality of poverty caused by uneven distribution of global wealth and resources.

The main theme of the WSF is the north–south issue, particularly the issue of just redistribution of wealth. The WSF is protesting against neoliberalism because it opposes the competitive principle of the market economy as the only standard and the commercialization of public services. The objectives of the have-nots are consistent with those of the WSF. In that case, why is the Social Forum of Have-nots held in rivalry with the WSF?

DAL representative Jean-Baptist Eyraud claimed that the WSF was already 'repeating the same arguments as last year's' at the second forum and 'had no concrete proposal or action as to how to achieve another world.'[7] He appealed for the formation of NoVox based on the criticism that the organization of the forum was led by TSMOs to the exclusion of the poor. In fact, many of the movements led by the have-nots were unable to participate in the forum and their views were not reflected in the WSF.

Starting with this perception and with the main objective of playing the role of the 'voice for the voiceless,' NoVox staged protests by bringing its repertoire of public space occupation into the WSF. At the 2003 WSF, NoVox occupied vacant land owned by the City of Porto

Alegre and held the Social Forum of Have-nots. Then, it occupied a vacant building owned by the city and moved homeless families in.[8] It took part in a march called by the Dalit in India. In 2007 it occupied Osaka City's Paris office in protest against the eviction of homeless people from Nagai Park in Osaka. At the 2007 WSF in Nairobi, it mounted daily protests jointly with local slum movements against the forum organizers who excluded the have-nots.

The WSF in itself is an event embodying the emergence of GCS and it could not have been organized if it was not for globalization. Many of the attendees use English, which is not their native tongue, and are the biggest beneficiaries of the Internet, make international calls on a daily basis, and fly all over the world to attend international conferences. Conference venues such as Porto Alegre and Nairobi are just some of the many destinations for their official trips. Although their agenda may be an opposition to globalization rather than promotion of it, they are no different from the global elite in that they are disconnected from the space of places.

Social movements exert influences through disruption of order (Tarrow 1989) but the WSF organizers seek forum venues that can maintain comfort and order, even though they are located in the global south. In this sense, the WSF in itself is closer to an ordinary international conference rather than an action staged by social movements. The venue changes each time but the attendees do not change very much. It is not a forum involving local social movement groups, and it is attended by the same members who discuss the same topics every time.

By contrast, NoVox proposes to make the WSF into a forum to meet face to face with local social movements. In Nairobi it acted together with the People's Parliament to demand free attendance by slum residents. On the opening day of the WSF, they blocked the road to the venue to force free admission for everyone. On the following day, they occupied the organizing committee office in protest. They also occupied the exorbitantly priced restaurant at the venue and distributed food.

These actions are nothing but inconvenient disturbances in the eyes of the WSF organizers, who are global resistance elites. However, the demonstration of the have-nots' solidarity with the locale through direct activism at the WSF is an inevitable consequence of the involvement in local movements by have-nots as participants. As far as the have-nots are concerned, their issue is treated as only one of the discussion materials at the WSF. Even if they offer the material of discussion, they are not given a chance to turn their resistance identity into a project identity. In that case, it is more meaningful for them to link arms with the local have-nots and expand their resistance identity.

Conclusion

How much common ground can the attempt of TSMOs for alter-globalization have with communal groups? On the one hand, the GCS argument recognizes that TSMOs are expanding the domain of decision-making beyond state sovereignty. On the other hand, new social movement theory had higher expectations for the development potential of resistance by communal groups rather than TSMOs. Examination of the relationship between TSMOs and communal groups will provide an answer to the difficult question of how to turn the resistance identity of communal groups into the project identity.

Returning to Castells, his own expression that resistance identity forms the basis of project identity is a valid one but it does not match the reality. He recognized international movements, such as feminism and environmentalism, and international NGOs, such as Amnesty International, as desirable movements based on project identities (Castells 1997). However, the supposed project identities of these TSMOs should be considered as direct products of GCS and they cannot be regarded as something evolved from the resistance identities of communal groups.

It is possible to think that the rise of TSMOs represents democratization of cosmopolitanism, which used to be a monopoly of the elite, and the formation of systematic foundations for cosmopolitan democracy. However, GCS only relatively democratizes cosmopolitanism of the elite and only a very few NGOs and social movement groups can be its constituents (Goodman 2002: xix; Pieterse 2001: 26–7). After pointing out potential problems of GCS in this distorted structure, we need to consider a possible relationship between communal groups and TSMOs.

The leaders of GCS have been offering a helping hand to many communal groups in their effort to establish civil society in the global south. Needless to say, such an effort has played a role in democratization of the global south. At the same time, however, there are many communal groups that are gaining power, even though they are not regarded as candidates for civil society and are receiving no assistance from the global north. Western India's Hindu-based

Swadaya movement or the basic Christian community movements in South America and the Philippines bring diversity to the universality-oriented civil society (Walker 1994). Islamism is another candidate (Peterse 2001: 31).

What is common among these movements is that they are deeply entrenched in the impoverished class, even though their leaders may come from the middle class. This is because they implement anti-poverty measures in a form that is compatible with non-Western traditions, and their identities and real interests match the needs of the poor. And the more deeply they are rooted in non-Western traditions, the farther they are from the global north's idea of civil society. If there is to be spontaneous resistance in the global south, it is likely to be based on these communal groups that are regarded as non-civil society.

If there is to be alternative globalism, it cannot be a simple extension of the global north's civil society. As Goodman (2002) argues, GCS may be forced to play the role of complementing globalism from civil society's side. However, it is no doubt the most influential subject that promotes conversion from globalism to global democratic control at this point of time. What can it do to avoid winding up as a complementary player in the present neoliberal globalism and at the same time avoid changing or excluding resistant identities of a myriad of communal groups under universalism?

Respect for diversity is a golden rule for GCS but the distance between each of the communal groups and TSMOs is hopelessly great in reality. Adjusting this diversity to a level that is acceptable to the universality of GCS represented a certain aspect of transnational social movement networks. Even at the WSF, it has been pointed out that the forum is founded on 'civil' political culture of the white, male, middle class, which contains processes of marginalization and exclusion (Waterman 2004). Sen points out contradictions in the movement that is often praised as 'global civil society' by sharply criticizing the 'conceit' of the WSF organizers, who think their 'analyses are necessarily correct' (Sen 2004).

In response, Santos (2004) proposes a way to overcome such contradictions. He urges people to reconsider the image of 'another world' that reflects the ideals of the global elite by presenting both Western values and the Hindu and Islamic concepts of human dignity, as well as orally handed down wisdom of Africa and so on, in mutually translatable forms instead of simply excluding movements that are inconsistent with the values (such as human rights and democracy) of

Western origin. It is essential to work on recasting GCS, rather than communes, in order to achieve alternative globalism. In other words, GCS will need to approach individual communes and allow them to enter into dialogue without modifying or excluding them.

Part II
Minorities in Asian Cities

6 Islam in Bali

Naoki Yoshihara

Introduction

On October 12, 2002 and again on October 1, 2005, terrorist bombs blasted Kuta, Bali's downtown area in the south part of the island. The bombs deeply shook Bali, 'island of the gods,' which, together with its Hindus, is renowned. Needless to say, the number of victims claimed by the bombs shocked the world. More importantly, the incident highlighted to the world that Bali can no longer remain untouched by the contradictions brought about by globalization. In fact, the substratum of Balinese society has been hit by seismic changes since these two events occurred—changes that are continuing to have an impact today. For example, walking down the streets of Denpasar, the capital, we cannot help but notice the brand new mosques, both big and small, that are being erected everywhere as if to eclipse the *pura* or Hindu temples that represent Bali. Indeed, when we enter the bookshop located in central Denpasar, we can also spot crowds forming in front of the shelves stacked with Koran-related books. I have been conducting fieldwork in Bali for over ten years now, and up until recently this was unthinkable.

Interestingly, these trends have been overlooked by the world. Based on my observations, I believe that the silent progression of Islamization occurring in Bali at present is intimately related to the development of global tourism. Incidentally, as at 2004 the number of Japanese tourists visiting Bali stands at over 325,000 annually, far surpassing the number of overseas tourists from any other country (BPS 2005). This situation remains the same in 2007. Furthermore, it is believed that the vast numbers of Japanese tourists headed for Bali on a daily basis are contributing to the development of global tourism. Nevertheless, most Japanese visiting Bali continue to cling to fixed images of Bali from the past, and seem completely disinterested in the Islamization of Bali, despite the fact that the Japanese are, in effect, contributing to Bali Islamization through their role in promoting global tourism.

Undoubtedly, the Muslims living in Bali are a minority when we consider their number. However, it is a fact that the Islamization of Bali, as described below, has started to cause disintegration in some parts of the cosmos order prescribed by Bali Hindu *adat* (customary law)[1]. In other words, Bali Hindu, the traditional thematic construction premised on a homogenous race, can no longer stand.

Based on information gathered during my recent fieldwork, this chapter elucidates how Islamization is actually taking place in Bali, and examines the impact it is having on Balinese society.

Development of global tourism in Bali

First, let us briefly examine how tourism developed in Bali. According to Scholte (1996), the start of tourism in Bali can be traced back to 1908 when the Dutch colonial government succeeded in forcing the Klungkung kingdom, which was stubbornly holding out against it, to capitulate. At this time, the Dutch army's massacre of locals (so-called *puputan*) was widely reported throughout the world. A policy for preserving Balinese culture was then adopted to evade mounting criticism. As part of this move, a tourism office endorsed by the colonial government was established in Batavia (now Jakarta), and the catchphrase 'Gem of the Lesser Sunda Isles' was used to promote Bali's allure. Later, in the 1920s, the colonial government deployed a policy known as Balinization, which urged Balinese youth to embrace their cultural heritage. The result drew outside interest to Bali. Incidentally, Bali became a household name after Balinese dance was shown at the Colonial Exhibition held in Paris in 1931.

In line with this development, regular ocean crossings connecting Surabaya, Semarang, Batavia, Singapore and Bali were established between the late 1920s and the mid-1930s. In addition, the number of visitors to Bali gradually increased after the establishment of hotels such as the Bali Hotel (Denpasar), Kuta Beach Hotel and Suara Segara ('Sound of the Sea'), among others. Incidentally, official records of the aforementioned tourism office show that the number of travellers visiting Bali increased rapidly from 213 people in 1924 to 1,428 people in 1929, and to approximately 3,000 in 1939 (Picard 1996). Bali thus experienced a tourism boom mainly through the workings of external agencies during the colonial period. However, the boom experienced during the colonial era was just the beginning. Locals were not yet actively involved in it.

It was only after the arrival of Suharto's *Orde Baru* (New Order) that the wave of tourism swept through Bali. Suharto, the hero of the independence movement and the first president, showed a sustained interest in Bali, partly because his mother was Balinese. However, the presence of foreign travellers was not very noticeable during his rule (1945–66) (Pringle 2004). It was after the Bali Beach Hotel was set up in 1966 (with war compensation funds provided by Japan) and the Ngurah Rai Airport was opened in 1969 that the basis for Bali's development as a focal point of international tourism was formed.[2] Indeed, the number of overseas tourists visiting Bali increased at an exponential rate from 86,000 people in 1969, to 313,000 in 1974, and to 642,000 in 1982. Furthermore, foreign currency earnings gained from tourism also increased rapidly from US$10.8 million in 1969 to US$359 million in 1982 (Erawan 1994; Government Tourism Office 1997).

The crucial factor in the development of tourism was the successive establishment of Nusa Dua Beach Hotel managed by the state-run Garuda Indonesia, and various world-class star-rated hotels (such as Club Med, Hilton, Hyatt, Sol, Sheraton, Shangrila, Ramada and Hard Rock Hotel) after the opportunity presented itself with the opening of the Bali Beach Hotel and Ngurah Rai Airport.

Neither can we overlook how, in line with this development, Garuda Indonesia and other airline companies (such as KLM, Lufthansa, UTA/ Air France, Lauda Air, JAL, ANA, Singapore Airlines, Cathay Pacific, Malaysia Air Service, Air New Zealand, Thai Airways, Qantas, Ansett Australia and Continental Micronesia) competed with each other in establishing regular flights to Bali. The first five-year development plan under *Orde Baru* (1969–74) acted as the underlying driving force. Tourism was incorporated into this five-year plan and the development of Bali's tourism was pursued as part of the national policy. In 1983 the move to allow tourists in without visas, for example, was implemented as part of this national policy.[3] Subsequently, business tycoons who joined hands with Suharto's family maneuvered behind the scenes, causing tourism to expand across Bali from the 1980s to the mid-1990s. The erratic development was not limited only to the uncoordinated building of hotels, but extended to the establishment of resorts and land reclamation for golf courses.

Such relentless expansion of tourism was part of a process that strengthened the notion that Bali was actually a 'colony of Jakarta' (Hitchcock and Putra 2007: 22). It was believed that the slump in tourism across the nation following the 1997 Asian financial crisis and the ensuing collapse of *Orde Baru* would also have a great impact on Bali. However, Bali did not slump to such levels. The reason behind this was that Japanese and Australian tourists, who enjoyed the benefits of a strong yen and strong Australian dollar against the rupiah, continued to arrive on the shores of Bali. The maelstrom surrounding East Timor's independence in the post-*Orde Baru* era and the Bali riots that occurred due to the opposition in the Indonesian Democratic Party of Struggle to the appointment of Abdurrahman Wahid (also known as Gus Dur) as president did little to stop the flow of tourists to Bali. It was the Bali bombings, carried out by terrorists in downtown Kuta on October 12, 2002, that saw the number of tourists sink to record low levels (see Table 6.1). The number of overseas tourists fell by 22.75% in one year from 2002 to 2003. Moreover, most of this fall was in the numbers of tourists from Australia and various European countries. In 2004 there was a shift towards an underlying upward trend, but once again it took a sudden turn for the worse when the second terrorist bombings occurred on October 1, 2005 in Jimbaran and Kuta.

While tourism in Bali developed under highly dubious circumstances when seen in this light, it has been, at least until recently, closely linked to globalization. It is evident that the establishment of air routes between Denpasar and major international cities, as well as the setting up of numerous hotel chains, acted as a driving force. Furthermore, it is also clear that the development of tourism brought about a domino (knock-on) effect, which encouraged the growth of restaurants and other industries, particularly art, handicraft and clothing, which serve foreign tourists and visitors (Hitchcock and Putra 2007: 23). Today, however, Bali represents even more than that. Bali is an international brand in its own right. It has turned into a base for exporting products made in central and eastern Java, as well as Indonesia's eastern islands (namely Lombok), to the world. Naturally, multinational corporations have gathered in Bali to cooperate in the pursuit of profit; the momentum of which is transforming it into a city of conventions.

Indeed, it is not the intent of this chapter to further elaborate on this point. The aim here is to show that the development of the aforementioned global tourism has destroyed, and indeed still *is* destroying, the ecosystem that Bali inherited from time immemorial; it is also drastically unsettling Bali's agriculture, which has served as its economic mainstay, as well as the closely linked Hindu-based society.

Table 6.1: Shifts in overseas tourist numbers (2001–05) (Unit: person)

	2001	2002	2003	2004	2005
Asia/Oceania	764,508	726,289	524,213	920,590	816,454
	(9.55)	(–5.00)	(–27.82)	(75.61)	(–11.31)
Australia	238,857	183,389	107,386	267,338	249,520
Japan	296,282	301,452	228,013	325,849	310,139
Europe	430,214	392,262	295,340	316,419	396,964
	(–2.42)	(–8.82)	(–24.71)	(7.14)	(25.46)
United States	97,828	76,064	54,489	67,566	76,903
	(–15.53)	(–22.25)	(–28.36)	(24.00)	(13.82)
ASEAN	54,664	70,146	97,432	128,450	114,823
	(69.55)	(28.32)	(38.90)	(31.84)	(–10.61)
Middle East	322	3,770	3,925	9,572	2,543
	(–86.52)	(1070.81)	(4.11)	(143.87)	(–73.43)
Others	1,791	11,156	13,180	23,915	5,043
	(–96.09)	(522.89)	(18.14)	(81.45)	(–78.91)
Total	1,356,7	1,285,642	993,185	1,472,191	1,419,269
	(0.07)	(–5.24)	(–22.75)	(48.23)	(–3.59)

Note: Figures in brackets indicate percent shifts from the previous year.
Source: based on BPS (1996, 2001, 2006).

For example, mangrove forests are being cut down and replaced with artificial culture ponds to keep up with the massive volumes of shrimps consumed by tourists. Coral reefs are being destroyed to fulfill the rising demand for lime in connection with the rush to build hotels. Mountain forests and wilderness are being flattened to create nature reserves to protect wild animals from tourist trekking tours. In relation to this, the aim of this chapter is to elucidate the impact of Islamization as a global phenomenon on Balinese society.

Influx and settling of Muslims in Bali

In examining the effect of global tourism on Bali's existing society through the study of Islamization, it is clear that it can be understood most plainly in terms of two phenomena. First, the phenomenal growth of hotels and restaurants means that the indigenous Balinese, particularly the young people, are being employed by the business

Table 6.2: Changes in Bali's workforce by industry (1970–2004) (Unit: person; ( ) indicates % distribution ratio)

Year	A	B	C	D	E	F	G	H	Total
1970[a]	(66.7)	(5.8)	(2.5)	(10.5)	(1.2)	(0.2)	(8.3)	(4.9)	(100.0)
1980[a]	(50.7)	(9.8)	(4.8)	(14.5)	(2.2)	(0.5)	(15.3)	(2.0)	(100.0)
2000	552,248	252,420	134,285	412,014	82,188	37,632	227,539	11,626	1,712,954
	(32.4)	(14.7)	(7.8)	(24.1)	(4.8)	(2.2)	(12.6)	(0.7)	(100)
2004	681,320	190,420	104,595	489,750	86,245	21,215	234,725	26,895	1,835,165
	(35.3)	(14.2)	(7.2)	(23.0)	(4.0)	(2.0)	(13.4)	(0.9)	(100.0)

Notes:
A = Agriculture, forestry and fisheries[b]
B = Manufacturing
C = Construction
D = Business, restaurant, hotel
E = Transportation, storage, communications
F = Finance, public health
G = Services[c]
H = Others[d]
a: Actual figures for 1970 and 1980 are unknown.
b: Includes farm workers.
c: Includes public services.
d: Others include mining and quarrying, as well as electricity and gas supply.
Source: Nagano (2007).

sector in droves. As a result, more and more young people leave the agricultural sector, thus causing a situation in which there is an acute scarcity of agricultural workers. Incidentally, a comparison of the workforce in the different industries between 1980 and 2004 (as shown in Table 6.2) reveals that while the distribution ratio of agricultural workers decreased from 50.7% to 35.3%, that of business, restaurant and hotel employees showed a gradual increase from 14.5% to 23.0%. Second, the expansion of tourism goes hand in hand with the birth of various related industries. In particular, the development of Bali as a brand saw the rise in demand for clothing and handicrafts, namely *batik* (fabric on which wax is applied to create a pattern after dyeing). Consequently, rows of *batik* factories were set up in the suburban area in South Denpasar, where many semi-skilled labourers where hired. Map 6.1 shows how the *batik* factories are located in groups, mainly in Desa Pemogan in the South Denpasar subdistrict of Denpasar city. The number of factories peaked around the year 2000.

Map 6.1: Location of batik factories

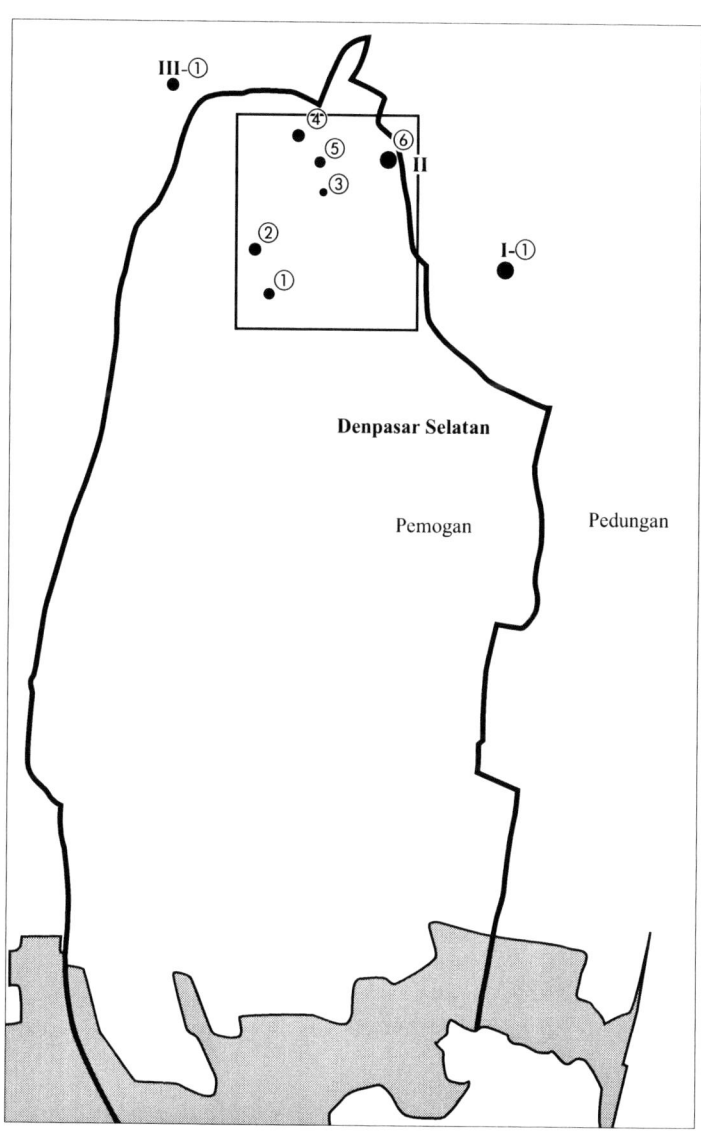

I Pendungan
① Three locations (1985)

II Pemogan
① Three locations (1991–96)
② Four locations (2001–06)
③ One location (1995)
④ Three locations (1985–2001)
⑤ Six locations (2006)
⑥ Fifteen locations (1998–2002)

III Pemecutan Kelod
①❽ Three locations (2000–06)

In relation with the first phenomenon, agricultural land surrounding Denpasar is being destroyed bit by bit, either to be turned into housing areas or to be used partly for building inexpensive accommodation called *losmen* to service low-paid workers (Hitchcock and Putra 2007: 23). What is most interesting, however, is the fact that many of the farmlands abandoned by the young people are being farmed by temporary residents from Java. They are generally farmers who have come from eastern Java as immigrant workers using their networks of relatives or acquaintances from the same hometowns. They rent the farmland from the Balinese, and do everything from rice planting to harvesting by hand. Once they finish, they move on to the next location.

Similar to the so-called seasonal immigrant workers, they send the money earned to their families back home, and sleep and eat (they do their own cooking) in tents set up either on vacant land they have rented or on the roadside (Photograph 6.1).

Now let us shift our attention to the second phenomenon. The *batik* factories themselves are mostly run by Javanese immigrants who have already registered as residents. The semi-skilled workers employed by these *batik* factories are also mainly Javanese from either central or eastern Java (there are virtually no Balinese involved). They are basically temporary residents working in jobs under dirty, hard and dangerous conditions. They are similar to the previously mentioned immigrant farmers in that they have come seeking jobs because they are no longer able to sustain themselves in their own home towns. Also, most of them find their jobs through their networks of acquaintances from their hometowns and relatives. Their workplaces are 'sweatshops' in every sense of the word—no ventilation, extremely hot and highly humid. They lodge in places that look like shacks next to the factories

Photograph 6.1: Tents inhabited by KIPEM

Photograph 6.2: Batik factory worksite (taken by the writer)

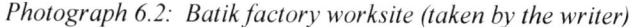

(refer to Photographs 6.2 and 6.3). Furthermore, in addition to the waste disposal issue, the *batik* factory waste fluid is also a major issue and recently involved neighbouring residents when it polluted the irrigation canals of the *subak* (irrigation association) and rice paddies (refer to Nagano 2007 regarding this matter).[4]

What further warrants our attention is that not only do the temporary residents from Java, as outlined above, support the progress of global

Photograph 6.3: Shack-like housing inhabited by batik factory workers (taken by the writer)

tourism from below, but, together with manual labourers (mainly in the tile factories) from Lombok called the *buruh Lombok*, they are also in the process of constructing a lower-class society in Bali. They are mostly Muslims, and are doubtless a minority group in the Bali Hindu-dominated Balinese society. At present, this minority group, which is made up temporary residents, is increasing in number in conjunction

Table 6.3: Population shift by religion (1996–2006) (Unit: person)

Year	Muslim	Hindu	Buddhist	Protestant	Catholic	Total
1996						
Bali	163,259	2,672,151	16,054	10,454	12,157	2,874,075
	(5.7)	(93.0)	(0.5)	(0.4)	(0.4)	(100.0)
Denpasar	43,119	312,667	6,743	2,497	6,388	371,424
	(11.6)	(84.2)	(1.8)	(0.7)	(1.7)	(100.0)
2001						
Bali	183,977	2,823,173	18,844	21,255	15,782	3,063,031
	(6.0)	(92.2)	(0.6)	(0.7)	(0.5)	(100.0)
Denpasar	44,626	357,684	7,653	8,295	7,755	425,983
	(10.5)	(84.0)	(1.8)	(2.0)	(1.8)	(100.0)
2006						
Bali	198,933	2,956,875	20,925	48,799	22,258	3,247,772
	(6.1)	(91.1)	(0.6)	(1.5)	(0.7)	(100.0)
Denpasar	68,705	342,629	9,329	32,350	10,902	463,915
	(14.8)	(73.9)	(2.0)	(7.0)	(2.3)	(100.0)

Note: Figures in brackets indicate percent changes compared with the previous year.
Source: BPS (1996, 2001, 2006).

with the development of global tourism. The influx and settling of this minority group is resulting in the creation of shanty towns, and the number of *ruko* (*rumah* = house, plus *toko* = shop) being erected through this trend is proving to be immense. Although they may return to their home towns in Java due to the temporary closures of the *batik* factories (as a result of the effect of the two terrorist bombing incidents, or the shadow cast by the entrance of the late bloomer China into the market), as long as Bali offers a place where people can avoid starvation, they will inevitably return.[5] Either way, as long as the Balinese want to avoid dirty, hard and dangerous jobs, and absolute poverty persists in the hometowns of the temporary residents from Java, then the influx and settling of the latter group in Balinese society is inevitable.

Needless to say, it is difficult to accurately trace the changes in the population of such temporary residents from Java due to their high mobility and migratory nature. Table 6.3 shows that since 1996 the growth of the Muslim population in Denpasar seems to outrival the growth of the Hindu population. However, the figures here only include Muslims who have been registered as residents, and does not include the temporary residents. Consequently, the actual number of Muslims living in Bali, especially Denpasar, is estimated to be a few times the number shown in Table 6.3. In fact, the inclination of the local community to label the temporary residents as illegal residents and expel them has had the adverse effect of 'sheltering' or hiding their existence, and thus allowing them to grow. This point is further elaborated upon in the next section.

Top-down population control and the community's flexible response

Bali's provincial government and the authorities in Denpasar city have, up until now, labeled the temporary residents from Java as KIPEM, and basically adopted a policy of curbing the influx of KIPEM. KIPEM (Kartu Penduduk Musiman, or seasonal residents identity card) originally points to an identification card. In Bali, however, the word KIPEM also refers to people who hold KIPEM –in many cases, immigrant workers. In this chapter, KIPEM refers to people. In 1998 KIPEM were divided into temporary residents, seasonal residents and visitors based on the 'Provincial regulations on population management in Bali,' and were differentiated from the residents who have settled there. Under the existing rules, they were required to either submit a change of address form or report to their administrative authority at the lowest level, such as the *desa* or *kelurahan* (non-autonomous village). Furthermore, the provincial governor's declaration, 'Policy on the execution of population registration in Bali,' dated February 27, 2002, which was sent out to the head of each district and city, stated that 'it has become increasingly necessary to carry out population control through population registration as the influx of KIPEM is causing the population in Bali to grow.' With this in mind, the declaration outlined the registration conditions for KIPEM, and enumerated the general principles (standards) such as, among others, the issuance of the certificate of immigration/change of address, creation of a register for immigrants, obligation of the (housing) tenant to report to the *banjar* (hamlet), and obligation for the employer of a KIPEM to report to the *desa* or *kelurahan*. However, up until this point the provincial authorities were overwhelmed in their attempt to gain an understanding of the trend in KIPEM influx, and the instructions relating to the general principles more or less failed to go beyond a mere afterthought.

The terrorist bombings on October 12, 2002 drastically changed this situation. The 'Policy relating to the population registration of immigrants' issued by the governor on November 14, about one month after the bombings, to the head of each district and city emphasized the 'restoration of social order.' It specifically pointed out that this should be achieved through the complete registration of the immigrant population. Detailed regulations, such as the requisites (the registration fee was first mentioned at this time), forms (format) and procedures concerning the general regulations were now determined. Yet, the response of the *desa* and *kelurahan* towards this policy was varied. For example, the registration fee they collected was not uniform. On the other hand, a move to expel the KIPEM strengthened at the community level. Incidentally, the *Kompas* newspaper reported on January 7, 2003 that indigenous vigilantes called *pecalang* were frequently forcing their way into houses in the middle of the night in Denpasar and demanding that residents show their temporary identification cards (referred to as KIPP). In the midst of all this, the central government ordered the adoption of a more systematic and effective population control measure/policy to curb KIPEM. Subsequently, on February 10 the governor issued Declaration Number 153 of 2003, entitled 'Agreement between the Bali provincial governor and the heads of all districts and cities on the implementation method of population control in Bali.'

The agreement detailed everything from the definition of population registration to matters regarding guarantors, procedures, administrative fees (registration fees) and others. In particular, it made the guarantors bear joint responsibility for the registration of KIPEM and their period of stay (valid for three months and only permitted to be extended once). It also included the fine details, such as prescribing a uniform administrative fee of 50,000 rupiah for the issuance of temporary identification cards (re-issuance of temporary identification cards in the case of extensions also incurs an administrative fee of 50,000 rupiah) as a measure to avoid confusion regarding the onsite population control system and regulations regarding the treatment of KIPEM. It was evident that this was an effort to force the burden upon both the KIPEM and those accepting the KIPEM. It also shows that there exists a thinly veiled intent to curb the influx of KIPEM. At the same time, we can also grasp the administrator's logic of trying to reorganize the population control system (which was made chaotic by the influx of KIPEM) in a top-down fashion by clarifying who is responsible and unifying the administrative procedures. Incidentally, the governor issued Declaration Number 3 of 2005 on January 20, entitled 'Regarding the information system relating to Bali's population control,' which instructed each level of administration from the head of the village/town/ward/city to the head of the district to put together a report on a daily basis containing information on population control and submit it to the higher authorities.

Now let us examine how the lowest levels of administration and the *banjar* actually handled the situation in the midst of the tightening population control from above, particularly the regulation of KIPEM. First of all, the registration fee is usually paid to the *desa* via the *kelian* (head of *banjar*). In the case of the abovementioned Desa Pemogan, the fee is 100,000 rupiah. Of the fee paid, the *desa* takes 50,000 rupiah, while the *banjar dinas* (the hamlet under the local government) and *banjar adat* (the hamlet under local customary law) each take 20,000 rupiah.[6] The remaining 10,000 rupiah is used to cover fees to maintain village security and running costs of teams assigned to collect unpaid identification administrative fees. Meanwhile, the registration fee for extending a identification for three months is 30,000 rupiah. Of the fee paid, the *desa* takes 15,000 rupiah, the *banjar dinas* and *banjar adat* take 6,000 rupiah each, and 3,000 rupiah is used to cover the running costs of teams assigned to collect unpaid KIPEM administrative fees. Regardless of the amount, the point is that as far as these administrative fees are concerned they generally fall within the framework determined from above.

Let us now refocus our attention on the form taken by the abovementioned teams that collect unpaid administrative fees from the point of view of the community's response. These teams were clearly formed at each *banjar* in response to requests received from above. At the *banjar* (a *banjar* under Desa Pemogan) where I conducted my fieldwork, the team would visit the temporary residence of the KIPEM in the *banjar* once a week on a Sunday to check each KIPEM's period of stay. The results were reported to the *desa*. The *desa* would conduct a *sidak* (spot check), and prosecute and fine those who had not paid or had overstayed. However, the team concerned never took any punitive measures. Instead, it would reduce the administrative fee, allow for payment in installments, or even provide loans to pay the fines if the KIPEM were having difficulties finding work or struggling with low pay.[7] In other words, the community is not responding to calls from above for tighter regulation as in the abovementioned newspaper article. Rather, the community tends to contribute by forming and rebuilding the safety net for KIPEM.

It goes without saying that this community response is no more than one example. However, we cannot overlook it as merely one example when we consider how it reveals that the top-down suppression of

KIPEM is not affecting the community in a uniform manner. At any rate, as long as global tourism continues to develop and the community response to the top-down intervention and regulation of KIPEM is varied and flexible, the influx and settling of Muslims within Balinese society will continue.

The *ajeg Bali* undercurrent

At the same time, it is also important to point out that the influx and settling of Muslims within Balinese society is turning into a fresh point of tension in Bali. Of particular interest in relation to this is the *ajeg Bali* ('sustainable and strong *Bali*') movement, which called for the preservation of Balinese tradition and was started by the *Bali Post* in April 2002. After going through some twists and turns, the movement later found sympathy among groups that responded negatively to the influx and settling of Muslims within Balinese society. While *ajeg Bali* has more than one origin, it is obvious that all members share the same spirit of post-*Orde Baru* decentralization. Decentralization introduced a new move in Indonesian society that aims to review the centralized system (prevalent up until then under *Orde Baru*) and establish local identity. In Bali the *Bali Post* group started the *ajeg Bali* movement when it called for the promotion of local culture as part of the move to establish identity (Hitchcock and Putra 2007: 173). However, for most Balinese the call made by *ajeg Bali* was not a novel idea, nor did it seem like a meaningful expression of culture.[8]

It was only after the terrorist bombings of October 2002 that *ajeg Bali* went beyond the simple promotion of an outdated tradition. The incident transformed *ajeg Bali* from a mere expression of culture into a social and political slogan. It began to clearly demand that the island be protected from terrorism. In other words, safety and security came to be prioritized above culture, and it was through this that the movement was linked to the development of tourism. But tourism brings about a negative impact in that it acts as an external agent that destroys the environment and increases the gap in living standards. Consequently, expelling such 'evils' and protecting and maintaining Bali became the main purpose of *ajeg Bali* as a movement. Incidentally, those who cry out for *ajeg Bali* perceive the 'evils' that have been pointed out and KIPEM as one and the same thing. This is why KIPEM are nothing more than the object of suppression and expulsion.[9]

Ajeg Bali, indeed, is not a monolith. As the term *ajeg Bali* floods Balinese society, various viewpoints that intersect in a complicated manner with one another have started to manifest themselves. Some see it as cultural propaganda, or as a political movement, while others see it as a market strategy adopted by media groups. Furthermore, it is not unusual for *ajeg Bali* to become a point of contention at the national government level. Some are starting to see *ajeg Bali* through an analogical perspective of 'unity in diversity' at the nation level. Yet, regardless of how broad the issue becomes, it still does nothing to stop the undercurrent that is running through *ajeg Bali*, and neither does it help ease the tension created with the influx of Muslims into Balinese society. At any rate, while the *ajeg Bali* movement started off by calling for the protection of Bali and preservation of Balinese tradition from outside influences, which have been brought on by the development of global tourism, it is now spreading in an ominous fashion by turning into a practical movement that is at one with the community in seeking to expel 'foreign elements' as a means to increase Bali's security.

The events reported by the *Bali Post* amidst this situation on June 4 and 6, 2007, as described below, cannot in anyway then be seen as a mere coincidence. According to the *Bali Post*, a group of Muslim youths from Kampong Islam Kepaon was trying to pass through the neighbouring Bali Hindu *banjar* of Jaba Jati on their bicycles in the early morning hours before dawn (3 am) on June 3 when they got into a fight with youths from Jaba Jati. The youths of Jaba Jati hastily hit the *kulkul* (wooden signal drum) when they realized they were about to lose, and awakened the whole *banjar* in an attempt to rally support. As a result, the residents of Jaba Jati rushed to the site en masse. Meanwhile, the youths in Kampong Islam Kepaon who heard this, especially the women, panicked and were overcome by fear that the residents of Jaba Jati were going to descend on them. While the incident itself is nothing more than something that arose from a quarrel between two groups of youths living in neighbouring areas, it is evident that there is a subtle link between its underlying cause and the call for *ajeg Bali*, or the social trend that operates by the same principles.

Conclusion

Bali, the 'island of the gods,' hitherto maintained a unique social construction in which the whole island was whitewashed with Bali Hindu under Indonesia's principle of 'unity in diversity.' Ironically, this played an important part in the nation-building endeavor of 'imagined communities' (Anderson 1983). However, the fall of *Orde Baru* and the development of global tourism, which piggybacked on it, undermined the very foundation of social construction that exists, or is believed to exist, only in Bali. Most significantly, the development of global tourism is forcing Bali to accept Islam, which represents an element that the traditional and dominant Bali has found difficult to accept. Bali is today facing the prospect of being engulfed by the wave of Islamization that is sweeping across the globe. Needless to say, this is precisely the reason why traditional Bali or conservative Bali is popping its head out of the ground in a frantic attempt to protect itself from this gigantic wave. These trends seem to take a stance of suppressing or expelling foreign elements, and carry with them an inherent inclination towards the locality by adopting a 'closed protectionist' principle. In other words, there is a force that is working to contain the Muslims living in Bali, regardless of their residential status, as a minority group. However, it does not take much to know that such reactions have already been anticipated by the trend of globalization.

In this chapter we took a brief look at the present state of Bali, which is struggling to come to terms with its exposure to the global phenomenon of Islamization. Even if the struggle between two different elements supposedly causes the 'emergent'[10] to arise from within Balinese society in the future, it will probably be a considerably long time before it happens. With regard to this matter, we can only continue to pay close attention and keep watch over it. However, I would like to finally touch upon the significance that the Islamization of Bali, as described above, has for the Japanese.

As mentioned in the beginning, the Japanese play the greatest role in assisting Bali's global tourism. Despite this, however, the Japanese are ridiculously ignorant of the Islamization of Bali that is progressing hand in hand with the advance of global tourism. A majority of them just accept as 'existent' the thematic construction of a homogenous race based on the image of Bali Hindu that they have been presented with, and merely act as its consumers. To these people, Islamization is virtually non-existent. Furthermore, they cannot not get past this notion because in their minds the Muslim presence in Bali will remain as an absolute minority group. Naturally, since Bali is, for them, merely a 'different group of people' who exist only to be gazed upon, it is probably impossible for them to even conceive of the idea of Islamization. However, the 'existent' is starting to fade away from Bali's reality. Conversely, that which was labeled as 'non-existent' is starting to take over as 'existent'. Consequently, it is imperative that the Japanese gain a deeper awareness of this matter, together with a sense that their own experience as tourists is, in fact, spurring on Islamization.

A deepening of such sense/awareness could, in a way, make more relative the way the Japanese presently perceive things in Japan. It may allow them to go beyond their conception of 'existent' (a homogenous society that has been tacitly solicited by the nation-state) to look at the social realities, and to be more critical of the way they blindly reject new trends that do not fit with their conception, especially the way they reject as 'non-existent' the emergence of 'ethnoscape' (Appadurai 1996), or the scape created by people who move around the globe. At present, here lies my main interest; that is, the potential that the Islamization of Bali offers the Japanese.

7 Unchanging Fortunes of Jakarta Informal Sector Workers

Raphaella Dewantari Dwianto

Introduction

No news on the Jakarta informal sector might be good news for informal sector workers, mainly for those who conduct micro-scale businesses selling foods, soft drinks, snacks and so on. News about them is mostly about how they and their fellow-workers are being kicked out (sometimes literally) from the places where they do business by the so-called 'executing troops' of the Jakarta government.[1] It is known that the government of Jakarta has been adopting a dual position regarding informal sector workers. In most cases these workers are treated as a problem for society. At other times they are expected, for example, to be a certain kind of attraction for tourists.[2]

Being positioned as the source of problems for the city of Jakarta and facing unequal treatment, it is evident that these informal sector workers have significantly less control or power over their own lives compared to workers in the formal sector. Even if the number of workers in the informal sector exceeds those in the formal sector, these workers have much less access to education, wealth and success. In short, informal sector workers in Jakarta belong to the minority.[3]

Amidst such positioning and condition, this chapter takes a closer look at Jakarta informal sector workers, focusing on *pedagang keliling* (hawkers). Through several cases of *pedagang keliling* in two contrastive residential areas in Jakarta, I show the struggle of these informal sector workers during a prolonged crisis in Indonesia.[4] Looking at their struggle, we will try to grasp their perceptions of their daily lives as hawkers and their survival strategies, not only during the crisis but also since then. Let us begin with some introduction of lives of *pedagang keliling*, which are based on real people's lives.

A tale of two *pedagang keliling* in South Jakarta

No-other choice: Karno

Three o'clock in the morning. forty-year-old Karno (not his real name) knows in his sleep that soon his wife will come to wake him up, meaning that he has to start preparing his push-cart. He has been a vegetable hawker for many years. As a young man he left his small village, near Pekalongan city, twenty-four years ago. When he left, he never imagined that his life in Jakarta would be this harsh. Before he left for the city, Karno, who had only finished primary school, worked in a textile factory. There were many textile factories in Pekalongan, which is not surprising, since the city in the north part of central Java is well known for its colorful *batik* (traditional dyed fabric). One day a friend from the same village who had left for Jakarta asked him whether he would like to go to Jakarta. Karno wanted a better life, so he opted for Jakarta. In Jakarta his textile factory experience helped him in getting a job at a garment factory, where he worked for seven years. However, he quit the job in 1990 and started to work as a *pedagang keliling*, selling fruits in the western part of Jakarta. This was the start of his 'career' as a *pedagang keliling*. In the mid-1990s another friend from the same village told him about a new elite housing compound in the south of Jakarta, and the friend convinced Karno that he could gain much more if he sold vegetables in the new housing compound. Karno believed his friend. In 1995 he borrowed some money from a friend and began hawking vegetables in the south. Karno was determined to obtain a good profit and to be a successful vegetable hawker.

As the sound of *azan subuh* (hail for Muslim early morning prayer) from a nearby mosque tails off, Karno goes out of his house, pushing his *gerobak* (cart) towards *pasar kemiri*, a traditional market nearby, to buy his stock of vegetables. From day to day, he feels his cart is getting heavier, even before he loads any vegetables on to it. It is different from when he was a fruit hawker. Being a vegetable hawker is much harder because most vegetables are more perishable than fruits. At the end of the day he often has to throw them away. Added to this, he still has not earned the profit that he once imagined when he started his vegetable hawker business in the elite housing compound. On his luckier days he can get a net profit of 50,000 rupiah in one day (about US$6). But there are days when he can only get half that much. On such days there is not enough money for his family, let alone to send to his ageing parents in his village. On such days Karno sinks down in despair, and he really wants to get another job. But this is the only job he can get. Karno has no other choice.

The teacher and the apprentice: Harto and Agus

In the market Karno always meets fellow hawkers who also do business in the same elite housing compound. On this morning he meets Harto (twenty-nine years old) and Harto's nephew, Agus (sixteen years old) (neither are their real names). Just like Karno, Harto started selling vegetables in the housing compound in 1995. And just like Karno, Harto was born as a poor farmer's son in a small village near Pekalongan. Dropping out of primary school, Harto helped with the farming work, but then decided that he did not want to be a farmer, so when he was nineteen years old he left his village to try to make his fortune in Jakarta. He was lucky enough to get a job at a *tempe* (fermented soybean) factory in Jakarta. To start his business as a vegetable hawker, the father of two children borrowed some money from a relative. At present he still has to spare some of his daily profit to pay the loan back, while also providing everyday necessities for his family. However, in contrast to Karno, Harto's daily profit is much more stable, with a daily profit of around 40,000 rupiah. The present condition seems to be more or less satisfactory for Harto, and he does not think of looking for another job or of returning to his small village. For now, his life consists of getting up very early every morning (without any holidays), going to the market to stock his cart with fresh vegetables, and starting to sell vegetables in the housing compound before six o'clock in the morning. Around noon he returns to his rented house, where he lives with his wife and children, and also with his nephew Agus. Agus is now learning from his uncle to be a vegetable hawker. That is why every morning Agus accompanies Harto selling vegetables in the housing compound.

Agus has just come to Jakarta from his village. Like his uncle, he did not finish primary school. When he was still in his village, one day a person from Jakarta came looking for anyone who was willing to go to Jakarta and work in a dressmaking factory in Bekasi, a town adjacent to Jakarta. When Agus heard this, he started to dream of making a success of himself in Jakarta. He left his parents and his six brothers and sisters, and went to Bekasi. However, Agus only lasted four months in this job. He then moved to Depok and lived with his

Photograph 7.1: Agus the apprentice

uncle. Rather then being jobless, he chose to help his uncle without receiving any payment. He is thinking of returning to his village when he is older. But until then he tries to master the know-how of vegetable hawking from his uncle, and will become a hawker himself if he can borrow some money to start his own business.

A tale of two *pedagang keliling* in Central Jakarta

The super-mom: Parti

At about the same hour when Karno, Harto and Agus are preparing their carts, about twenty kilometers away a middle-aged woman of strong frame starts her day by loading her cart with fresh fish to be sold in a densely populated residential area, usually known as an urban-*kampung*.[5] In contrast to the elite housing compound where Karno, Harto and Agus do business, the people in this urban-*kampung* are of low and middle income. Everyday, and without a single day off, fifty-three-year-old Parti (not her real name) goes around the urban-*kampung* with her cart, selling fish. Parti has been working as a hawker since 1966, the year she left her small village near Pekalongan. Born as a daughter of a small-land farmer, she had to quit primary school and work as a farm labourer. When an acquaintance invited her to leave her village and go to Jakarta, she accepted, thinking that there might be a better chance in the capital city of Indonesia. However, for a person without any formal educational, such as Parti, it is difficult to find a job in an office. So she started her own business as a vegetable

Photograph 7.2: Parti the super-mom

hawker. She borrowed some money from an acquaintance and started selling vegetables.

In the urban-*kampung* where she usually does her rounds, the hawkers do not always use carts, since the alleys are often narrow. A female hawker will often put her merchandise in a big rattan basket, and carry the basket on her back, using a cloth slung over her shoulder and around her waist. With her strong-boned figure, the young Parti did her rounds in the urban-*kampung* with a heavy basket of vegetables on her back. During more than thirty years of working every day as a vegetable hawker, Parti still managed to find time to fall in love, get married and give birth to eight children, who still live with her and her husband in their rented house. But even a super-mom such as Parti can get tired. That is why, in 2001, she decided to quit selling vegetables and switched to selling fish using a push-cart. She never thinks of quitting her work as a hawker because she knows very well that her big family needs all the income it can get, and being a hawker is the only thing that she can do. And she never stops dreaming of going back to her village and having a quiet retirement some day when her children can manage their own lives.

The sales woman: Lestari

Another female hawker in the *kampung* area, although with a different kind of merchandise, was pushing her bicycle loaded with *jamu* (Indonesian traditional herbal drinks). Thirty-two-year-old Lestari (not her real name) has a rather different appearance compared to other female hawkers. She has a beautiful face and long black hair loosely tied in a rather stylish ponytail. She has always been stylish since her high school years in Solo, a city in Central Java well known

Photograph 7.3: Lestari the sales lady

for its beautiful and classy women. It is a pity that Lestari could not finish her high school due to her parents' financial difficulties. Like almost all of her fellow hawkers, she was also born into a farming family. When her parents decided to move to Jakarta to seek a better life, she went along, leaving her hometown in 1989. She was lucky enough the following year to get a job as a door-to-door salesperson at a big national cosmetics company. With her job she could support her parents in Jakarta. For two years Lestari worked there. It was unfortunate that in 1992 she had to leave the company. Since she needed income, she started her own business selling *jamu*. She continues the business still, working five or six days a week. Part of the profit she earns as a *jamu* hawker supports her own family (she is now married with one child), while some of it is sent to her parents in Solo, since they decided to return to the city. Lestari still hopes to get a job at a company in Jakarta; however, for the time being, she tries to put up with being a *jamu* hawker.

Urban informal sector

These stories of Karno, Harto, Agus, Parti and Lestari are stories of workers in the informal sector in urban Jakarta. There have been abundant academic studies on the informal sector in general, which results in various explanations and viewpoints. Starting with the term 'informal sector' itself, the terminology of the informal sector was introduced by an economic anthropologist, Keith Hart, in the early 1970s. From findings from his field study on slums in the city of Accra in Ghana, Hart introduced the concept of an informal economy through his division of income opportunities. He mentioned three income opportunities—formal income opportunities, legal informal income opportunities and illegal informal income opportunities (Hart 1973).

However, the informal economy actually existed long before the terminology was introduced. The study on the informal economy also has a longer history than its terminology. One of those earlier studies is the study on the dual economy and was carried out by a Dutch scholar, Julius Herman Boeke, in the 1930s. Boeke focused on economic activities of the Dutch East Indies (the present Indonesia), where he found that there were economic activities based on the principles of capitalism (represented by enterprises and firms), while at the same time there were contrastive activities (which he described as oriental economy) (Boeke 1942).

More than half a century since Boeke's research, a Japanese scholar, Fujimaki, also tried to clarify various economic activities through categorizing them into four domains of activities—formal, informal, illegal and criminal (Fujimaki 2001: 17). Based on Fujimaki's observation, big enterprises conduct economic activities mostly in the formal domain, sometimes in the informal domain and, in some cases, in the illegal domain. While smaller enterprises and subcontracting firms tend to operate in the formal domain—although to a very limited degree—they are more active in the informal domain of the economy. Although a very few hawkers conduct economic activities in the formal domain, most of them are in the informal domain and, to a certain degree, in the illegal domain, such as when they are using spaces that are not designated for economic activities. The illegal and criminal domains are for smugglers, drug dealers and the like.

To be added here are the viewpoints of two German sociologists, Hans-Dieter Evers and Rudiger Korff (2000), who highlight the informal sector as a strategy of survival for people living in urban areas. Despite its significance for surviving life in cities, it is neither recorded nor included in the country's balance sheet. It is therefore regarded as a 'shadow economy,' meaning that it is beyond the reach of the policies of the ruling government. In contrast with the formal sector, because the informal sector belongs to the 'shadow economy' it is often positioned as being against nation building. And in relation to this, among scholars of social sciences there is a tendency to make a dichotomy of the formal sector and the informal sector, in which the latter is regarded as the economy in a traditional society.

By looking at the abovementioned studies on the informal sector, it is beyond argument that there have been various concepts of the informal sector, depending on the viewpoint of each scholar. Bangasser (2000: 1–2) sees a kind of evolution in the concept of the informal sector during the past three decades, mainly in policy-oriented studies, and then tries to see it in a historical flow by putting the evolving concept into three phases. The first phase is the decade of the 1970s, when the concept of the informal sector was developed and took root. The second phase is the decade of the 1980s, when the concept of the informal sector was taken up by many different actors. These are also the years when the informal sector began to be incorporated into various programs by various actors. The third phase is the decade of the 1990s, when the concept of the informal sector was recognized internationally and then incorporated into official international schema.

With its integration into the official international schema, the most-often adopted definition of the informal sector is the one prepared by the International Labour Organization and the United Nations Development Program. The definition refers to the informal sector as the non-structured sector that has emerged in the urban centre as a result of the incapacity of the modern sector to absorb new entrants. The indicators for the informal sectors are that it (1) is easy to get in and out of, (2) is based on traditional resources, (3) is carried out by family members, (4) is small or micro-scale, (5) is labour intensive, (6) only requires skills obtained from informal education, and (7) is a competitive, unregulated market.

Informal sector in Indonesia

Previous studies

To get to know the informal sector workers in Indonesia we can refer to the work of Hugo (1973). From his field study covering a rural area in West Java, Hugo tries to see the geographical move of labourers from those rural areas to Jakarta and Bandung. He shows that access to job opportunities depends on each person's network of relatives or acquaintances from the same village who have previously moved to the city. Such networks not only bring new labourers from the same village to the city, but also form layers of informal workers from the same village who are engaged in the same labour. Furthermore, according to Hugo, among West Javanese who move to urban areas there are those who then live in the city, and there are those who go back and forth between their villages and the city. The former tend to obtain jobs in the formal sector, whereas the latter work in the informal sector for a certain period of time and return to their hometowns. They then return to the same city, and again work in the informal sector, often doing the same thing as they did before. Therefore, if there is a certain vertical mobility among these people, it does not come from a change of jobs, but from the change in the mode, place or scale of the same informal sector work.

If Hugo focuses on the geographical mobility of informal sector workers in West Java, Jellinek minutely studies informal sector workers in inner areas of Jakarta, covering *becak* (pedicab) drivers, workers in home-based industries, micro-scale traders, construction workers and workers in the service sector in *kampung* areas (Jellinek 1977a, 1977b, 1988, 1991). From her field studies in Jakarta, Jellinek concludes that these workers in the informal sector are swallowed by the process of economic development of the government, which then gives them the characteristic of being temporary. The change of spatial structure in the city, the decreasing number of inhabitants in the center of the city, and the shift in government policy to economic development all contribute to the temporary characteristic of the informal sector and, furthermore, drives the people who can only depend on the informal sector for their livelihoods into poverty.

The studies of Hugo and Jellinek were conducted in the 1970s, although their findings can still be applied to the present Jakarta. More recent studies are those by Ngadisah (1987), Somantri (1990) and Taqiyyah (2002). These three studies focus on personal networks of informal sector workers in urban areas. In the studies of Ngadisah and of Somantri, we can see patron–client relationships between informal sector workers in micro-scale trading in traditional markets of Jakarta. Both researchers conclude that being workers in the informal sector puts them in an unstable and insecure position. Such workers then seek protection from patrons, and often they find it in people of the same informal sector. It can be said that patrons are the bare necessity of life for informal sector workers. According to Ngadisah, there are various roles of patron, but in most cases a patron functions (1) as a source of funding, (2) with help in stocking merchandise or as a provider of merchandise, (3) as an intermediary between informal sector workers and local administrative staff, and (4) as a religious or spiritual guide. Adding to Ngadisah, Somantri concludes that patrons in informal sectors not only take leadership in financial matters such as providing capital or providing merchandise, but also provide leadership in cultural and social matters.

Rather different from Ngadisah and Somantri, who conclude that relationships between patrons and clients are vertical, Taqiyyah finds that this is not always the case. She studies the patron–client relationships between informal sector traders, local gangsters and local administrative officials in a traditional market in Jakarta. This patron–client relationship is also influenced by where the person came from. An informal sector trader who was born in the area and whose parents and grandparents were native to the area wins respect from local gangsters, and sometimes becomes a kind of 'father' to the local gangsters. An informal trader who is not native to the area will seek protection from local gangsters by giving them some kind of protection fee. Taqiyyah concludes by finding that relationships between informal sector traders, local gangsters and local administrative officials are multi-layered and complex.

Based on the various conclusions of findings from the above studies on the informal sector, we can see some characteristics of the informal sector as summarized in Table 7.1.

The first characteristic is that the informal sector has a range of activities that spread across a wide spectrum, with retailing as the dominant activity. And in this wide spectrum several activities can be found almost simultaneously in a single unit; that is, products are made and sold in the same place. In its micro or small scale, the workers usually consist of family members or casual employees, with flexible—but long and unprotected—working hours. With workers from family members, it is very usual to see the use of personal and domestic assets, with capital also obtained from family or friends, and in some cases from money lenders. These workers get their skills from informal apprenticeships, since only low skills are required.

Informal sector and economic crisis

Even though one characteristic of the informal sector is its invisibility, this sector contributes much to the economy of the country. Before looking at the present condition of the informal sector in Indonesia,

Table 7.1: The characteristics of the informal sector as represented in current literature

Characteristics	Comments
Range of activities	Few activities, spread across a wide spectrum. Retailing is dominant. A few in almost any conceivable activity, especially niche markets. Transport is often dominated by the informal sector.
Combinations of different activities	Several activities are in a single unit, simultaneously, or by frequent change. Products are made and sold in the same place.
Small	Most are without regular employees; some have a few workers.
Internal organization and employment relations	Flexible, casual, family-run; unprotected workers. Long working hours.
Invisibility: informal relationships with suppliers, clients and the state	Few licences or formal contracts, flexible hours, irregular contacts. Tend to be 'invisible,' unregulated and uncounted, avoiding taxes, licence fees and standards.
Informal skills acquisition and limited skills needed	Skill gained through informal apprenticeships; a few have received vocational training. Few barriers to entry; low initial capital and skill required.
Operators have low incomes	Income not far above minimum wage for most.
Low initial capital, limited access to formal credit and an under-capitalized process of production	Informal capital from family, friends, money lenders and other business interests. Limited technology may hamper efficiency and limit investment and improvement.
Consumption and production are not separated	Use personal and domestic assets; business expenditures, income, assets and labour are linked to those of the household.

Source: Tipple (2005: 614).

let us first get a glimpse of the informal sector in Asian countries. According to Table 7.2, which shows revenue data of ten countries in Asia, even in Vietnam, where the amount of revenue is the lowest among other Asian countries, the informal sector contributes a total of US$48.9 million. In China the informal sector contributes up to US$1,395.5 million, or around thirty times as much. When compared to gross national product (GNP) of the country, we can see that more than half of Thailand's total GNP comes from its informal sector, while in the Philippines, Bangladesh and Malaysia the informal sector contributes more than one-third of each country's GNP. According to

Table 7.2: Percentage of revenue from informal sector in Asian countries

Country	Total revenue from informal economy ($US million)	Percentage of GNP
Thailand	634.1	52.6
The Philippines	344.2	43.4
Bangladesh	166.9	35.6
Malaysia	256.2	31.1
South Korea	1,251.30	27.5
India	1,046.80	23.1
Indonesia	276.8	19.4
Vietnam	48.9	15.6
China	1,395.50	13.1
Singapore	128.9	13.1

Source: Size and Measure of the Informal Economy in 110 Countries Around the World, Friedriech Schneider, (July 2002) as quoted in *Kompas* daily edition of April 15, 2006.

Table 7.3: Percentage of workers in informal sector in Indonesia

	1982	1985	1987	1990
informal sector workers as % of total working people	66.0	68.7	72.8	71.4
male				
urban	34.6	38.2	40.6	40.6
rural	67.9	72.9	77.2	77.2
female				
urban	55.3	51.9	53.1	51.4
rural	77.9	81.1	85.0	84.4

Source: Gunawan (1992: 26).

the table, Indonesia's informal sector contributes almost 20% of its GNP, with a total amount of US$276.8 million.

Compared to other countries in Asia, Indonesia's informal sector cannot be said to contribute much to its GNP; however, when we see the number of Indonesian people working in the informal sector, we can understand than the informal sector in Indonesia absorbs more people of productive age that the formal sector. As shown in Table 7.3, during the 1980s until the early 1990s, the percentage of people

Table 7.4: *People of productive age in informal and formal sector in Indonesia*

Sector	2000		2001		2002		2003		2004		2005	
	No	(%)	No	(%)	No	(%)	No	(%)	No	(%)	No	(%)
Informal	58.3	71	55.8	61	57.9	63	60	64	59.2	63	60.6	64
Formal	31.5	29	35	39	33.6	37	32.7	36	34.5	37	34.3	36

Note: No. is the amount of people (millions).

Source: Size and Measure of the Informal Economy in 110 Countries Around the World, Friedriech Schneider, July 2002) as quoted in *Kompas* daily edition of April 15, 2006.

working in the informal sector showed an increase of 4.4% each year. In 1982 the percentage of workers in the informal sector reached 66%. It kept increasing to 68.7% in 1985, and to 72.8% in 1987. In 1990 the percentage slightly decreased, but the decrease was not significant.

More recent data can be seen in Table 7.4, which shows the tendency of workers in the informal sector during several years following the economic crisis in Indonesia.

Looking at Table 7.4, it is clear that more than two-thirds of working people in Indonesia belong to the informal sector. A closer look tells us that during the year 2000 (that is about two years after the economic crisis that hit the country in 1997 and 1998), the percentage of those who worked in the informal sector reach 71% of the total number of people of working age. During the years following the crisis, the number of workers in the informal sector was still about two times the number of those in the formal sector. After seven years (that is, in 2005), the percentage of those in the informal sector was still much higher than in the formal sector.

Looking at types of employment (see Table 7.5) in the informal sector, agriculture, forestry, hunting and fishery were dominated by informal workers during the crisis (in 1998) and in the years afterwards (2002). Following these types of employment is employment in wholesale trades, retail trades, restaurants and hotels. Next come employment in transportation, storage and communications.

In some types of employment, such as finance, insurance, real estate and business services, there are many more workers in the formal sector than in the informal sector. Yet, even in such businesses there are informal workers. As a consequence, the number of informal workers is much higher than formal workers.

Table 7.5: Workers by employment type in Indonesia

Employment type	1998					2002				
	formal	informal	total	formal %	informal %	total	formal	informal	total	formal %	informal %	total
agriculture, forestry, hunting, fishery	5,674,348	33,740,417	39,414,765	14.39	85.61	100	3,281,861	37,351,766	40,633,627	8.08	91.92	100
mining, quarrying	382,768	291,829	674,597	56.74	43.26	100	276,852	354,950	631,802	43.82	56.18	100
manufacturing industry	6,152,120	3,781,502	9,933,622	61.93	38.07	100	7,745,354	4,364,643	12,109,997	63.96	36.04	100
electricity, gas, water	128,995	18,854	147,849	87.25	12.75	100	161,101	17,178	178,279	90.36	9.64	100
construction	2,829,228	692,454	3,521,682	80.34	19.66	100	1,962,207	2,311,707	4,273,914	45.91	54.09	100
wholesale trade, retail trade, restaurants, hotels	2,862,075	13,952,158	16,814,233	17.02	82.98	100	3,902,501	13,892,529	17,795,030	21.93	78.07	100
transportation, storage, communications	1,692,692	2,461,015	4,153,707	40.75	59.25	100	1,598,606	3,073,978	4,672,584	34.21	65.79	100
finance, insurance, real estate, business services	589,418	28,294	617,722	95.41	4.59	100	931,529	60,216	991,745	93.93	6.07	100
other services (community, social, personal services)	10,019,402	2,374,870	12,394,272	80.83	19.17	100	7,976,008	2,384,180	10,360,188	76.99	23.01	100
Total	30,331,046	57,341,403	87,672,449	34.6	65.4	100	27,836,019	63,811,147	91,647,166	30.37	69.63	100

Source: Sakernas 1998 and 2002, as quoted in Firnandy (2004: 4).

Table 7.6: Worker in informal sector by employment status

employement status	1998 number	%	2002 number	%	2006 number	%
self employed	20,523,338	23.41	17,632,909	19.24	19,504,632	20.44
self employed assisted by family members or temporary helpers	19,690,059	22.46	22,019,393	24.03	19,946,732	20.9
employer with permanent workers	1,525,625	1.74	2,786,226	3.04	2,850,448	2.98
labourer or employee	28,805,421	32.86	25,049,793	27.33	26,821,889	28.1
family worker (unpaid worker, casual employee in agriculture and non-agriculture)	17,128,006	19.53	24,158,845	26.36	26,333,234	27.58
total	87,672,449	100.00	91,647,166	100.00	95,456,935	100.00

Source: Sakernas 1998, Sakernas 2002, BPS 2006.

According to a survey by Sakernas (the National Labour Force Survey), the status of employment of those in informal sectors can be grouped into five employment statuses—self-employed; self-employed assisted by family members or temporary helpers; employer (in informal sector) with permanent workers; labourer or employee; and family worker (which includes unpaid worker, and casual employee in agriculture and non-agriculture). Based on this, Table 7.6 shows that the percentage of those in the informal sector who are self-employed—regardless of whether he/she works alone or assisted by family members or temporary helpers—is more than 40% (45.87% in 1998, 43.27% in 2002, and 41.34% in 2006).

Looking further into the profile of workers in the informal sector (Table 7.7), it is not surprising that the lower the educational attainment, the higher the percentage of workers in the informal sector. There is no significant difference between the situation in 1998 and in 2002. The percentage in 2002 is even higher for lower-educated people who work in the informal sector.

When it comes to urban areas in Indonesia, the percentage of people who work in the informal sector keeps increasing. In 1971 the percentage of workers in the informal sector in urban areas was around 25%, which then increased and reached 36% in 1980, and

Table 7.7: Formal and informal workers by educational attainment in 1998 and 2002

Educational attainment	1998						2002					
	formal	informal	total	formal %	informal %	total	formal	informal	total	formal %	informal %	total
under primary school (no education)	1,236,347	6,710,659	7,947,006	15.56	84.44	100	423,654	6,210,376	6,634,030	6.39	93.61	100
primary school—unfinished	3,546,694	13,095,750	16,642,444	21.31	78.69	100	1,835,155	12,769,576	14,595,731	12.57	87.43	100
primary school—graduate	8,779,547	24,081,274	32,860,821	26.72	73.28	100	6,644,366	27,961,272	34,605,638	19.2	80.8	100
junior high school—graduate	4,489,714	7,708,620	12,198,334	36.81	63.19	100	5,128,757	10,213,713	15,342,470	33.43	66.57	100
senior high school—graduate	5,272,596	3,726,196	8,998,792	58.59	41.41	100	5,890,033	4,183,259	10,073,292	58.47	41.53	100
senior vocational school—graduate	3,961,425	1,583,889	5,545,314	71.49	28.51	100	4,057,191	1,957,879	6,015,070	67.45	32.55	100
junior college—graduate	1,476,300	175,968	1,652,268	89.35	10.65	100	1,737,939	226,570	1,964,509	88.47	11.53	100
university—graduate	1,568,423	259,047	1,827,470	85.82	14.18	100	2,118,924	297,502	2,416,426	87.69	12.31	100
total	30,331,046	57,341,403	87,672,449	34.6	65.4	100	27,836,019	63,811,147	91,647,166	30.37	69.63	100

Source: Sakernas 1998 and 2002, as quoted in Firnandy (2004: 6).

Table 7.8: Labour market structure in Indonesia by urban/rural area and by sex in 2002 (%)

	urban	rural	male	female	total
Share of employment					
Agriculture	13.0	65.6	43.7	45.4	44.3
Non-agriculture	87.0	34.4	56.3	54.6	55.7
Total	100.0	100.0	100.0	100.0	100.0
Non-agriculture					
Informal	43.7	65.9	48.2	58.6	51.9
Self-employed	32.2	44.4	36.2	37.7	36.7
Family worker	6.5	11.1	2.9	17.8	8.2
Casual wage	5.0	10.4	9.1	3.1	7.0
Formal	56.3	34.1	51.8	41.4	48.1
Regular wage	52.5	30.9	47.0	40.1	44.5
Employer	3.8	3.2	4.9	1.2	3.6
Total	100.0	100.0	100.0	100.0	100.0

Source: Sakernas 2002, as quoted in Alisjahbana and Manning (2006: 240).

further increased to 42% in 1990. The peak was in the year 2000—or around two years after the economic crisis—when it reached 65% of the total working people in urban areas (Firnandy 2004). In the following years, the number of people working in the informal sector does not show any significant decrease, which means that, even after the economic crisis, there are more people in the informal sector compared to the formal sector.

From the statistical data in Table 7.8, it can be said that the informal sector in Indonesia functions as a receiver of an abundant number of people who are at a productive age. In the case of Indonesia, the informal sector also functions as a survival strategy during an economic crisis.

Now knowing the general profile of informal sector workers in Indonesia, mainly during the years of economic crisis and during the following years, in the next part the focus is on one type of informal sector worker—the *pedagang keliling*. The data introduced in the following part is based on field studies of hawkers whose business routes are in residential areas in Jakarta. Two contrastive residential areas are covered in this study. One is an urban-*kampung*, the other is a newly developed elite residential area. Field work for these cases was done in 2001 for both residential areas.

Real lives of informal sector workers in Jakarta

The areas: Menteng Atas and Depok

As mentioned briefly in the above paragraph, two areas covered in the studies of informal sector workers for this chapter are two contrastive areas in Jakarta. The urban-*kampung* in this study is a residential area known as Menteng Atas. It covers around 1.47 square kilometers, with a density of 5,100 people per square kilometer.[6] The people who inhabit this area mostly earn middle to lower incomes. Even though a few are native to Betawi,[7] most people are immigrants, and some are seasonal immigrants, which results in diverse customs and habits of the people in the urban-*kampung*. The other area is an elite residential area developed in the early 1990s. The residential area is situated in the main street of a city called Depok, a city adjacent to the south part of Jakarta. Depok city itself covers around 67.13 square kilometers, and the development of the city follows that of Jakarta, as it was initially designed as a sleeper town for people who commute to Jakarta for their work. Depok has experienced significant development since the 1980s, when several universities—including the national university, Universitas Indonesia—moved their campuses to the city. With a population of more than 600,000 people, the city now has its own department stores and super-malls.

Pedagang keliling in Menteng Atas: type of merchandise

In Menteng Atas urban-*kampung*, various merchandise is sold by *pedagang keliling*, but the most common merchandise is food, whether in the cooked form, to be cooked when the transaction takes place, or as ingredients for cooking. This confirms Schoch's (1985) argument that hawkers provide goods or services for all kinds of daily life necessities. In Menteng Atas urban-*kampung*, from morning until around noon, we can see *pedagang keliling* who sell vegetables, bread, *kerupuk* (Indonesian crackers), *kue* (small cakes), *bubur nasi* (rice porridge), *bubur kacang ijo* (bean porridge), *ketoprak* (cold rice noodle, bean sprouts and fried bean curd with peanut sauce), *jamu* and kerosene. In the afternoon, between midday and six o'clock, it is even easier to find food, since almost all *pedagang keliling* who circulate during these hours sell food. We will meet *pedagang keliling* who sell *bubur sumsum* (sweet sticky rice porridge), *mie bakso* (meat ball soup with noodles), *pecel* (cooked vegetables with spicy peanut

Map 7.1 Jakarta with Menteng Atas and Depok

Photograph 7.4: Ketoprak hawker in Menteng Atas

sauce), *rujak* (fruit salad), *es cincau* (a kind of jelly with frappe ice), *kembang tahu* (bean curd for drinks), bread, *tape* (fermented rice for drinks), *agar-agar* (gelatin drinks) and *kue ape-ape* (small pancakes). Apart from meat ball soup, all food or drinks are cold. In the evening,

Table 7.9: Menteng Atas pedagang keliling *based on type of merchandise ([number of persons])*

morning
bread [5], *jamu* [3], *kerupuk* [1], *kue* [1], kerosene [3], vegetables [3], *bubur nasi* [2], *bubur kacang ijo* [1], *ketoprak* [1]

afternoon
bubur sumsum [2], *cincau* [1], *kembang tahu* [1], *mie bakso* [1], bread [2], *tape* [1], *pecel* [2], *kue ape ape* [1], *agar agar* [1], *rujak* [1]

evening
shiumai [2], *sekoteng* [1], *nasi goreng* [3], *sate* [1], shoe repairer [1], curtain maker [1]

Note: survey done on May 25, 2001.

Photograph 7.5: Kerosene man in Menteng Atas

after 6 o'clock, when the people return to their homes after a day at work, warm food can be seen more often. There are *pedagang keliling* who sell *shiumai* (dumplings), *nasi goreng* (fried rice), *sate* (chicken or mutton kebabs with peanut sauce) and *sekoteng* (a warm ginger drink). There are also *pedagang keliling* who do not sell food, but offer services such as shoe repairs or curtain-making. From merchandise being sold in this area, we can also see the tendency to eat out (in this case, buying food, rather than cooking food). This reveals that the urban-*kampung* has temporary residents who are seasonal immigrants to Jakarta.

Pedagang keliling in Menteng Atas: demographic features

Having interviewed twenty-five *pedagang keliling* in Menteng Atas urban-*kampung*, it turns out that the youngest is twenty-one years old, while the oldest is fifty-six years old, which means there is a wide range of age among *pedagang keliling*, with an average age in their late twenties to early thirties. These *pedagang keliling* do not have high educational attainment. Except for a very few of them, most did not finish junior high school, and some did not go to school at all. All of the interviewees were born outside of Jakarta; half came from West Java, the other half came from Central or East Java. They left their hometowns and their parents, who worked as agricultural labourers or as small landowner farmers. This explains the dependency among vegetable *pedagang keliling* on their networks from their farming-background villages. Among hawkers in this area, the one with the longest experience as a hawker left his hometown in the 1960s and has been a hawker in Jakarta since then. Some moved to Jakarta in the 1990s. A few moved to Jakarta after the economic crisis. When it comes to their working experiences, there is a similarity among them: they find work that needs almost no special skills at all, resulting in a reproduction of unskilled labour. In short, *pedagang keliling* as informal workers are immigrants from West and Central/East Java who have low educational attainment and are unskilled labourers.

Another interesting point to be highlighted here is that *pedagang keliling* tend to live very near to the area where they peddle, and the places where they live are usually rented or are provided by their 'bosses.' When it comes to housing, it seems that the existence of the 'boss' is significant, since the 'boss' is the one who supports them in finding a place to live, or even provides the place. We can see that there is a certain patron and client relationship between *pedagang keliling* and the person they call their 'boss.' And in such houses, among *pedagang keliling* who are married, there are two groups—those who live together with their spouse and children, and those who live separately from their family. The latter reveals the fact of seasonal immigrants who leave their families and come alone to

136 Chapter 7

Table 7.10: Menteng Atas demographic features (a)

no	merchandise	age	sex	educational background	place of birth	present address	type of housing	ethnic group	religion	marital status	present family structure	occupation of parents
1	bread	40	male	primary	Brebes	Menteng Pulo	boss's place	Javanese	Islam	married	wife, 2 children (live separately)	land-owner farmer
2	bread	56	male	primary	Indramayu	Menteng Atas	bread factory	Sundanese	Islam	married	wife, 9 children (live together)	land-owner farmer
3	kue	37	female	none	Subang	Pedurenan	rented house	Sundanese	Islam	married	4 children (live with 2nd child)	agricultural labourer
4	kerupuk	29	male	junior high	Ciamis	Menteng Atas	rented house	Sundanese	Islam	married	wife (live together)	micro-scale sundry goods seller
5	gorengan	23	male	primary	Cirebon	Gang Muria	boss's place	Sundanese	Islam	single	parents, 5 siblings (live separately)	vegetables seller in traditional market
6	vegetables	50	female	none	Pekalongan	Menteng Atas	rented house	Javanese	Islam	married	husband, 3 children (live with husband)	land-owner farmer
7	vegetables	50	female	primary	Pekalongan	Kober	rented house	Javanese	Islam	married	4 children (live with 3rd child) (husband died)	agricultural labourer
8	vegetables	44	female	primary	Pekalongan	Menteng Atas	owned house	Javanese	Islam	married	husband, 2 children (live separately)	land-owner farmer
9	fish	53	female	primary[a]	Pekalongan	Menteng Pulo	rented house	Javanese	Islam	married	husband, 8 children (live together)	land-owner farmer
10	kembang tahu	29	male	primary	Cirebon	Tebet	boss's place	Sundanese	Islam	married	wife, 1 child (live together)	land-owner farmer
11	otak-otak (fish patties)	27	male	primary[a]	Purwakarta	Tenggulun	boss's place	Sundanese	Islam	married	wife, 1 child (live together)	land-owner farmer
12	ketoprak	23	male	junior high	Brebes	Menteng Pulo	high school building	Sundanese	Islam	single	parents, 4 sisters (live separately)	teacher (ustadz) in Islamic school
13	bakwan	27	male	primary	Jombang	Menteng Atas	rented house	Javanese	Islam	divorced	(live alone)	land-owner farmer
14	bakwan	22	male	primary	Ngawi	Menteng dalam	boss's place	Javanese	Islam	single	parents, 4 siblings (live separately)	agricultural labourer

15 shiumai	30	male	primary	Pekalongan	Menteng Atas	rented house	Javanese	Islam	divorced	sister, sister's child (live together)	labourer in fish-cultivating pond
16 shiumai	29	male	primary	Karawang	Tegal Parang	rented house	Sundanese	Islam	married	wife, 2 children (live separately)	broker in land-selling
17 es cendol (rice flour drinks)	NA	male	junior high	Cilacap	Menteng dalam	rented house	Javanese	Islam	married	wife, 1 child (live together)	land-owner farmer
18 jamu	32	female	senior high[a]	Solo	Menteng Atas	rented house	Javanese	Islam	married	husband, 1 child (live together)	land-owner farmer
19 sundry goods	33	male	primary	Cirebon	Lapang Ros	rented house	Sundanese	Islam	married	wife, 2 children (live separately)	land-owner farmer
20 kerosene	42	male	primary[a]	Pemalang	Menteng Pulo	boss's place	Javanese	Islam	married	wife, 3 children (live separately)	fruit hawker
21 kerosene	30	male	senior high[a]	Pemalang	Menteng Pulo	relatives' house	Javanese	Islam	married	father, wife, 1 child (live with father)	sundry-goods hawker
22 curtains	30	male	senior high[a]	Bandung	Manggarai	rented house	Sundanese	Islam	married	wife, 1 child (live separately)	land-owner farmer
23 cloth-dye	21	male	primary	Madura	Klender	rented house	Madouranese	Islam	single	(live alone)	bull / cow seller
24 ashes	47	male	primary[a]	Bekasi	Menteng Atas	boss's place	Betawi	Islam	married	wife, 3 children (live together)	ashes seller
25 shoe-repairing	26	male	primary[a]	Garut	Kampung Melayu	rented house	Sundanese	Islam	married	wife (live separately)	NA

Notes:
1) Time of field research is May 26, 2001, from 8 am to 11 am, and from 3 pm to 6 pm.
2) Explanation for language written in Indonesian language: kue = baked, kerupuk = traditional crackers, gorengan = deep-fried sweets, kembang tahu = bean curd, otak-otak = fish patties, ketoprak = Jakarta-style salad with rice noodles, bean sprouts and bean curd, bakwan = meat balls and fried wantons, escendel = traditional cold drinks made from rice flour, jamu = traditional herbal.

Table 7.11: Menteng Atas demographic features (b)

no	work experience
1	labourer in coffee plantation in Sumatra (1985-87) ⇒move to Jakarta (1987)→bread hawker (1987–present)
2	construction worker ⇒move to Jakarta (1960)→satay hawker (1960–62)→bread hawker (1962–present)
3	agricultural labourer ⇒move to Jakarta (1992)→*kue* hawker (1992–present)
4	⇒move to Jakarta (1995)→*krupuk* hawker (1995–present)
5	vegetable hawker in Cirebon ⇒move to Jakarta (1976)→*gorengan* hawker (1993–present)
6	agricultural labourer ⇒move to Jakarta (1980)→vegetable hawker (1980–present)
7	agricultural labourer ⇒move to Jakarta (1975)→vegetable hawker (1975–present)
8	agricultural labourer (?–1971)→vegetable hawker (1972–76) ⇒move to Jakarta (1976)→vegetable hawker (1976–present)
9	agricultural labourer ⇒move to Jakarta (1966)→vegetable hawker (1966–2000)→ fruit hawker→fish hawker (2001–present)
10	agricultural labourer ⇒move to Jakarta (1989)→selling tabacco in kiosk (1989–91)→ construction worker (1992–93)→bicycle taxi →*kembang tahu* hawker (93–present)
11	bull herder (?) ⇒move to Jakarta (1990)→*otak otak* hawker (1990–present)
12	⇒move to Jakarta (?)→cinema ticket seller (→; 1 year)→gardener (→)→*ketoprak* hawker (→–present)
13	agricultural labourer→construction worker in Banyuwangi (→) ⇒move to Jakarta (1994)→gardener(1994–2001)→*bakwan* hawker (2001–present)
14	bread hawker in Kalimantan (1992–95)→farmer in Ngawi (1995–96) ⇒move to Jakarta (1996)→*bakwan* hawker (1997–present)
15	⇒move to Jakarta (1990)→vegetable hawker with elder sister (1990–92)→*shiumai* hawker (1999–present)
16	agricultural labourer (?) ⇒move to Jakarta (2001)→second-hand goods seller and *shiumai* hawker (2001– present)
17	construction worker in Tangerang (1990–91) ⇒move to Jakarta (1992)→ *es cendol* hawker (1992–present)
18	⇒move to Jakarta (1989)→employee of Sari Ayu cosmetics (1990)→*jamu* hawker (1992–present)
19	⇒move to Jakarta (1987)→construction worker in Cilandak (1991)→sundry goods hawker (1992–present)
20	⇒move to Jakarta (1975)→employee of a dress maker in Grogol (1975–78)→driver of three wheeled vehicle Bajaj vehicle in Grogol (1978–83)→kerosene hawker (85–present)
21	bus driver in Pemalang (1997–98)→employee in *Bandung* (1998–99) ⇒move to Jakarta (1999)→kerosene hawker (also taxi driver) (1999–present)

22 teacher of Islamic junior high school (1989–92) ⇒move to Jakarta (1992)→curtain hawker (1992–present)

23 cloth-dye hawker in Surabaya (?) ⇒move to Jakarta (1995)→cloth dye hawker (1995–present)

24 agricultural labourer (?) ⇒move to Jakarta (1971)→kerosene hawker (1971; 3 months)→ashes hawker (1971–present)

25 construction worker in Garut (1995–97) ⇒move to Jakarta (1997)→shoe repair hawker (1997–present)

Note: signs in working experience; ⇒ shows year of moving to Jakarta, → shows change of jobs in Jakarta.

the city to do unskilled informal work, such as becoming *pedagang keliling*. The former group shows that even those who settle in the city with their families continue to work in the informal sector.

Pedagang keliling in Menteng Atas: situation

To know about the present situation of *pedagang keliling* in Menteng Atas urban-*kampung*, we should first know about the network that brings them to Jakarta. Siblings or relatives and acquaintances are an important source of information and mutual help when it comes to starting a business as a hawker. This also explains why some *pedagang keliling* have siblings or relatives working in the same kind of informal sector business. Yet, there are more important reasons why they become *pedagang keliling*. They became hawkers to support their families or because there is no other choice of work for them in the city. Life is not easy for these *pedagang keliling*. Some have to work seven days a week, and most can only have one day off in a week. Hardship is not only about their working days; their incomes as *pedagang keliling* are also contrary to their hopes. And looking at their daily profit, there is a wide gap even among *pedagang keliling* of the same merchandise. This tells us that informal sector workers also face rivalry among themselves, which can result in a significant decrease in income.

It is not only the food and drink hawkers who have to deal with tight competition for customers; in Menteng Atas kerosene hawkers also have similar problems of rivalry. Among relative newcomers such as *bakwan* (meatball and fried wonton soup) hawkers, not only does the number of *pedagang keliling* of the same merchandise increase, but they also face the problem of decreasing numbers of customers. Adding to these difficulties, the rise of prices following the economic

Table 7.12: Menteng Atas situation of pedagang keliling

	person depend upon after arrived no in Jakarta	reason for becoming a hawker[a]	future plans	reason for answer	method for getting capital	place procure merchandise	other hawkers in family	ownership of utensils	revenue per day (rupiah)[b]	usage of revenue[c]	working days	plan to return
1	nobody	1,3,5,7,9,11	want to change job	want to gain more success	borrow from boss	boss's place	siblings	borrow from boss	200,000	6,7	7 days	yes
2	nobody	1,11	want to quit	want to return to hometown	from bread factory	bread factory	none	borrow from factory	120,000	2,6,7	NA	yes
3	siblings/relatives	1	plan to continue	better income compared to in hometown	none	pedurenan	none	borrow from boss	55,000–60,000	1,2,3,7	5 days	no
4	siblings/relatives	1,3,7	want to change job	present job is too tiring	hawker's own money	agent	father-in-law	borrow from boss	60,000	2,3,6	4–5 days	no
5	acquaintance	3,11	plan to continue	present job suits the hawker	borrow from boss	boss's place	elder brother	hawker's own	100,000	2,3,7	6 days	yes
6	husband	1,3,6	plan to continue	the hawker knows the job well	borrow from husband's relative	pasar rumput	none	hawker's own	110,000	2,5,7	3–4 days	no
7	siblings/relatives	1,3	plan to continue	present job suits the hawker	borrow from friend	pasar rumput	several people	hawker's own	NA	2,7	6 days	no
8	nobody	11	want to change job	want to do a bigger business	borrow from parents and friend	pasar rumput	husband, son-in-law	hawker's own	300,000	1,2,3,5,7	5–6 days	yes
9	acquaintance	1,2,11	plan to continue	no other choice of job	loan	pasar rumput	none	hawker's own	200,000	1,2,3,4	every day	yes
10	siblings/relatives	1,2,3,11	pan to continue	can live both in Jakarta and in hometown	borrow from boss	boss's place	brother-in-law	borrow from boss	50,000–55,000	2,3	7 days	yes
11	acquaintance	3	want to change job	want to be otak-otak maker (not hawker)	borrow from boss	tenggulan	uncle	hawker's own	varies	1,2,3,6	every day	yes
12	NA	1,2,6,9	want to change job	want to try various jobs	borrow from parents and ketoprak agent	pasar baru	none	hawker's own	125,000–170,000	1,2,4,5,6	4–5 days	yes
13	acquaintance	1,2,3,8	want to change job	want more income, want to try various jobs	none	boss's place	none	borrow from boss	20,000–50,000	2,3,7	every day	yes
14	nobody	1,2,8,11	want to change job	NA	borrow from boss	NA	none	borrow from boss	60,000	2,4	6 days	no
15	siblings/relatives	1,2,11	want to change job	want to work in a factory	borrow from friend	pasar baru	nephew	NA	20,000–30,000	2,3,6	6 days	yes

#	lives with	a	plan	reason	money source	origin	relative	place	income	c	days	?
16	nobody	1,11	plan to continue	enough income	from uncle	uncle's place	NA	hawker's own	20,000–30,000	2,3	3–4 days	yes
17	nobody	1,11	plan to continue	enough income	hawker's own money	menteng dalam & pasar	elder brother	hawker's own	50,000–85,000	2,3,5,6	6 days	no
18	parents	2,11	want to change job	NA	hawker's own money	hand-made	none	hawker's own	NA	2,3,7	5–6 days	no
19	acquaintance	1,11	want to change job	want a better job	borrow from parents	pasar mester	elder brother	hawker's own	50,000	2,3	varies	yes
20	acquaintance	1,8,11	plan to continue	can pay children's school fees	from kerosene agent	agent	elder brother	borrow from agent	200,000–275,000	2,3	7 days	no
21	nobody	1,7,11	want to change job	not enough income	none	kerosene agent	father	hawker's own	205,000–397,000	1,2,3,4,5,6	6.5 days	yes
22	nobody	1,3,11	plan to continue	present job suits the hawker	borrow from parents	bandung	2 siblings	hawker's own	15,000 (net profit)	2,3,5	6 days	yes
23	acquaintance	1,2,3,6,8	plan to continue	no other choice of job	hawker's own money	Surabaya	none	hawker's own	30,000	2,3	5 days	no
24	siblings/relatives	11	want to change job	saving for old age	borrow from boss	jatinegara	father	rent	25,000	1,2,3,4,7	5+ days	yes
25	acquaintance	1,2,11	plan to continue	NA	hawker's own money	pasar jatinegara	none	hawker's own	25,000–85,000	2,3,6,7	6 days	yes

Notes

a: 1. to support family's life; 2. to contribute to family's income; 3. no other choice of job; 4. lost previous job; 5. to pay back loan; 7. to save for next job; 8. invited by friends; 9. recommended by siblings and relatives; 10. no reason at all; 11 other reasons.

b: US$1 = 9,000 rupiah

c: 1. payback loan; 2. everyday living cost; 3. sending to family in hometown; 4. leisure; 5. buying materials for business; 6. savings; 7. other.

crisis makes it harder for *pedagang keliling*. All of these add up to a decrease in income.

With a decreasing income, hawkers still try to meet their families' daily needs, and some still manage to send some money to their parents or families in the villages. If possible, these *pedagang keliling* want to do better jobs that bring better incomes. Yet, it is not always possible, or it is almost impossible to change jobs with their very limited skills. With all these hardships, some of them dream of going back to their villages. But this is also impossible for the time being, since they picture Jakarta as the place that has jobs for them. They hold to this dream, hoping that they really can return to their villages and live quiet 'retirement' lives.

Pedagang keliling in Depok: type of merchandise

Pedagang keliling in the Depok elite residential area are not very different to their fellow workers in Menteng Atas urban-*kampung*, yet there are some points to be highlighted, since these reveal characteristics of *pedagang keliling* in each area. If we look at their merchandise, we can also see much food and drink, but some of their merchandise cannot be seen in the urban-*kampung*. In the morning, before noon, we can see *pedagang keliling* selling bread, *bubur ayam* (chicken porridge), *ketoprak*, *kerupuk*, bean curd and vegetables. The peddlers not seen in the urban-*kampung* but who can be seen in this elite residential area are *pedagang keliling* selling morning newspapers, flowers and house plants, and fertilizers for gardening. In

Photograph 7.6: Hawkers in Depok elite residential area

Table 7.13: Depok pedagang keliling *based on type of merchandise ([number of persons])*

morning
bread [5], *tahu bandung* [1], vegetables [3], flowers & house plants [2], fertilizer [1], *bubur ayam* [1], morning news paper [4], *ketoprak* [1], *kerupuk* [1]

afternoon
gorengan [1], *es doger* [1], ice cream [1], *jamu* [3]

evening
shiumai [2], *bakpao* [1], *mie bakso* [1], *rujak* [1], *nasi goreng* [1], *mie goreng* [1], bread [2], *kue* putu [1]

Note: survey done on March 23, 2001.

the afternoon, almost the same as in the urban-*kampung*, we can find *jamu*, *gorengan* (deep-fried sweets) and *es doger* (frappe ice). We also can buy ice-cream of various flavors. And in the evening, there are *shiumai, mie bakso, rujak*, bread, *nasi goreng, mie goreng* and *bakpao* (meat-filled buns). We can notice that there is no *pedagang keliling* selling kerosene, since in this residential area there are no houses that use kerosene stoves (all households here use gas stoves). The selling of morning newspapers also shows that people living in the area have middle to upper incomes and are used to getting written information such as that provided by newspapers. And, while it is impossible to garden in Menteng Atas urban-*kampung* because of the lack of land, each house in the Depok elite residential area has its own garden (although most are not very large gardens). This is why we can find *pedagang keliling* selling flowers or house plants.

Pedagang keliling in Depok: demographic features

Of seventeen *pedagang keliling* interviewed in Depok, there are several similarities with their fellow workers in Menteng Atas urban-*kampung*. However, some other points contrast with Menteng Atas. The first is the range of ages of Depok *pedagang keliling*, who tend to be younger (more are in their teens and early twenties). The younger age tendency also parallels the tendency of higher educational attainment. There are no *pedagang keliling* who did not go to school at all. At the least they went to primary school, but a person with a high school background is still a very rare case. We can say that even though *pedagang keliling* in Depok are slightly better educated compared to those in Menteng

Table 7.14: Depok demographic features (a)

no	merchandise	age	sex	educational background	place of birth	present address	type of housing	ethnic group	religion	marital status	present family structure	occupation of parents
1	bread	23	male	senior high	Semarang	Depok Timur	company's dorm	Javanese	Islam	single	parents, 3 siblings (live separately)	land-owner farmer
2	bread	23	male	primary	Bogor	Depok Lama	bread factory	Javanese	Islam	married	parents, wife, 6 siblings (live separately)	Islamic prayer teacher
3	bread	NA	male	primary	Rangkas Bitung	Depok Lama	boss' place	Sundanese	Islam	married	wife, 4 children (live separately)	land-owner farmer
4	*krupuk*	35	male	senior high[a]	Ciamis	Cijujug – Bogor	rented house	West Javanese	Islam	married	wife, 1 child (live together)	land-owner farmer
5	vegetables	40	male	primary	Pekalongan	Depok I	rented house	Javanese	Islam	married	wife (live together)	employee
6	vegetables	29	male	primary[a]	Pekalongan	Depok I	rented house	Javanese	Islam	married	wife, 2 children, nephew (live together)	land-owner farmer
7	vegetables	16	male	primary	Pekalongan	Depok I	uncle's house	Javanese	Islam	single	parents, 6 siblings (live separately)	land-owner farmer
8	vegetables	24	male	primary	Pekalongan	Depok I	rented house	Javanese	Islam	single	father, 4 siblings (live separately)	land-owner farmer
9	vegetables	40	male	primary[a]	Pekalongan	Lenteng Agung	rented house	Javanese	Islam	married	wife, 3 children (live together)	construction worker
10	porridge	30	male	junior high	Bekasi	Taman Baru —Depok	rented house	Bekasi	Islam	married	wife, 1 child, sister-in-law (live together)	agricultural labourer
11	*shiumai*	20	male	primary	Bekasi Timur	Gg Pertanian —Depok	boss' place	Betawi	Islam	married	parents, wife, 5 siblings (live separately)	land-owner farmer
12	*shiumai*	19	male	junior high	Bekasi	Depok Lama	rented house	Betawi	Islam	NA	parents, 2 siblings (live separately)	vegetable hawker
13	*shiumai*	25	male	junior high[a]	Bekasi	Margondak —Depok	boss' place	Betawi	Islam	married	parents, 3 siblings (live separately)	agricultural labourer
14	*shiumai*	23	male	primary	Bekasi	Tanah Baru —Depok	rented house	Betawi	Islam	married	wife, brother (live together)	agricultural labourer

15	shiumai	19	male	primary	Bekasi	Tanah Baru—Depok	boss' place	Bekasi	Islam	single	parents, 2 siblings (live separately)	land-owner farmer
16	newspapers	13	male	junior high[b]	Depok	Depok II	parents' house	West Javanese	Islam	single	mother, 5 siblings, grandparents (live together)	house maid (mother)
17	newspapers	14	male	junior high[b]	Bogor	Depok II	parents' house	West Javanese	Islam	single	parents, 7 siblings (live together)	jobless

Notes:

Time of field research is March 24, 2001, from 8 am to 11 am, and from 3 pm to 6 pm.

Table 7.15: Depok demographic features (b)

no	work experience
1	construction worker in Semarang (1996; 1 month) ⇒move to Jakarta (Depok) (1996) → bread hawker in Depok (1996–present)
2	⇒move to Jakarta (1996) → electric fan hawker in Grogol (1997–99) → bread hawker in Depok (1999–present)
3	⇒move to Jakarta (1976) → bread hawker in Depok (1997–present)
4	labourer in Tasikmalaya (1985–90) → labourer in poultry farm in Citeureup (1990–93) → labourer in rubber plantation in Banten (1993; 6 months) ⇒move to Jakarta (1993) → storehouse guardman (1993–94) → *krupuk* hawker in Bogor (1994–present)
5	factory worker (1980) → textile factory (1981–82) ⇒move to Jakarta (1882) → garment factory (1982–90) → fruit seller in Serpong (1990) → vegetable hawker in Depok (1995–present)
6	farmer ⇒move to Jakarta (1991) → worker in tempe factory (1991–96) → hawker in Depok (1996–present)
7	apprentice in dressmaking factory in Bekasi (4 months) ⇒move to Jakarta (2001) → vegetable hawker in Depok (2001–present)
8	⇒move to Jakarta (1991) → vegetable hawker in Lenteng Agung (1991–95) → vegetable hawker in Depok (1995–present)
9	⇒move to Jakarta (1972) → vegetable hawker in Lenteng Agung with brother (1972–96) → vegetable hawker in Depok (1996– present)
10	⇒move to Jakarta (1993) → chicken porridge hawker in Depok (1993–present)
11	⇒move to Jakarta (2001) → *shiumai* hawker in Depok (2001–present)
12	⇒move to Jakarta (1995) → *shiumai* hawker in Depok (1995–present)
13	shop attendant in market(→) ⇒move to Jakarta (1993) → *shiumai* hawker in Ciledug (1993) → *shiumai* hawker in Depok (?–present)
14	street vendor 'asongan' in Bekasi (1992–93) ⇒move to Jakarta (1993) → vegetable hawker in Klender (1993) → *shiumai* hawker in Depok (?–present)
15	*shiumai* hawker in west Bekasi (1996–97) ⇒move to Jakarta (1997) → *shiumai* hawker in Depok (1997–present)
16	(newspaper selling is his first job; he is a class mate of no. 17)
17	(newspaper selling is his first job; he is a class mate of no. 16)

Note: signs in working experience; ⇒ shows year of moving to Jakarta, → shows change of jobs in Jakarta.

Atas, they are still from a low-level educational background. In relation to their hometowns, one interesting thing to note is that all the vegetable hawkers come from the same village, which is a village near Pekalongan city in Central Java. If we look again at vegetable hawkers in Menteng Atas urban-*kampung*, we can also see that they come from the same area. Regarding hawkers from West Java, most of them come from the area known as *Bodetabek* (Bogor, Depok, Tangerang and Bekasi, which are cities in the greater metropolitan area of Jakarta). Whether they come from Central Java or from areas nearer to Jakarta, most of them come from farming families, some of whom were landowner farmers and others agricultural labourers. Looking further into their present family structures, more than half of them live away from their families. This is more obvious in the cases of those from West Java. We can say that these *pedagang keliling* leave their families to do the farming work in their villages while they come to the city to work as informal sector workers. The place where they were born also tells us another fact. Networks of people from the same village selling the same type of merchandise can be seen among vegetable hawker in Depok, just like their fellow workers in Menteng Atas. Similar network can also be found among *shiumai* hawkers who are of Betawi origins. Most *pedagang keliling* in Depok moved to the area (or moved to Jakarta) during the 1990s, the years when the city was undergoing rapid development and turned from a small town into an urban area. Among these informal sector workers, we can also find a second generation of immigrants who joined the informal sector. Their housing is not very different from Menteng Atas, where they tend to live near the place where they peddle. In Depok *pedagang keliling* also choose to live near their business routes. Most of them also live in rented houses (or rooms), or in places provided by the 'boss.' Although most *pedagang keliling* live separately from their families, there are some who live together with their spouses and children. These immigrants families are becoming permanent residents of Depok.

Pedagang keliling in Depok: situation

As in the Menteng Atas case, we begin by looking at the network that brings these *pedagang keliling* to Jakarta. Although siblings/ relatives and acquaintances are still important, there are more people (compared to Menteng Atas) who have come to the city on their own. These informal sector workers in Depok tend to depend less on a 'boss' or relatives when seeking resources to start their hawker businesses. The tendency can also be seen in the way they secure materials and utensils for their businesses. However, once they have started working as *pedagang keliling*, siblings or relatives who also work in the informal sector and with the same type of merchandise become the most important network and source of information concerning their

Table 7.16: Depok situation of pedagang keliling

	person depend upon after arrived no in Jakarta	reason for becoming a hawker[a]	future plans	reason for answer	method for getting capital	place procure merchandise	other hawkers in family	ownership of utensils	revenue per day (rupiah)[b]	usage of revenue[c]	working days	plan to return
1	nobody	2	plan to continue	present job suits the hawker	none	branch in Depok Timur	none	hawker's own	150,000–200,000	2,3,6	7 days	yes
2	acquaintance	1,2,3,7	plan to continue	easy job compared to other job	none	Usman Street	nephew	borrow from boss	140,000	2,3,6	7 days	no
3	acquaintance	1,3	do not know	NA	none	branch in Kemuning street	none	rent (400rp/day)	varies	2,3	5 days	yes
4	nobody	1,3,5,7,9,11	want to change job	now saving for the next job	none	branch in Depok	father	borrow from factory	120,000	1,2	3–4 days	no
5	acquaintance	1,3,8,11	want to change job	do not get enough profit	hawker's own money & borrow from someone	pasar Kemiri	younger brother	hawker's own	250,000–500,000	2,3	7 days	no
6	nobody	1,11	plan to continue	NA	borrow from relative	pasar Kemiri	younger brother	hawker's own	400,000	1,2,5	7 days	no
7	labourer seeking person	11	plan to continue	want to be independent	none	pasar Kemiri	two uncles	hawker's own	(belongs to uncle)	NA	7 days	yes
8	siblings/relatives	3	plan to continue	no other choice of job	got from parents	pasar Kemiri	brother, brother-in-law	hawker's own	400,000	2,5	7 days	yes
9	NA	1,3	plan to continue	present job suits the hawker	borrow from boss	pasar Kemiri	brothers-in-law	hawker's own	500,000	2,3,5,6	6 days	yes
10	nobody	1,2,8,11	plan to continue	NA	money from harvest	pasar Kemiri	younger brother	hawker's own	80,000–100,000	2,5	7 days	no
11	nobody	2,3,7	do not know	-	boss's money	Margonda Street	cousin	borrow from boss	20,000–30,000	2,7	7 days	no
12	siblings/relatives	1,2,7	want to change job	present job too tiring	borrow from brother	home made	brother	hawker's own	50,000–80,000	2,6	4 days	no
13	cousin	1,11	want to change job	enjoy being hawker	borrow from boss	Pertamina Street	none	borrow from boss	80,000–100,000	2,3,6	6.5 days	no

14	siblings/relatives	1,2,3	do not know	-	borrow from friend	from rented house	none	hawker's own	80,000–90,000	2,3	6.5 days	no
15	acquaintance	2,11	want to quit	want to continue study	borrow from boss	Tanah Baru	none	borrow from boss	60,000–80,000	3,6	varies	no
16	-	1,8,11	plan to continue	NA	none	Osa branch	relative	hawker's own	10,000–25,000	7	7 days	-
17	-	2,8,11	want to change job	present job too tiring	none	branch in Proklamasi street	elder brother	hawker's own	32,000	6,7	6 days	-

Notes

a: 1. to support family's life; 2. to contribute to family's income; 3. no other choice of job; 4. lost previous job; 5. to pay back loan; 7. to save for next job; 8. invited by friends; 9. recommended by siblings and relatives; 10. no reason at all; 11 other reasons.

b: US$1 = 9,000 rupiah.

c: 1. pay back loan; 2. everyday living cost; 3. sending to family in hometown; 4. leisure; 5. buying materials for business; 6. savings; 7. other.

work. Even though the hawker situation in Depok is slightly different from Menteng Atas, *pedagang keliling* in Depok also enter the informal sector because there is no other choice of work for them, yet they need to fulfil the daily needs of their families. Life as *pedagang keliling* in Depok is certainly not easier than in Menteng Atas. The fact that more of them have to work seven days a week tells us that it is a hard life. And the economic crisis also made it worse for them, since they now have more rivals in the same business; also, those who sell cooked food, such as bread or cakes, and those who sell fresh vegetables, often have to throw away their unsold merchandise at the end of the day, since these things are perishable. *Pedagang keliling* in Depok can be said to be newcomers in the business, with no significant presence of a 'boss,' but more rivals and longer working hours make their situation more unstable, compared to their fellow workers in Menteng Atas.

Yet, *pedagang keliling* in Depok still try to support their families' daily lives while sending some money to their hometowns, and in some cases they even try to save for their future. However, even if the life in the city is hard and unstable for them, most of them choose to stay and continue working in the informal sector. They think that if they return to their hometowns there will be no work for them, even as *pedagang keliling*. It means that, even if in the city they have to work hard to make ends meet, they see that city life still has more prospects than village life.

The unchanging fortunes of the Jakarta informal sector

As the capital city of Indonesia, Jakarta underwent (and is still undergoing) extremely vast urbanization and urban development. Until 1997 (that is, before the economic crisis), urbanization and urban development in Jakarta were characterized by the restructuring of physical and economic activities, in which the core of the city had changed from a manufacturing centre to a services and financial activities centre. Jakarta's urbanization has been a complex process, accompanied by intensive borderless flows of investment, goods, information and people (Firman 1999). The abundant numbers of workers in the informal sector in Jakarta were part of this intensive flow of people to Jakarta. Prior to the economic crisis Jakarta experienced two intensive flows of people from outside the city. The first occurred in the period between the late 1950s and the early 1960s, and the second in the period between the 1980s and the 1990s (Tomagola 2002).

During the first period, immigrants to Jakarta were not only from the island of Java but also from other islands in Indonesia. These people were mostly from West Sumatra, North Sumatra and South Sulawesi, with some from the Mollucas. They were of higher educational attainment, compared to other Indonesians at the time, and of middle or higher class. At the same time, immigrants from West, Central and East Java were of lower class and low educational background. The number of immigrants from the latter group was more significant compared to the former. The pattern of migration was a chain migration pattern, in which the head of the household went to Jakarta first, leaving behind his family. He would stay with a relative or acquaintance until he found a job and a place to live. After a while, he would invite members of his family (including relatives) to Jakarta. The pattern was then repeated, and usually resulted in members of families or people of the same village living nearby and doing similar work.

The second period of vast immigration to Jakarta (that is, during the 1980s and 1990s) was one of the results of world globalization, which promoted striking economic development in Southeast Asia (and also produced the economic crisis in 1997). In this second period of immigration, people who came to the city were unskilled and from lower-class rural areas. With the repeat of the chain migration pattern, the areas in Jakarta that functioned as receivers of people from the first period of immigration and that have become urban-*kampung*, were also the destinations for immigrants of the second period. This resulted in more densely populated urban-*kampung*.

The economic crisis in 1997 slightly changed the tendency of this rural–urban migration (Firman 1999: 77). It is reported that the crisis led a large number of immigrant urban workers to return to their hometowns as they lost their jobs in the cities. Or, immigrant urban workers began to send their family members back to their villages, since living expenses in the cities rose significantly. However, since the economic crisis also hit rural areas (causing rural people to look for additional sources of income), there were still large numbers of immigrants to urban areas, despite decreasing opportunities of jobs in the urban areas. Harvey (2006: 98) says that 'capital rich regions tend to grow richer while poor regions grow poorer' (caused by circular and cumulative causation within the economy), and this prevailed even in the middle of the economic crisis that severely hit the whole country. This economic crisis migration marks a third period of migration to Jakarta. From the real stories of informal sector workers in this chapter, it can be said that some of these workers belong to this third period of immigration to Jakarta, while some are second-generation immigrants from the previous periods.

Jakarta has seen three periods of vast immigrations, each with its own kind of people and mode of migration. Yet the result of these migrations is similar; to be exact, each migration contributed more to the density not only of the population of Jakarta, but also to the population of workers in the urban informal sector. Shrinking opportunities for places to live, as well as for finding jobs (whether in the formal sector or the informal sector), seem to be perceived by those informal workers as part of their daily lives, and have to be accepted as they are. Moreover, they still see that working for a living in Jakarta is better than going back to their villages. They have clung to the idea of staying in the city and continuing their work—not only before Indonesia was hit by the severe financial crisis in 1997 and 1998, but also during the prolonged crisis, and even after the country began to recover very slowly from the crisis. And for survival, informal sector workers depend mainly on their hometown networks, which consist not only of relatives but also of acquaintances who often do the same kind of informal sector business.

From the lives of Jakarta informal sector workers in this chapter, we can see at least two points to be highlighted. The first is that their position as a minority has not changed, be it before the 1997 economic crisis, during the crisis, or in the years following the crisis. They still hold to their dreams of succeeding in the city, but their opportunities for success, education and wealth are still very narrow. Such conditions resonate with the minority group characteristics proposed by Schaefer (2006). However, if the typology of minority groups is divided into racial, ethnic, religious and gender minority groups, then these informal sector workers can be said to involuntarily enter a minority group that is based on economic factors.

Related to the above point, the lives of Jakarta informal sector workers in this chapter also tell us that it is certainly not a recent trend that capitalism has reached every part of the everyday lives of these workers. Therefore, it is relevant to understand the adjustments and adaptations that occur in their daily lives as a path that leads to an understanding of how capital accumulation is working on the global stage (Harvey 2006: 80). Furthermore, Harvey (2006: 113) affirms that:

> Capitalism treats as commodities many of the fundamental elements within the web of life that are not produced as commodities. This

applies to labour, to all of what we often refer to as 'nature' as well as specific forms of our social existence. Once the body becomes a blatant 'accumulation strategy,' then alienation follows (though whether this is greeted by revolt or passive resignation is an open question).

However, looking at the unchanging fate of these workers, it can be said that workers in the informal sector in Jakarta accept passively the alienation that follows commodification of labour by capitalism. Even with their dreams of becoming more successful in life, the facts tell us that it is an unchanging fortune for Jakarta informal sector workers.

8 Street Homeless as an Urban Minority: A Case of Metro Manila

Hideo Aoki

Introduction

In cities of industrial countries, the numbers of homeless people have increased and their existence has become a social problem since the 1980s. In cities of developing countries, the numbers of street homeless who cannot live even in squatter areas have increased since the end of the 1990s. These people have many serious problems in surviving on the streets. They are an *urban minority* deprived of human rights and excluded from society. However, the problem of the street homeless has not yet been constructed as a social problem in developing countries because it is overwhelmed by the large scale of the squatter problem. The street homeless have been regarded as a part of the squatter homeless. Therefore, government reports and academic papers about them are very few. Based on my information, this chapter clarifies the actual situation of the street homeless in Metro Manila, and extracts the fundamental problems and analyzes them. Four concrete topics are proposed. First, I enumerate the various people on the streets and classify them into categories, and give a tentative definition of the street homeless. Second, I analyze the actual situation of the parents/families of street children, and a picture of the street homeless is shown indirectly. Moreover, I analyze the process by which inhabitants have been evicted from the squatter areas (squatters are the biggest source of the street homeless). Third, I show an overall picture of the street homeless in Metro Manila. I discuss in particular the conceptual relationship of the street homeless and the squatter homeless. Finally, I explain how globalization produces the street homeless; that is, the process forming the street homeless as a symbolic phenomenon of the transformation of the urban structure brought about by the economy of neoliberalism. I extract two factors that induce poor people to the streets (*pull-factors*) and three factors that push poor people to the streets (*push-factors*). Increases in the numbers of the new homeless in industrial countries and of the street homeless in developing countries are simultaneous processes that continually exist in globalization.

Subject and method

The new types of homeless people emerged almost simultaneously on streets in the cities of the world. They have emerged in the new era of industrialization. In cities of the United States (like Los Angeles and New York) since the 1980s, in cities of Japan (like Osaka and Tokyo) since the second half of the 1990s, in cities (like Warsaw and Prague) of former socialist countries that transferred to capitalism, and in cities (like São Paolo and Jakarta) of developing countries since the end of 1990s, the numbers of new homeless people have increased.[1]

The new homeless are the most deprived people and the most discriminated-against people in contemporary cities. They are an *urban minority*. The problem of the new homeless has been constructed as a *social problem* and has become a policy issue in industrial countries. In the United States since the 1980s the numbers of homeless people traditionally composed of middle-aged white males drifting around the downtown skid rows of cities have decreased, but there has been an increase in the number of homeless people who are diversified in sex, age and ethnicity, and who spread out across the whole city and became visible to the citizens (Levinson 2004: 108, 392). In Japan, since the second half of the 1990s, there has been a decrease in the number of day labourers who sometimes sleep on the streets around the so-called *yoseba* (the special district where day labourers live and get jobs from the recruiters) when jobs, especially in the construction industry, are unavailable. In contrast, there has been an increase in the numbers of homeless, the *nozyukusya* (rough sleepers), who cannot return to their work sites once they have been pushed on to the streets. Various people from miscellaneous occupations at the bottom of society have joined them. These homeless people live in station precincts, parks and on riverbanks, and are thus visible to other citizens.

It is said, too, that the numbers of homeless people living on the streets, the *street homeless*, have increased in cities of developing countries (Levinson 2004). They are at the bottom of urban society in developing countries, and cannot live even in the squatter areas. According to a professor of the University of São Paulo, in São Paulo, Brazil, the numbers of street homeless increased in the 1990s and reached more than 100,000 people at the beginning of the 2000s.[2] In Metro Manila (hereafter Manila), as in other cities in developing countries, there have been many street homeless in the past, and their numbers are increasing rapidly now. However, in developing countries the street homeless have not attracted strong attention because their existence has been overwhelmed by the large-scale problem of the squatters, and they have been referred to only as part of the squatter problem. Only in recent years have the street homeless been recognized as a peculiar problem in some developing countries. But their actual situation is still unknown in most countries. The existence of the street homeless was not constructed as a *social problem* in Manila. Therefore, administration reports and academic research about the street homeless are very few, except those that concern street children.[3]

Arnold Padilla pointed out that extremely poor families have recently increased in number in Manila and that people who can afford neither to build nor to rent houses in the squatter areas have become noticeable in various other places; they can be seen with their push carts along the seawall, on the sidewalks, under bridges and flyovers, in the middle of traffic islands, on the empty streets at night, on the lawns of cathedrals and in parks (Padilla 2000: 5–6). And he called these people the 'visible homeless,' the 'permanent homeless' (which seems to mean that people are unable to return to the main society again) and the 'modern nomads', discriminating them from the squatter homeless.

In such circumstances this chapter aims to make clear the actual situation of the street homeless in Manila and to analyze the basic problems they have, based on my fieldwork. The street homeless in cities of developing countries are the product of globalization, as is the case in industrial countries (Aoki 2006: 1–13). In other words, the transformation of urban structures through globalization is intensively reflected in the situation of the street homeless. Their appearance symbolically expresses the polarization of the urban class structure under globalization. The reason this chapter focuses on the street homeless rather than the large-scale squatter problem is to investigate the strategic importance in studying the street homeless.

This chapter is based on data from books and papers written about the urban poor, on my observations of the street homeless, and on face-to-face interviews I conducted with them, with administrative officers and with staff members of non-government organizations (NGOs) in Manila between September 2006 and February 2007.

People on the street

What kinds of people are on the streets of Manila? I will enumerate them based on my observations.[4]

People working on the streets

There are many people engaged in various informal jobs on the streets—vendors selling goods such as newspapers, cakes, dusters, *sampaguita* (flowers), tobacco and so on; porters carrying shoppers' bags from the markets; drivers of buses, *FX* taxis (taxicabs of medium-size), *jeepneys* (twin-benched jitney buses) or *tricycles* (three-wheeled motorcycles); bus conductors; barkers shouting out to passengers to ride buses, *FX* taxis or *jeepneys*; and blind buskers playing electric guitars and singing. These people have houses mostly in the squatter areas. They take to the streets in the morning, work there during the daytime and return to their houses in the evening. Therefore, they are not strictly homeless. However, among them are some people who do not have houses and who sleep on the streets at night—these are the homeless people. The street homeless cannot survive on the streets without working some kind of job. Therefore, it is not easy to distinguish the street homeless from the non-homeless people.

People evicted from the squatter areas

The number of people evicted from squatter areas has increased in Manila (I will explain the background of eviction in detail later). Among them are people who have been evicted from the squatter areas without being given relocation lots, and people who reject the relocation sites even if they are compensated with land. People who have jobs in the places around the former squatter areas cannot move to the relocation sites. Some people return from the relocation sites. It is not easy for them to find jobs in the relocation sites because there are very few employment opportunities.[5] They cannot commute from the relocation sites to Manila because it takes money and time to commute. As a result, some people leave their wives and children in the relocation sites and 'migrate' to Manila; others sell the houses in the relocation sites and return to Manila. People who do not have relatives to rely on end up on the streets.

Squatter areas are areas of public or private land that people occupy without the permission of the land owners. They do not have the legal right to live on the lots. Therefore, the squatter inhabitants are homeless, too. I call them the *squatter homeless*.[6] The squatter homeless appear to be the biggest source of the street homeless in Manila. Therefore, the squatter homeless give us important information with which we can infer the situation of the street homeless.

People migrated from the provinces

Many people are still migrating from the provinces to Manila, though the numbers of migrants is reducing.[7] In general, most of them live temporarily with relatives in the squatter areas—there is an indication that 80% of newcomers from the provinces enter the squatter areas in Manila (URC 1997: 25). However, as the eviction of squatters in inner-city Manila proceeds, the numbers of newcomers who cannot enter even these areas increase. These people are forced to stay with their baggage in station precincts, in parks, cemeteries and so on. They are the street homeless. They are divided into three categories. First, there are people who intend to migrate to Manila.[8] Second, there are people who have houses in the provinces near Manila—they leave their families, live in parks, cemeteries and so on, and periodically return to their provinces. They are the circular migrants who go to Manila and return to the provinces every week/month/year. They are not the street homeless strictly because they have fixed jobs and permanent houses in the provinces. Finally, there are refugees of calamities and political persecution. The Philippines is a country where natural calamities such as typhoons and earthquakes occur regularly. In addition, wars between government troops and rebel armies continue in the provinces. Affected by these disasters and wars, people lose their houses and are confronted with a life crisis and become domestic refugees. They escape their home towns with no possessions and go to Manila to seek help from relatives. Those who do not have relatives become the street homeless. In Manila there appear to be many refugees.

Ethnic minority people migrated to Manila

Another group migrating to Manila comprises people who come from the communities of tribal minorities such as people from Cordillera, Aeta in Luzon, and Moro in Mindanao and Palawan Island. They migrate to Manila because they have no means of livelihood in the provinces. And they live on the streets in downtown areas and become vendors and beggars.⁹ According to an activist of NGO$_3$, there is a syndicate of beggars composed of Cordillera people around EDSA Street in Cubao of Quezon City. Especially during the seasons of Christmas and New Year, there is an increase in the number of people, counting on the booming economy, who come to Manila for vending and begging. When these seasons pass, some people return to their provinces, some enter their ethnic communities in Manila and some people remain on the streets.[10] The last group of people become the permanent homeless.

Street children

In the Philippines the misery of the street children has attracted the interest of national/local administrations, NGOs and researchers as a symbol of Philippine poverty. Therefore, there are many reports and papers about street children. The problem of the street homeless has been regarded as part of the problem of the street children. The street children are defined as infants and adolescents under eighteen years old who stay on the streets during most of the daytime (Ruiz 2005: 5). They are classified into four types. First, there are the children who work on the streets after school and go back to their parents/families (parents and families are used interchangeably hereafter) at night (the children *on* the street). They work on the streets and contribute to their families' livelihoods. They comprise 70% of the street children. Second, there are the children who live on the streets and only sometimes go back to their parents (the children *of* the street). They comprise 20% of the street children. Third, there are the children who are abandoned and ignored by their parents. These children have completely broken, or have had broken, the bonds with their parents. They comprise 5% of the street children. Finally, there are the children of the *street families*. These children push carts with their families, move downtown and sleep on the streets at night with their families.

Tentative definition

The above classification of street dwellers was possible just by enumerating people on the streets by each category. There is some overlap between these categories, which also include the non-street homeless. To summarize the above, the street homeless comprise the following people: people working on the streets, people who have been evicted from the squatter areas, people who come to Manila, ethnic minority groups of people who work as seasonal workers, and street children and their families. Thus, a tentative definition of the street homeless is given as such: *the street homeless are people who do not have permanent and fixed houses, who do not have relatives with whom they can live, and who live alone or in a family unit on the streets in a fixed spatial range.* They are contrasted against the squatter homeless, although the border between the poorest part of the latter and the street homeless is blurred.

Families of street children

Information about the street children is important data from which we can see the whole picture of the street homeless. Therefore, my interest is in the parents of street children rather than the street children themselves. The families of street children of the fourth type, which I referred to above, are the street homeless. And large parts of the families of street children of the second and the third types are the street homeless, too.

Number of families

We have no reports that enable us to know the population of the street homeless in Manila.[11] But some reports show the real conditions of the street children. UNICEF made a nationwide survey in 1991 and counted 107,005 street children in Manila (NYC 1998: 144). In 2000 the Council for the Welfare of Children counted 44,435 street children, who were understood to be street children simply by viewing them (CWC 2006). Emma Porio reported that there were 50,000 to 70,000 street children in Manila in 1988 (Porio 1994: 112). The last number is often cited in other reports and papers as the population of street children in Manila. As I have already written, many street children live with their families (75%) or have some contact with their families (20%). From these facts, we can infer that many families of the street children also may be homeless or almost homeless. Moreover, there are many single street homeless who do not have children. Many people who have migrated from the provinces to Manila appear to sleep on the streets alone. As a whole, there are many single street homeless in Manila (as I discuss later in this chapter). Adding the number of the single street homeless to the number of the street children's families, we can infer that there are many more than 100,000 street homeless in Manila.[12] I regret that I cannot specify an accurate number of the street homeless.

Spatial distribution of families

The street homeless have to find the basic necessities of life in order to survive on the streets. The places where they can find such necessities anytime are the places where many people gather and where goods circulate all the time. According to the nationwide survey made by the Department of Social Welfare and Development (DSWD) in 1998, the main spatial distribution of street children was as follows: 36.5% on the street, 8.0% in the market, 12.4% around churches and amusement districts. Street children were numerous in the entertainment district, the business district, bus terminals and parks (Ruiz 2005: 5). According to the DSWD-NCR report (DSWD-NCR 2006a), the spatial distribution of street homeless who were given relief by DSWD-NCR was as follows: 40.8% in Manila City, 18.9% in Quezon City, 7.1% in Taguig, 6.9% in Pasay City, 5.5% in Parañaque City, 5.0% in Mandaluyong City, and 15.8% in other places. The street homeless who were given relief were numerous in municipalities with big downtown areas. The places where the street homeless seek life necessities are sometimes different from the places where they sleep at night. The places where the street children work and sleep are sometimes different from where the adult homeless work and sleep, too. With the adult street homeless, dangerous places such as cemeteries, riverbanks and canals are added to their places of work and sleep. However, we may consider that the places where the street homeless work and sleep are almost the same as those of the street children. The families of the street children live near their children. As far as I observed, the places where many street homeless sleep and live are Quiapo, Cubao, Baclaran, Santa Ana, Santa Mesa, Divisoria, Navotas, Luneta Park/Rizal Park and North Cemetery.[13] According to a representative of a drop-in centre for street children in Quiapo, more than 1,500 people live on the streets between Quiapo Church and the Pasig River. Among them at least 1,200 to 1,300 people appear to be homeless.[14]

Jobs of families

How do the street homeless earn their livelihoods on the streets? The information about the street children's families is important in order to know the realities of the street homeless. DSWD-NCR conducted a rehabilitation project for 606 street children and their parents between April and June 2005 (DSWD-NCR 2006b). In Quirino Avenue in the City of Manila, thirty street children and their parents who sold *sampaguita* participated in this project. They were the families who were almost homeless because of evictions by the improvement project of the Philippine National Railway (PNR), and they were going to transfer to relocation sites. The jobs of children's parents were as follow: dishwashers, cooking assistants, *jeepney*/tricycle drivers, barkers, laundrymen/women, and tobacco and duster sellers. Most families earned 50 to 200 pesos per day and three families earned more than 250 pesos. (The set minimum wage of a worker in Manila in 2006 was 300 pesos per day.) In Parañaque City twenty-one street children participated in the project. Among the parents, ten were *sampaguita* sellers (among them four parents earned 200 to 300 pesos per day) and eleven were food sellers who received the scraps from the restaurants in Baclaran (some of them earned 200 to 300 pesos per day). They lived in shanty houses on the streets around the church. In Pasay City ten street children participated in the project. The jobs of their parents were as follow: two parents were *balut* (boiled duck's egg) sellers and earned 100 to 200 pesos per day, four were food sellers and earned 200 to 300 pesos per day, one parent was a fish seller and earned 200 pesos per day, one parent was the owner of a *sari-sari* store (small general store) and earned 300 pesos per day, one parent was a *sampaguita* seller and earned 300 pesos per day, and one parent's job was unknown. In Quezon City fifteen street children participated in the project. Twelve parents were *sampaguita* sellers and earned 150 to 200 pesos per day, and three parents migrated to Manila's suburbs (Bulacan) with their children. All of these families were the victims of the squatter evictions and lived in rental rooms arranged by the National Housing Authority. In San Juan City ten street children participated in the project. Their parents were *sampaguita* sellers and some were mineral water sellers.

These children are only some of the street children in Manila and the samples are biased because they were the street children who participated in the project. However, it can be understood from the report that the street children's parents were homeless or almost homeless. Most of them were street vendors. Their average earnings were 200 to 250 pesos and their living conditions were extremely poor (the minimum cost of living in Manila was 590.3 pesos per person per day in 2000) (NSO 2000). Their dwellings were on the streets or in temporary rental rooms. There were many families who lost their houses because of evictions from the squatter areas.

Squatters

Many street homeless were from outside Manila. According to a report of the Jose Fabella Center, a public facility for the street homeless, more than half the street homeless were born outside Manila (JFC 2006). However, led by young people, the nature of the street homeless is changing to a generation that was born in Manila. In other words, *a mechanism producing the street homeless as a social stratum is continually formed in the economic and social structure of Manila.* To explain this mechanism is the very objective of this chapter. In doing so, squatters become the most important part because they are the biggest source of the street homeless. We do not have any proof to testify this hypothesis at present. Even so, it can be pointed out that the number of the street homeless seems to increase steadily and that many street homeless are the product of the squatter homeless. What is the process? I will clarify some aspects of the process producing the street homeless through the analysis of squatters.

Urban redevelopment

The squatter population in Manila increased in the 1990s. According to government statistics there were 432,450 squatter families in 1995 (MMHP 1996: 11), 577,291 squatter families in 1999 (Padilla 2000: 5) and 716, 387 squatter families in 2000 (NHA 2001: 13). Three general processes are contributing to this increase. First, the number of poor people in Manila increased. The rate of poverty incidence in Manila was 8.5% in 1997 and 11.4% in 2000 (NSO 2000). Second, land and house prices soared. For example, the land price in the business district along Makati Avenue was 60,000 pesos per square meter in 1990 and 220,000 pesos per square meter in 1998 (URC 1998: 1.3). Third, the housing policy by the government became deadlocked. The number of houses that the government needed to build in Manila between 2005 and 2010 was set at 496,928 (Karaos and Payot 2006: 67–8). However, only one-third of those houses were targeted to be built. It is unclear if this target will be achieved.[14] Manila's economy has been activated, and investment in land has been accelerated, by globalization. As a result the land price has soared. This has brought three results. First, squatters on areas of land that had been not used or devastated were evicted. Second, the squatter areas were marginalized from the inner-city (with high land prices) to the suburbs (with low land prices). Third, the government could finance and construct houses and relocate only some of the people affected by the policies. At the same time, the government implemented land privatization. Finally, the government started to improve the urban infrastructure with large-scale projects. The improvement of dangerous districts and the beautification of the streets were urged, too. People were prohibited from constructing houses within ten meters of riverbanks and within fifteen meters of railway lines.

Eviction from squatter areas

All of these events resulted in the eviction of squatters. Many squatter areas were originally designated by the government as the priority areas for the evictions. Of the squatter areas in Manila in 2000, 13.2% were in dangerous zone such as the seashore, riverbanks, along railway lines and at dumpsites (NHA 2004: 13); 22.9% were in government-designated sites of infrastructure development; 44.9% of squatter areas were situated on public lands; and 19.1% of squatter areas were situated on private lands. That is, 36.1% of squatters in Manila were waiting to be evicted at anytime. Thus, the eviction of squatters has been repeated. There were evictions from eighteen squatter areas in Manila and 10,048 families were evicted in 2001 alone (Padilla 2002: 6). In 2004 there were evictions from 341 squatter areas in Manila (Karaos and Payot 2006: 75). According to NGO_1, 4,591 families and 22,295 people were evicted from squatter areas between October 2005 and April 2006 (Karaos and Payot 2006: 75). In 2005 the government started to improve the Philippine National Railway line running from the northern part of Manila (Caloocan North, Malabon, Valenzuela, Mandaluyon) to the southern part of Manila (Caloocan South, Manila, Makati, Taguig, Parañaque, Muntinlupa). At the same time, the government started to improve the riverbanks and the waterways in Manila. The total number of families that were evicted by 2005 and that were planned to be evicted by 2010 are shown in Table 8.1 (Karaos and Payot 2006: 76). According to the table, more than 130,000 families will be evicted in the next five years.

To the streets

The Urban Development Housing Law regulates that the eviction of squatters should be prohibited in principle except in the districts given priority for eviction, that finance for housing should be given

Table 8.1: Families that were relocated and are planned to be relocated

	Planned	Relocated	Not yet relocated
North PNR	38,588	22,318	16,270
South PNR	50,013	6,753	43,260
Pasig River	10,827	6,095	4,732
Esteros	26,120	5,073	21,047
Others	7,495	7,127	368
Total	133,043	47,366	85,677

Source: Medium Term Philippines Development Plan and National Housing Authority (Karaos and Payot 2006: 76).

precedence for evicted families, and that relocation sites should be given to families evicted from public land. However, many squatters have been evicted without any compensation. The tragedy is that people have been evicted from the squatter areas and pushed to the streets, but not enough counting has been done. Although 20,116 families were evicted from the squatter areas in Manila between 1992 and 1995, only 43% of them were given relocation sites (Karaos 1996: 10–12). None of the 1,600 families evicted from squatter areas in Muntinlupa City in 1999 were given lots to which to relocate (Padilla 2000:16). A pamphlet produced by a research company discusses eighteen cases of evictions under the Arroyo government in 2001 (IBON Foundation Inc. 2001). Finally, 1,591 families (this number does not include families along the railways of PNR) were evicted from the squatter areas: 23.8% of those families were given lots to relocate to and 37.0% of those families were given the money for relocation (Karaos and Payot 2006: 77). As a case that I witnessed, about 300 families were evicted from the squatter area in Quiapo and more than 1,500 people became homeless in February 2007.

People who are not given lots to relocate to have to look for substitute places to live. People who cannot afford other places are forced to be homeless. But what happens to people who are transferred to the relocation sites? Often the relocation site is far from Manila, and there are no job opportunities there. Often they cannot live comfortably in the relocation sites because they do not have electricity or water supplies, or schools and hospitals.[15] As a result, many relocated people are forced to return to Manila. People who can secure their lives in Manila are fortunate: others cannot but be homeless. The total numbers of people who were not given lands to live, people who returned from the relocation sites and people who became homeless are unknown. However, it is not difficult to infer that these people are the biggest source of the street homeless.

Street homeless

Who are the street homeless? I have to refine the concept of the street homeless based on my discussion until now: the street homeless are people working on the streets, parents of street children, and people evicted from the squatter areas. Next, I show a whole picture of the street people based on data collected by the Jose Fabella Center.

Concept of street homeless

We do not have a definition of the street homeless in which we can discriminate them from the squatter homeless clearly. The National Housing Authority discriminates the (street) homeless people from the squatter inhabitants as shown in Table 8.2 (NHA 1993). According to the table, the squatter inhabitants are regarded as people who live in fixed places; in contrast, the street homeless are regarded as people who always change the places they sleep and who live everywhere. However, four problems result from this discrimination. First, there is a problem about what the shelter is. There are no squatter homeless without any shelter. But if spaces beside trees and buildings, fences made of pieces of wood, carts covered with sheets or scrapped cars can be called shelter, we can say that many street homeless have shelters. Second, there is a problem about what is meant by the words 'fixed' and 'move.' The squatter areas are the areas where people continuously occupy the lands. Therefore, the spatial bases for the occupants' lives are fixed. On the other hand, the street homeless are regarded as always moving the places they sleep. However, the street homeless mostly sleep in some constant areas. The street homeless who move without any concern about where to sleep every day are actually very few. It is surely not easy for the street homeless to look for safe places to sleep everyday. Third, there is a problem about what is meant by 'live' on the street. The word 'live' can mean 'to spend most of the daytime on the street' and 'to sleep on the street.' There are many vendors who return to their houses at night. They are not homeless. I call the street homeless the people who sleep on the streets at night. The term 'street dweller' is ambiguous, too, because it

Table 8.2: Differences of squatter inhabitants and homeless people

Squatter inhabitants	Homeless people
have shelter	do not have shelters
have fixed places to sleep	always change the places they sleep
live in the downtown areas, riverbeds, dump sites etc.	live everywhere (streets, parks, cemeteries, under bridges, etc.)

contains these two meanings. Finally, there is a problem about what is meant by the words 'collectively' and 'separately.' The squatter area is an area where people live collectively. The places that they can secure are limited. In contrast, the living places of the street homeless are not limited because they move alone or in each family unit. On this account it is easier for them to secure living places 'everywhere', as we can see in the table.[16]

In summary we have no criteria with which to discriminate the street homeless from the squatter homeless perfectly. They are borderless. It is difficult to define the street homeless generally.[17] We have to define the street homeless case by case as per the objective of the study. With this in mind, I can say the next point at least. The squatter homeless are people living in *permanent* and fixed shelters. In contrast, *the street homeless are people who have no permanent, fixed shelters and who move on the streets (outdoors) of a constant area alone or in a family unit.* The street homeless are people who cannot live even in the squatter areas and thus are ranked socially below the status of the squatter homeless.[18]

Picture of street homeless

According to a Jose Fabella Center report about the street homeless (JFC 2006), most of the residents of the facility (75.2%) were homeless, and were found on the streets and brought to the Center by the Sidewalk Operation Group of the Metropolitan Manila Development Authority. The Center accepted 2,794 street homeless between January and June 2006. They were composed of vagrants (461 people), beggars (86 people), people living on the street (2,193 people), victims of squatter evictions (42 people) and others (12 people). Their age composition was as follows: 34% were less than seventeen years old (infants and adolescents), 19% were eighteen to twenty-four years old, 44% were twenty-five to fifty-nine years old, and 3% were more than sixty years old. According to the director of the Center, most children have parents.[19] Many parents were the street homeless and other parents lived in the squatter areas. The civil status of the residents was as follows: 69 were divorced, 189 were junior, 231 cohabitated, 1,718 were single, 499 were married and 73 were widows (total 2,779). The gender of residents was 72% male and 28% female. Finally, 46% were born in Manila, and 54% were born outside Manila and came from across the whole country.

We can deduce three points from this information. First, the residents of the Jose Fabella Center were distributed over a broad age hierarchy from infant to advanced ages. Second, related to this, their civil status varied from junior to widows. Many residents were single (61.8%). Most of the people who were married and who cohabitated appeared to be single when they entered the Center. Finally, people who were born in Manila comprised almost half of the residents, an unsurprising result since there were many infants, children and minors among them. This situation shows that the street homeless are not only from the provinces.

The spatial distribution of residents' living places just before they came to the Center was as follows: 6% came from the First District of Manila, 30% came from the Second District (Mandaluyong City, Marikina City, Pasig City, Quezon City and San Juan), 8% came from the Third District (Caloocan City, Malabon, Navotas City and Valenzuela City), 21% came from the Fourth District (Las Piñas City, Makati City, Muntinlupa City, Parañaque City, Pasay City, Pateros and Taguig), and 35% came from out of Manila. As we can see, 65% were from the various districts of Manila, especially the Second and the Fourth Districts. Thus, it is inferred that the street homeless may diffuse from the metropolitan central area (the First District) to neighbouring areas, though we do not have any methods to test this. Next, it is inferred that the street homeless may be pushed from the Third District, the poorest region in Manila, to the rich region, where it is easier for them to get the necessities of life.

The composition of work that people did before coming to the Center was as follows: 19 were drivers, 5 were driver assistants, 53 were beggars, 12 were parking boys/girls, 8 were car dispatchers, 96 were workers (meaning day workers who go to a work place from the street), 43 were various kinds of helpers, 41 were barkers, 113 were vendors, 99 were scavengers, 63 were juniors, 6 were street children, 9 were students, and 133 had other jobs (total 700 inmates). The vendors, scavengers, beggars, car dispatchers, barkers, drivers and driver assistants were all engaged on the streets. Thus, it is concluded that the homeless people earn their livelihoods *on the street, by the street* and *through the street.*

The street homeless mostly gain their livelihoods as vendors, scavengers, car dispatchers, barkers and by illegal activities as snatchers, pickpockets, drug dealers and prostitutes. There are many street homeless who are hired by bosses or who borrow the goods for selling. The street homeless who commit illegal activities are relatively few. The most numerous street homeless are engaged in scavenging and begging. The scavenger is further classified into four groups: the scavenger buying cans, bottles, paper, hardware and so on using money that he/she borrows from a dealer; the scavenger picking up cans, bottles, paper, hardware and so on that are thrown away; the scavenger picking up anything such as used shoes, bags, toys and so on; and the scavenger picking up edible things from waste material. There is a status ranking from the scavenger who has money or a cart to the scavenger who has nothing. The beggar is classified in groups, too: the beggar earning money by playing an instrument or showing arts, the beggar embracing a child in order to provoke sympathy from other people, and the beggar begging just by hand.[20]

Formation of street homeless

New homeless

The street dwellers are not the new people who appeared recently in Manila. Newcomers from the provinces, who lived on the streets because they were jobless, have been seen from the old days. They could not secure places in the squatter areas. They drifted around and begged food and money. The numbers of these people were not few. However, these people have been regarded as a part of the squatter homeless. But the street homeless have increased much more since the end of the 1990s. Such recognition has been shared among the citizens. The street homeless have become noticeable everywhere in the urban center of Manila. Thus, they were called the 'visible homeless' and were discriminated from the squatter homeless. It is only a matter of time that these street homeless will continue to increase in number, and that their existence will be recognized as a particular social existence. Manuel Castells wrote that the occupation of urban space by the new marginality produced the *new poverty*, which takes two forms. First, a connived ghetto where people 'left behind' by mainstream society are permitted to live in marginalized places. Second, a dangerous strategy but at the same time a technique for survival, street people with no fixed abodes openly appear at the urban central area (Castells 1997: 236).

Globalization

The increase in the numbers of the street homeless is not only a phenomenon that occurs in cities of developing countries—it also corresponds to the increase of new homeless in cities of industrial countries.[21] What lies beneath these phenomena and produces them is the so-called globalization. The increase in the numbers of street people in Manila has its unique process prescribed by the (urban) economic history in the Philippines. Why is the Philippines' (Manila's) economy not able to take off? Why is the Philippines' (Manila's) government unable to resolve the problems of poverty and housing? What political, social and cultural conditions are there behind these problems? These questions have to be answered one by one.[22] Keeping this in mind, I ask why globalization has resulted in the increase of the street homeless. And I explain its general process in Manila, one of the cities of the developing countries. The process is composed of five sub-processes, which are functional and related to each other.

Increase of life chance

Globalization has brought about the expansion of the service economy in Manila and has resulted in an increase in the supply of basic life necessities for the street homeless. First, the numbers of business facilities, convenience stores, family restaurants and so on have increased drastically,[23] and provide necessities such as food for the street homeless. More so, they have also provided opportunities for the street homeless to beg. I call this process the *first pull-factor* that induces poor people to the streets.

Second, the expansion of the service economy has urged the 'informalization' of the economy; that is, the increase of the new informal types of occupations that people can engage in with a small equity capital and without any special knowledge and skills (Aoki 2003: 113–119).[24] The existing informal sector has expanded, too. As a result, jobs on the street such as vendor, scavenger, barker and the carrier have increased at the bottom of the informal sector.[25] These jobs have increased the life chances of the street homeless. I call this process the *second pull-factor* that induces poor people to the streets.

Downward pressure on the worker's status
Globalization made the labour market shrink through neoliberalism and resulted in labour becoming more flexible (workers are required to have the ability to perform various jobs) and the contractualization of employment, which limits the worker's employment period to between three to six months. It made the worker's employment status unstable and cut back the worker's real wage. As a result, there has been an increase in the number of workers who are paid the minimum wage, even in modern companies including multinational corporations. These conditions have worsened the worker's situation. Some workers had part-time jobs with the informal sector, other workers transferred from companies to informal occupations. And other family members were set to work mostly with informal occupations (Aoki 2003: 113–119). All of these conditions strengthened the downward pressure on the worker's economic status, and this labour situation became the general background against which people at the bottom of society became homeless.[26] I call this process the *first push-factor* that pushes people to the streets. But not all economically depressed people become homeless. Only some people who do not have safety nets with their relatives are forced to go to the streets.

Eviction of the squatters
Among capitalists globalization has accelerated the competition and urge to redevelop land. The real estate market has expanded. Unused and desolated lands have been redeveloped. And the gentrification of the inner-city has proceeded.[27] Government policies such as privatization of public land, the improvement of dangerous areas and the beautification of the streets have accelerated these processes. People who were not given relocation lots on which to live, who rejected transferring to the relocation sites, who returned to Manila from the relocation sites or who did not have relatives with whom they could live were pushed to the streets. I call these processes the *second push-factor* that pushes people to the streets.

Deadlocked policies
Globalization has given birth to a financially slim government through neoliberalism, and has accelerated the financial crisis of the developing country. As a result the policies concerning the homeless

became deadlocked. First, the policies of job creation for the urban poor, especially the squatter inhabitants, were deadlocked. Second, the policies to secure relocation lots and the construction of houses for squatter inhabitants were deadlocked. Compensation to those evicted was only paid to some of the squatter inhabitants. Third, the policies for preventing people becoming paupers and the street homeless were also deadlocked. Finally, employment and welfare policies to provide relief to the street homeless were deadlocked. There are no homeless measures worthy of special mention except the emergency aid for medical treatment and six temporary small facilities for the street homeless in Manila.[28] I call these conditions the *third push-factor* that pushes people to the streets.

Study of the street homeless in developing countries

This chapter is an interpretation of how globalization has brought the street homeless to Manila. The street homeless have been formed as a social stratum through the processes of various factors that induced/pushed people to the streets—that is, the *pull-factors* and the *push-factors* that operate together. The circumstances in which the homeless people emerge are different in every country, every city. However, the 'new homeless' appeared almost at the same time in cities of the industrial countries and the developing countries. The same process has gone on in Manila, too. This fact is absolute. The new homeless is a symbolic product brought about by globalization. So, how have labour conditions and the housing of urban people at the bottom of society been transformed under globalization? How and which way is the character of poverty transformed? As a result, how are the poorest urban people reorganized? The study of the new homeless people gives the clues to answer these questions.

9 The Reorganization of Ethnic Chinese Groups in Thailand, and the Background to this Reorganization

Kazuo Yoshihara

'The World Lin Clansmen Convention' was held in Honolulu in mid-November 2002. It was an event at which a large number of Chinese and ethnic Chinese individuals with the surname 'Lin' gathered from around the world. Such events are not limited to those with the surname Lin. Gatherings where those with the same Chinese surname from around the world come together have been gaining popularity since the end of the 1970s. In 1986 roughly 8,000 individuals (as indicated by the event promoter) with the surname Lin met in Bangkok, Thailand.

The start of China's reform policies and the sense of expectation it generated towards China's expansive domestic market represents one reason why overseas Chinese and ethnic Chinese from around the world with the same surname, who are from the same birthplace, or who speak the same dialect have started up activities that foster mutual networking and exchanges. Up-front economic activities are rarely included in the official schedules of these same-surname conventions. However, many dinners and tourist activities are incorporated into the conventions, providing opportunities for exchanging relevant information and building personal trust, which serves as the foundation for trading and investments. Of course, this is not to say that personal trust can be easily established simply based on the fact that people are ethnically Chinese and share the same surname. The fact that one has the same surname and may share distant ancestry is merely an 'entrance' for building a trust relationship. There are many such selectable entrances, and the possibility of meeting a variety of individuals has great value. Using the Lin group as a case study, let us examine the process by which these ethnic Chinese surname groups, which are an anchor for making such activities possible, are generated.

It is widely known that there are many Chinese-Thais in the urban areas of Thailand, and that their assimilation into Thai society has been rapidly advancing since the 1950s. However, it is not well known that the ethnic activities of middle-aged and elderly ethnic Chinese, revolving around first- and second-generation immigrants, were being rejuvenated at the same time. In an era when the Chinese market economy is developing and Chinese-Thai economic relations are becoming ever closer, how will the Chinese-Thai behave?

Although the Chinese are definitely not a demographic majority in Thailand, it cannot be denied that their economic power has made large contributions to Thai economic development since the Ayutthaya Kingdom in the mid-fourteenth century up to the present kingdom. As a foreign immigrant group with economic power, the Chinese in Thailand form a visible ethnic group. Although they do not form an absolute minority group, they have been pressured to assimilate by indigenous majority groups since the rise of nationalism during the period of economic development in the 1960s.

A study of the number of Chinese immigrants during the twentieth century reveals major differences in the periods before and after the establishment of the new China. During the thirty-year period from 1918 to 1949, the yearly average number of immigrants was approximately 67,300, while the number of emigrants was 17,700. In other words, the net increase was approximately 50,000 per year. By comparison, after the establishment of the Communist regime, from 1950 to 1955 the yearly average number of immigrants was approximately 8,300, while the yearly number of emigrants was 6,800. This marks a sharp decline to a net increase of approximately 1,500 per year (Skinner 1957; Walwipha 1995). The number of permanent immigrant Chinese residents (overseas Chinese nationals, as opposed to the ethnic Chinese who have obtained Thai nationality) reached its peak in 1937 at approximately 540,000 people. The number then decreased year by year to approximately 400,000 in 1960, to 310,000 in 1970 (Wilson 1983) and to 290,000 in 1980. By 1987 the number was down to 180,000.

Each ethnic Chinese group has a different level of influence based on its population size and economic strength. In view of the principles underlying group formation, it can be said that same-township and same-dialect groups that are formed on the basis of differences in birthplace in China (based on the administrative units of village, township, county, prefecture, municipality, and province) and dialect (the Cantonese (Guangtong) dialect, Chaozhou dialect, Fujian dialect, Hainan dialect, Kejia dialect, and so on) have long exerted a strong presence.

Although the population proportion per dialect is difficult to obtain, according to Skinner (1957), the Chaozhou group is the largest. It comprised 56% in 1955, followed by the Kejia group at 16%, the

Hainan group at 12%, the Cantonese and Fujiangroups at 7%, and others at 2%. In terms of the relationship between these groups and occupational structure, specific dialect groups came to dominate the management echelon of specific industries from the nineteenth century onwards. From the time of the Great Depression until the Second World War, sectors dominated by the Cantonese group were gradually taken over by the Chaozhou group. The board member composition of the Chinese Chamber of Commerce is also roughly proportional to the population distribution of the dialect groups. That is to say, the difference in influence among the dialect groups is based on population and economic strength.

The organizations controlling each of the township/dialect groups are associations known as *huiguan* (associations). The organizations preceding the *huiguan* came into being as early as the latter half of the nineteenth century, but they became known as *huiguan* only in the twentieth century. The Fujian Club, which preceded the Fujian Huiguan, was established in 1871, and the Qiongzhou Club, which preceded the Hainan Huiguan, was established in 1875. At roughly the same time, in 1877, the Guangdong Guangzhao Club was formed, and later became the Guangzhao Huiguan. Later, in 1896, the temple that enshrines the Statue of Song Dafeng (which is still revered by many Chaozhou residents today) was built as an assembly hall for the Chaozhou group. In 1938 this group developed into the Chaozhou Huiguan. The Keshu Club was formed in 1910 and later became the Keshu Zonghui (Keshu Huiguan) in 1926. In 1923 the Jiangzhe Huiguan was formed as a group for residents from Jiangsu Province and Zhejiang Province. As observed above, the reason dialect groups with small populations generally formed earlier reflects their need to promote mutual aid and cooperative protection due to their weak status. Presently, the most powerful group is the Chaozhou group.

Although sub-ethnic groups based on such dialect differences came to articulate ethnic Chinese communities, a principle of group formation that further articulated the sub-ethnic groups also existed: Chinese surnames. In traditional Chinese society, family and kinship organizations are constructed on the principle of patrilineal descent. The members of these groups are all individuals with the same surname, excluding the females in the family of the woman entering the marriage (the wife, mother and grandmother). Consequently, if those with the same surname trace their ancestors back, they can assume that they share common patrilineal ancestors. Same-surname associations with voluntary membership represent familial organizations reconstructed in immigrant communities on the grounds of such an ideology.

Same-surname groups formed by immigrants and their descendants began to appear within the same-birthplace/same-surname groups at the beginning of the twentieth century. Although these same-surname groups are known as *zongqinhui* (clan associations), this term is not necessarily included in the names of the organizations. It was around the 1960s, in tandem with this trend, that many same-surname groups known as *zongqinzonghui* (clan general associations) began to be formed by those with the same surname from different birthplaces and who spoke different dialects, transcending the traditional birthplace/dialect groupings (Yoshihira 1998: 268–9).

What are same-surname groups?

Same-surname groups evolved in overseas ethnic Chinese communities separated from their native China. Many exist in various Southeast Asian countries, as well as in Taiwan and Hong Kong. There are also many in the United States and Canada. Although there are many groups with names like 'The X Surname Zongqinhui' and 'The X Surname Zongqinzonghui,' there are also many groups with names that are confusing at first glance, such as the 'Hainanese Chen Family Association' and 'Huang Jiang-xia Dong' in Thailand. The phrase 'same-surname group' was conceived as a research term in order to give a generic name to all groups with voluntary membership based on the ideology that having the same surname confirms the existence of patrilineal blood relationships.

In recent years same-surname family organizations have been re-emerging with a new look in China, particularly in the southern region of Fujian Province. In regions where lineage organizations have firmly developed, as they have in Fujian Province and Guangdong Province, many same-surname lineages have collaborated and merged to form clans based in cities. The reason for this is that social prestige is increased when same-surname clans merge. These clans are founded on the basis of having the same-surname and common ancestors that have produced successful candidates for the high-ranking state examination system for bureaucracy. They aim to cooperatively compile integrated genealogies, build ancestral halls in order to enshrine the ancestral plates of common patrilineal ancestors, and so forth.

Such same-surname clans seen up until the end of the Republic of China period lost nearly all of their formative underpinnings with the socialist reforms carried out after the era of the People's Republic of China began. However, since the reform era began at the end of the 1970s, a phenomenon closely related to the same-surname clan alliances emerged; it is a type of private organization that complements local administration as part of a policy to pursue foreign capital. In practical terms, these new organizations can be seen as a way of establishing the clans in former days. Groups that identify themselves as research organizations and *zongqinhui* for researching the prestigious ancestors in a family emerged in China as a result of the influence of overseas ethnic Chinese communities (Pan 2002). Same-surname groups that evolved in Hong Kong and in overseas ethnic Chinese communities were either formed as voluntarily joined groups modeled on the patrilineal descent organizations found in the Chinese hometowns of the overseas Chinese, or for the purpose of inheriting the collective property (owned in Hong Kong prior to the establishment of the People's Republic of China) of patrilineal descent organizations.

Types of same-surname organizations

Although the actual state of same-surname groups that exist in ethnic Chinese communities throughout the world has not yet been sufficiently elucidated, it is believed that there are several types of these groups. The following are the Lin surname groups found mainly in Thailand. I examine them using their relationships with their lineages and clans in their Chinese hometowns as criteria.

Same-surname groups are all joined voluntarily, and can be considered associations. They contrast with the lineage communities in the hometowns. Unlike the lineages, which are geographically limited as groups consisting of those living in the same area, an organization takes on associational characteristics when volunteers from several same-surname lineages collaborate to build an ancestral hall enshrining a common ancestor, irrespective of the fact that they live far away from each other.

Type A
Same-township organizations (formed by immigrants and their descendents from villages and townships—the administrative unit above villages) comprising lineages in which the inhabitants have the same surname often have group names that contain the name of the township and village; the members of these groups are thought to share

patrilineal ancestors from relatively recent generations. Naturally, all members have the same surname. There are ten groups containing members from Chaozhou, Guangdong Province, such as the Chenghai Huxin Lin Family Association and the Chenghai Nansha Xiangqin Association of Thailand, which is discussed later. The individuals involved in the formation of the Lin Clansmen General Association of Thailand were already playing active roles in small-scale groups such as these.

Type B

This type has larger-scale membership than Type A. Type B groups seem to have been formed through the revival of clanship relations on the strength of same-surname lineages within a county having cooperated to build ancestral halls. In the past some volunteers from a same-surname lineage from a municipality or from several counties would provide funding for the cooperative building of a large-scale ancestral hall in their central city. Clan alliance was devised for the purpose of political and economic benefits on the pretext of the enshrinement of common ancestors.

The historical evidence of common patrilineal relationships between related lineages is weaker than it is within a lineage. The existence of *zongpu* created by artificially integrating genealogies in order to compensate for this weakness served as their primary justification. Accordingly, in present-day immigrant communities, groups are formed with the basic membership qualification simply being that the individuals have the same surname. Groups formed with members who speak the same dialect often use the group name 'The X Surname Zongqinhui.' The Hainanese Lin Clansmen Association of Thailand, which is discussed later, took the name for its organization directly from the ancestral hall it built, and represents one example of this type.

Type C

These are same-surname groups formed through the merging of Type A and Type B *zongqinhui*, and are named 'The X Surname Zongqinzonghui.' The Lin Clansmen General Association of Thailand (Lin Surname Zongqinzonghui) discussed in detail in this chapter is a Type C group. Almost all *zongqinzonghui* in Thailand are structurally larger-scale than the *zongqinhui*. Although the key board members of the Type A and Type B *zongqinhui* also hold posts as board members in the *zongqinzonghui*, the general *zongqinhui* members do not automatically become members of the *zongqinzonghui*. However, they can participate in the events held by the *zongqinzonghui*. When same-surname Chinese (overseas and ethnic Chinese) form organizations based on the belief that having the same surname means having common patrilineal ancestors, these *zongqinhui* are often formed by individuals for whom communication is easy—in other words, by those who share the same dialect and similar lifestyle customs because they come from the same hometown. They then network with other *zongqinhui* of the same surname that use different dialects to form a *zongqinzonghui*.

However, Type A and Type B same-surname groups are sometimes formed after a Type C *zongqinzonghui* has been formed, most likely in order to have more intense and adaptable activities by further limiting a group to individuals from the same hometown. Further, organizations formed in regional cities are called *lianluosuo* (offices) during their small-scale stage, and then become known as *zongqinhui* when the organization is completed. However, *zongqinhui* that sustain relationships with *zongqinzonghui* often become regional affiliates of the *zongqinzonghui*. In the case of the Lin surname, there are six groups within such regional *zongqinhui* that formed earlier than the *zongqinzonghui*, and eighteen groups that formed after the formation of the *zongqinzonghui*.

Type D

These are groups formed through the coalition of multiple surnames, on the basis that patrilineal blood relations exist between the different surnames because their ancestors in ancient China were brothers. It is thought that they merge when the scale of each surname is small to take advantage of the larger scale. Examples include the Liuguitang Clansmen Association of Thailand (contains six surnames: Hong, Jiang, Weng, Fang, Gong and Wang; founded in 1965) and the Longkong Association of Thailand (contains four surnames: Liu, Guan, Zhang and Zhao; founded in 1961). The former was formed on the basis that a father with the surname Weng had six sons during the Song Dynasty, all of whom became *jinshi* (successful top-class candidates who have passed the exam given by the emperor) and adopted separate surnames thereafter. The latter was formed on the basis of a blood brother relationship and close friendship between characters in The Story of Three Kingdoms, but it seems that the patrilineal blood relationships and surname relationships in this group have been given an extremely extended interpretation. Type D groups are called *lianzonghui* or *dongzonghui*. There are no Type D groups involving the Lin surname.

Lin same-surname groups

Before the formation of Lin *zongqinzonghui* in Thailand, several Lin surname groups were established. The groups believed to have formed the earliest were those established between the end of the Qing Dynasty and the Republic of China period. One such group was an organization that preceded the Hainanese Lin Ancestral Hall organization, a *zongqinhui* of Lins from Hainan Island (whose native language is the Hainan dialect). Although this group has already been classified as a Type B same-surname group, it was called the Lin Family Association at its inception at the end of the Qing Dynasty. After the Second World War, in 1947, preparations were begun in Thailand for the formation of an official Hainanese Lin organization in concert with the establishment of the Hainanese Lin Association of Singapore for Hainanese Lins living in Singapore. It was originally named the Hainanese Lin Clan Club of Thailand, but its name was soon changed to the Chang Lin Clansmen Friendship Association of Thailand.

The development of the Hainanese Lin Clansmen Association of Thailand as a *zongqinhui* roughly coincided with the establishment of the Lin Clansmen General Association of Thailand. In the fall of 1961, land for the construction of an ancestral hall was purchased. In 1964 the ancestral hall was completed, and an opening ceremony was held. Lin Lairong (an individual who belongs to the Chaozhou group), the Chief Director of the Lin Clansmen Association of Thailand, attended the ceremony. In July that same year, registration of the board members with the Thai government was completed.

This *zongqinhui* built the Temple of Goddess Tianhou in 1975. This temple enshrined the Lin Mazu (sea goddess) as its guardian deity. Up until then the Mazu had been housed in a different location, but it was moved to this temple's ancestral yard in 1983. This group actively interacts with similar overseas groups. For example, it holds international friendship meetings with Hainanese Lins in Singapore, Malaysia and Thailand. The group began holding such meetings once per year in 1981 on a rotational basis between the groups in each country. The Chief Director of the Lin Clansmen Association of Thailand participates in the major events, which show that even though these are Hainanese group activities, the network between the Lins exceeds the confines of hometowns and dialect groups.

During the Republic of China period at the end of the Qing Dynasty, several Lin organizations sprung up in rural areas, as well as in Bangkok. In 1910 the Ancestral Hall of the Lins was established by Lins from Fujian in the central coastal Samut Songkhram Prefecture (now known as Yegong-fu in Chinese) in Thailand. Like the Hainanese Lins in Bangkok, the Ancestral Hall of the Lins is an ancestral hall, as well as the organization that built and maintains the hall. The organization continues to run activities promoting reciprocal aid and interaction between kinsmen of the same surname. Such activities are centred on the annual birthday ceremony of the first ancestor who settled in Samut Songkhram and are held in the eighth month of the lunar calendar. In 1979 the organization joined the Lin Clansmen Association of Thailand in Bangkok.

In 1916 a religious building known as the Tianhou Temple of the Lins was built in the Thonburi district on the shore of the Chao Phraya River in Bangkok. Three individuals from Chaozhou raised an amount valued at approximately 5,000 baht at the time for the construction of the temple, and then established a Board of Directors in order to operate and maintain the temple thereafter. The group headed by this Board of Directors focused on faith in the female Lin deity and events to demonstrate this faith, but interaction with other Lins was also a point of focus for them. When the temple was due to be rebuilt in 2000, donations were collected from various Lin groups throughout the country, as well as from individuals. Temples were first constructed as assembly halls for individuals from the same hometown within ethnic Chinese communities, and same-hometown groups centred on these activities were formed. Consequently, the fact that an organization that enshrines Mazu as an ancestor was formed as a same-surname group for the Lins and continues to exist is quite interesting. The Board of Directors is still today comprised entirely of individuals born in the Chaozhou region in Guangdong Province and their descendents. The buildings where individuals can go to worship are open to the public.

After the Second World War several Lin groups were formed in the central and southern regions in Thailand. These groups were formed by individuals from Chaozhou in those regions. They include the Ancestral Hall of the Lins in Samut Sakhon Prefecture (completed in 1984), the Ancestral Hall of the Lins in Nakhon Pathom Prefecture (completed in 1959) and the Ancestral Hall of the Lins in Songkhla Prefecture (completed in 1960). In each case, before these large buildings can be completed, the organizations are established, and fundraising is then conducted for several years to raise the money for construction. Each organization has a Board of Directors in order to operate and maintain the temple, fulfilling the function of a *zongqinhui*.

It is interesting to note that overseas lineage organizations had already been established by certain individuals from Chaozhou, Guangdong, in Bangkok during the 1950s and 1960s. This was the period in which socialist reform for a new China was being advanced by the Communist Party, and the disbandment of even collective landowner lineages was progressing. There were halls for ancestor worship called *dazongci* (great ancestral halls) in villages, where ancestral plates of the villagers' common patrilineal ancestors were enshrined. In Chaozhou the ancestral halls for all lineages are called *dazongci*, while branch ancestral halls for subordinate lineage organizations are called *zuci*. Overseas Chinese who abandoned the idea of returning home and decided to settle in Thailand and continue assimilating form the backdrop to the establishment of such groups. Points (i) through (iii) below are examples of such groups. Several groups also formed after the period of reform and liberalization policies in China. Point (iv) gives two examples of such groups.

(i) Chenghai Huxin Lin Family Association

This is a group formed by Lins from Huxin in Chenghai County, Chaozhou. It was established in Bangkok in 1956 by the descendents in Thailand of the first settler Wenzhi Gong, who belonged to the lineage branch of the ancestor Heyi Gong. Among the founders of this association is Lin Maosan, who is currently the President of the Lin Clansmen General Association of Thailand. The group promotes friendship by hosting a dinner party on the birthday of Tianhou on March 23. After the *zongqinzonghui* of the Lins was established, the group began to participate in the *zongqinzonghui* events and produced a lot of *zongqinzonghui* board members. Many of its members are also dedicated to improving schools, hospitals and ancestral halls in the group members' native hometown in China.

(ii) Chenghai Nansha Xiangqin Association of Thailand

This group was formed by Lins from Nansha in the same Chenghai County of Chaozhou. As expected, its members are the Lin descendents belonging to the lineage branch of Heyi Gong. Because the Lin lineage makes up most of the Nansha population, the same-hometown association of individuals from a township administrative unit consisting of multiple villages overlaps perfectly with the Lin organization. This organization was established in Bangkok at the beginning of the 1960s. A tour group for return visits to the ancestral village was recently established, and sends public investment and tourist parties back home. As an association of villagers sharing the same ancestor, it also contributed funds to repair the Lin *dazongci* in Nansha.

The hometowns of both abovementioned groups are located at the mouth of the Hanjiang River, one of the two large rivers in the Chaozhou region of Guangdong. Heyi Gong, the common ancestor of the two groups, was the father of Wenzhi Gong (the progenitor of Lins in Huxin) and Wensou (the progenitor of Lins in Nansha). He lived in Min County in central Fujian Province. He moved to Chaozhou, Guangdong, approximately 320 years ago. The fifteenth to eighteenth generation descendents of these founders of Huxin and Nansha who moved to Thailand were the initial board members of the respective kinship associations they formed.

(iii) Lins from Jieyang County in Chaozhou

There are also many groups of Lins from Jieyang County in Chaozhou, of which seven have been confirmed. Although they carried out sociable activities after the Second World War, it was not until the latter half of the 1960s that they became official organizations.

Xihe Lin Nanshan Gong Clansmen Association of Thailand

Like the Hainanese Lin Ancestral Hall, this group built a large ancestral hall that is comparable to a *zongqinzonghui* ancestral hall. In November 1965 on the birthday (the eighth day in the ninth month of the lunar calendar) of Nanshan Gong, the first ancestor, twenty volunteers began making preparations for establishing a Board of Directors in Thonburi, Bangkok. Approximately 200 participants gathered for ancestor worship and a dinner party. They then established a committee for constructing an ancestral hall in 1968, which was completed in June 1971. Nanshan Gong was the branch founder of the Jianhang Village of Jieyang County, and moved there from Putian County in Fujian Province. Lin Futian, a central figure in the Board of Directors, was also a leader in the Ancestral Hall of the Lins in Nakhon Pathom Prefecture.

It is worth noting that the initial leaders of *zongqinzonghui* and those of the Xihe Lin Nanshan Gong Clansmen Association overlap. The board members of this group, which can make its presence felt with a rather firm financial base, generally do not demonstrate leadership in the Lin Clansmen General Association formed at the national level. Although the reason for this is unclear, it is still something worth noting.

Hanxue Gong General Association
This association was formed by individuals from Jinhangin Jieyang County in the former Chaozhou municipality. The ancestor of the association is the eldest son Hanxue (thirty-third generation of the Lins) of the second wife of a *jinshi* from the Song Dynasty (thirty-second generation), and his name is used as the name of the group. He lived in Xianyou County in Fujian Province. Many thirty-fifth generation descendents moved to Jieyang in Chaozhou, Guandong Province. The number of descendents who moved to Thailand increased, beginning with the fifty-fourth generation, and there are approximately 100 households residing in Bangkok.

Dongyuan Xiang Lin Clansmen Association of Thailand
Formed by Lins from Dongyuan (presently a part of Jiexi County), Jieyang County. The ancestor of the group moved from Putian County in Fujian Province at the end of the Ming Dynasty or beginning of the Qing Dynasty, settling in Jieyang County.

Jieyang Donglin Xiang Lin Clansmen Association of Thailand
This group comprises Lins from Donglin, Jieyang County. The group began social gatherings after the Second World War. It hosts an international friendship meeting on the eighth day in the first month of the lunar calendar. In 1985 it organized its first dinner party in the *dazongci* of the Lin Clansmen General Association of Thailand. The eighth day in the first month was also the day on which Youshenhui (a procession with god statues) was held in the group's hometown. This is also the day on which the group runs a *zoucaiqi* (a parade with colorful flags) to celebrate the births of all male children over the past year. Interaction through rites of passage in life is the main activity. Lin Zuomou, one of the key figures who organized the establishment of the *zongqinzonghui*, is a leading member. Although one current board member of the Ancestral Hall of the Lins of Southern Thailand,

located in Songkhla Prefecture, was born in the Thai prefecture, he holds membership and is a board member of this clansmen association because his father is from Donglin Xiang.

Jieyang Tongkeng Lin Clansmen Association of Thailand
This association was established in 1976 by the descendents of Huashan Gong, who was from Tongkeng, Jieyang County. Even before its establishment, interaction through rites of passage in life for each descendant in Thailand has existed over a long period of time. Since its establishment the organization has hosted an international friendship dinner party on the Sunday following Yuanxiaojie (January 15 on the lunar calendar) every year. Clansmen scattered throughout various regions attend the event.

(iv) Two Lin groups were established during the 1980s.

Puning Shuihou Clansmen Association of Thailand
The ancestor of this association moved from Putian County, Fujian Province, to Jieyang County in Chaozhou, Guangdong Province, and then moved again to Shuihou in the neighbouring Puning County. Fourteenth-generation descendants and onwards have lived in Thailand. A preparatory roundtable discussion was held in February 1989, and the association was inaugurated in April of the following year. The association holds dinner parties once every other month. The main purpose of these dinner parties is to exchange information regarding member get-togethers and commercial pursuits, as well as to introduce descendents. More than seventy members participate in the friendship meeting held during the New Year holidays of the lunar calendar. This is an activity that follows the Yuanxiao festivities (January 15 on the lunar calendar) in the association's hometown. The members of the association also solicit donations in order to improve ancestral shrines, temples and schools in their hometown.

Huilai Lin Family Friendship Association of Thailand
This association was established in about 1983. The group's Chief Director was born in 1928, and moved to Thailand at age eighteen in 1946. He is one of the key members of the Huilai same-township association, and also holds a directorial position in the Lin Clansmen General Association of Thailand.

The establishment of the Lin Clansmen General Association of Thailand and the building of its *dazongci*

While introducing the Lin Clansmen General Association of Thailand (*zongqinzonghui*), let us also examine the background as to how the *zongqinzonghui*, which is of a larger-scale than the *zongqinhui*, is established.

The launch of the *zongqinzonghui*

Preparations for the establishment of this *zongqinzonghui* were made by key members of various Lin groups that were already established, such as the Nanshan Gong Clansmen Association of Thailand, the Jieyang Donglin Xiang Lin Clansmen Association of Thailand, and the Ancestral Hall of the Lins in Nakhonpathom, as well as by financial leaders in the country with the surname Lin. It was established in January 1962, although preparations for its establishment had begun in the 1950s. The *zongqinzonghui* was officially inaugurated in the spring of 1963.

Tracing the background to the establishment of this association reveals that individuals from Jieyang County called upon Lin Lairong, an individual from Chaoyang County who had demonstrated his capability as a Chaozhou businessman, to establish the *zongqinzonghui*. Individuals from Taiwan are also included in the register because many same-surname groups supported Taiwan's Kuomintang government, and were also affected by the Campaign for the Restoration of Chinese Culture promoted by the Kuomintang. Furthermore, people who speak the Chaozhou dialect can also easily understand Taiwanese, which has roots in the southern region of Fujian Province.

The building of the *dazongci*

Land for building the *dazongci* was purchased for approximately 1,330,000 baht by the *zongqinzonghui* in 1965. Construction began in 1967, and the *dazongci* was completed in 1970. An opening ceremony was then held. Construction expenses totaled approximately 5,840,000 baht (one can understand how large this value is knowing that the average monthly income in Bangkok in 1968 was approximately 476 baht per person). The ancestral hall was designed in accordance with the traditional Chinese architectural style. Carpenters and painters were brought from Taiwan for the construction work.

The purchase of the land and construction expenses were covered by donations from the board members and general members. Of the fifty-four main contributors, forty-six were from Chaozhou. Among these, Jieyang County members featured prominently with twenty people, followed by eight Chaoyang County members, six Chenghai County members, and six Chao'an County members. There were one Hainanese, one Taiwanese, and one member from Fujian Province.

It is obvious that Lins who speak the Chaozhou dialect as their native language, and who are the overwhelming majority in terms of their population size and economic force, cooperated with the minority of Lins who speak other dialects in order to establish the *zongqinzonghui* and build the *dazongci*.

Zongqinzonghui activities

The ancestral plates of great ancestors, starting with the primogenitor from China and direct ancestors of those living in Thailand, are enshrined in the altar for ancestral tablets of the *dazongci*. It is here that scholarship award ceremonies and sociable banquets for younger members and non-members who have the same surname are held during the Chunqiu ancestor memorial rites in spring and in the fall. The construction of the cemetery was completed in 1979, and was named the Jiulong Cemetery. In 1997 a second cemetery, the Xihe Cemetery, was finished beyond the *dazongci*, which offers a hall for ancestral worship where the ancestral plates are enshrined as a resting place for the souls of the ancestors. The completion of these cemeteries had great significance, as the Chinese believe that spiritual stability in the other world after death can be secured by offering a safe place for the ancestors' bones to be buried.

Another successful key activity of the association was the compilation and publication of the Taiguo Xihe Lin-shi Zupu (Thailand Xihe Lin Genealogy), a comprehensive genealogy of the Lins beginning with the primogenitor, which was published in 1986. Beyond activities related to ancestor enshrinement such as these, the association was also established for the purpose of the mutual assistance of its members, such as publishing congratulatory and condolence advertisements in various local Chinese newspapers, and offering relief money to victims.

A scholarship foundation was established by the ninth Board of Directors of the Lin Clansmen Association in 1978, and began offering scholarship benefits. Initially, the objective was to provide aid for educational expenses to young people from less-fortunate families, but the foundation eventually began providing scholarship benefits without regard to the financial strength of the parents. The scholarships were not limited to members of the association; they allowed any young individual with the surname Lin to apply. According to the 1993 record, the total foundation amount of money donated by volunteer members exceeded 23,000,000 baht, allowing grants of 1,800 baht for every elementary school student, 2,200 baht for every junior high school student, and 3,200 baht for every university student. From 1979 until 2001 a total of 27,250,000 baht was provided to approximately 12,300 students. In 2001 the money from 273 donations (by individuals, regional *zonghui* branches and so on) and that from the General Association itself totaled 36,630,000 baht. Like lineages and clans in ancient China that placed importance on producing individuals from the same family who would pass the state examination system for bureaucracy, same-surname groups located overseas also work to develop talent by emphasizing the importance of providing educational support.

The intentions of and historical backdrop to the establishment of *zongqinzonghui*

Both *zongqinhui* and *zongqinzonghui* have organization establishment principles that purpose the promotion of interaction and mutual aid between individuals who are believed to be blood-related through common patrilineal ancestors, and the enshrinement of these ancestors is the foundation of such activities. However, were the *zongqinzonghui*, which have a larger organizational scale than *zongqinhui*, established purely due to advantages of scale? In the case of Thailand, the establishment of each surname *zongqinzonghui* began around the 1950s, and by the 1990s, fifty-five groups had been established and were still active. The highest proportion of groups was established during the period beginning in the latter half of the 1960s and ending in the first half of the 1970s. The building of *dazongci* by raising huge amounts of funds through money donated by volunteer members is held as an ideal, and *zongqinzonghui* that have accomplished this goal gain the attention of Chinese communities.

As was the case with the Chen surname, many board members who enthusiastically partake in the activities of the Lin *zongqinzonghui* came to Thailand during the period of their infancy to adolescence (that is, around the Second World War). Even those who were born in Thailand have the experience of returning to the hometowns of their Chinese paternal ancestors to be educated. Their families went to Thailand with the hopes of making their livings there as overseas Chinese guest labourers, but after the Communist regime was established and the socialist reforms began they abandoned the idea of returning home and were naturalized in Thailand, making it their permanent place of residence. This marked the start of the assimilation process of the overseas Chinese. Leaving China has been restricted since this time, so the number of new Chinese emigrants has dropped drastically. Furthermore, measures to contain Chinese in Thailand were exchanged for measures for the promotion of assimilation since the mid-1950s. Thai assimilation of the curriculum in Chinese schools was promoted, and it started to become difficult to pass down Chinese culture to the descendents of overseas Chinese (first-generation immigrants with Chinese nationality). In the 1960s nationalism was strengthened by Prime Minister Sarit Thanarat as a plan to integrate people in Thailand in order to promote nation building.

Those who developed the businesses they inherited from their parents and those who succeeded in establishing businesses in one generation expect their children and grandchildren to become proud members of society as Thai nationals. At the same time Chinese immigrants expect their children to build upon their character as Chinese-Thai who can carry on the traditions of Chinese culture. The concept at the foundation of ancestor enshrinement is filial piety, which places importance on family and kinship. The Chinese believe that after they die, if their descendents do not continue to inherit and preserve a Chinese worldview and continue to worship their ancestors, then there is no guarantee for their lives in the other world after death.

Scholarship award ceremonies held at *dazongci* are reminiscent of activities that aimed to have the younger members of a family clan pass the state examination system for bureaucracy in China. Social upward mobility due to an emphasis on education is a value system shared among ethnic Chinese, and the construction of human relationship networks founded on same-hometown, same-surname and same-school relationships is considered necessary for success in life and work, as well as something that should be communicated to one's descendents.

Chinese immigrants were ahead of the times in their creation and implementation of a global network. Same-surname groups have completely different principles of social connection than same-township groups, the Chinese Chamber of Commerce, same-school organizations, Lions Clubs and Rotary, but they mutually complement one another and form large, multi-layered networks. *Zongqinzonghui* are established in order to function as a node that establishes closer ties between networks in the Chinese community. *Dazongci* can also be interpreted as being monuments constructed with the expectation of becoming foundations for activities that transmit Chinese traditions to others.

In Thailand the executive managers of each surname *zongqinzonghui* periodically gather to interact with one another and exchange information, and undertake several joint projects as well. Such activities offer international partnerships for all types of domestic and overseas Chinese groups

10 The Bangladeshi Community in London: Social Enterprises and the Transnational Development of Community Empowerment
Yaeko Nishiyama and Shiho Nishiyama

Introduction

Economic globalization has caused the concentration of wealth in a small number of cities and in the wealthy class. It has also generated new poor groups, including the underclass and the working poor, who cannot escape from poverty cycles. The resulting disparity and inequality issues have become serious concerns, particularly among immigrant workers. Since the 1950s the economically advanced European nations have accepted large numbers of immigrant workers to deal with the shortages of labour for industrial production. However, the shift of an industrial structure towards information industries has caused unemployment of many of these immigrant workers. The advanced nations have begun to adopt neoliberal policy and are beginning to find their immigrant workers a heavy burden. Immigrant workers generally come from developing countries in the peripheries of the global economy and are faced with difficulties in escaping from poverty. Neither their home countries nor host countries can provide them with much prospect for employment opportunities or economic success.

This chapter focuses on the global city of London, which historically has serious immigrant problems. It discusses the actual situation of poverty in the Bangladeshi community in the city's inner areas and the possibility of solving the poverty problem. We particularly focus on the fact that understanding the concept of poverty from the aspect of 'social exclusion' leads to potential solutions to the problem that are fundamentally different from those drawn from conventional understanding. Specifically, we attempt to understand poverty not only from the aspect of shortage of material resources (such as income and housing environment), but also from the aspect of the situation where individuals have lost the desire to live, have lost the ability to make a living, or have been socially isolated. The potential solutions to the problem drawn from this understanding are to enhance individual ability to live and to help individuals to build social relations, and to achieve these goals in the process of reconstructing their communities. In other words, the potential solution is to achieve individual empowerment and, by enhancing the autonomy of the communities to which these individuals belong, to achieve community empowerment.

In Britain Development Trusts have been in operation since the 1970s—that is, since before social exclusion became an issue, even a policy issue. Development Trusts are voluntary organizations that work to solve problems with community regeneration. Grassroots voluntary organizations have worked on inner city problems in large cities in manners that suit the local situations, and this movement has spread nationwide. Through trial and error these organizations have devised solutions, which are currently attracting attention as 'social enterprises.' We discuss the significance and potential of these social enterprises as a solution to social exclusion. We take as an example the Development Trust that has striven to regenerate the London Bangladeshi community, which has suffered from social exclusion.

The Bangladeshi community providing the foundation for London's globalization

The poverty problem in the Bangladeshi population

In Britain poverty is concentrated in ethnic minority groups. According to a recent Joseph Rowntree Foundation report (Platt 2007) that analyses ethnic groups and poverty from an income viewpoint, ethnic groups with the highest poverty rates include the Bangladeshi, Pakistani and black African populations. By any of the various indicators to measure poverty, the Bangladeshi population is ranked poorest.

Table 10.1 shows a comparison of full-time workers' weekly wages among ethnic groups. The weekly wages of Bangladeshi workers are 54% of the average wage and Bangladeshi workers have the very lowest of all employment. This means that Bangladeshi households, which depend on men for their income, are never well off, even if men can get one of the few full-time jobs.

The size of the Bangladeshi population in Britain was 283,063 in 2001, accounting for 0.5% of the total population. The Bangladeshi population is unevenly distributed in the country, with 54% living

Table 10.1: Comparison of weekly wages of full-time workers (£)

Ethnic group	Men	95% confidence intervals	Women	95% confidence intervals
All ethnic groups	497.89 (56,073)	494.89–500.89	375.80 (36,212)	373.52–378.08
White British	498.57 (49,553)	495.49–501.65	372.79 (31,313)	370.36–375.22
Indian	523.68 (880)	499.81–547.55	396.56 (587)	376.79–416.33
Pakistani	390.24 (337)	361.56–418.92	321.56 (134)	289.20–353.92
Bangladesh	270.22 (104)	232.04–308.39	324.48 (43)	280.83–363.13
Black African	445.15 (288)	412.43–461.14	372.65 (261)	352.71–392.59
Black Caribbean	436.79 (369)	412.37–475.93	393.71 (394)	376.47–410.95

Source: Platt (2007: 46).

in London and 22.8% (65,553 people) living in the Tower Hamlets borough of London. At primary schools in Tower Hamlets, 87% of the students are ethnic Bangladeshi. In order to specifically analyse the poverty problem in the Bangladeshi population, the following discussion focuses on the London Bangladeshi population.

During the 1980s under the Thatcher administration, deregulation was promoted in London under neoliberal policy, resulting in a rapid increase of redevelopment projects to enhance the financial functions of the city, including the development of London Docklands. The London Bangladeshi population is concentrated in the Tower Hamlets borough in the East End[1] of London, in particular in the Spitalfields/Banglatown area, which is located between Docklands and the City of London, the two major districts in which the international functions of the city are concentrated and which are directly affected by globalism (Map 10.1). The nearby Liverpool subway station saw rapid redevelopment of its surrounding areas.

The East End includes the Spitalfields market, once famous as a fruit and vegetable market; Whitechapel, where slum areas are concentrated; and Brick Lane, which is famous as the 'curry street.' Historically, as an area heavily populated by unskilled workers, the East End has received major influxes of Jewish and Bangladeshi immigrants. The area now has a multi-ethnic community, including 15,000 Somalis from Africa. The 65,000 Bengali residents[2] in the area are immigrants from the Bengal region of Bangladesh. Bengali immigration began around 1950 and first peaked in the 1970s. These immigrants have been engaged mainly in Indian restaurant,

Map 10.1: Location of Spitalfields/Banglatown

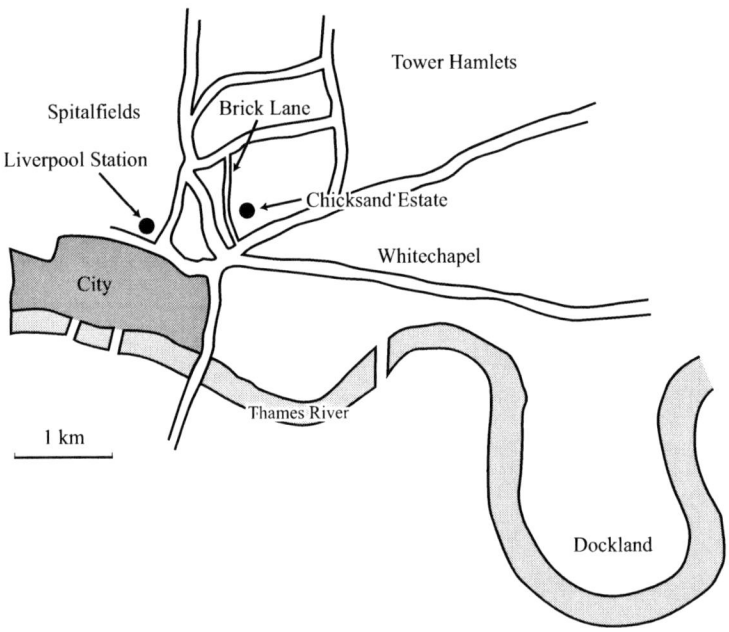

craftwork, design and printing businesses and have formed ethnic communities that are collectively known as 'Banglatown.' They are poor Asian communities packed in a valley between postmodern skyscrapers.

The area around Spitalfields was designated as the most disadvantaged area in London in 1980 (Forman 1989). This area is adjacent to the Chicksand Estate, the largest public housing estate in London. Many of the housing units in this estate are crowded, with four or five families from the home country often dwelling in one unit. In general, Islamic households are strongly inclined to have conservative values in life. They tend to think that men should work outside the home and women should run the household. As a result, women tend to stay home all the time, and few domestic violence or abuse cases are reported outside the home. Social problems are as serious as the economic poverty in the Bangladeshi population. This estate and the community at large must strive to solve poverty.

Only a small number of Bangladeshi residents have had professional education. For unskilled women and young minority adults, it is extremely difficult to get stable jobs in British society. While the unemployment rate in 2005 was 8.4% for the entire Tower Hamlets borough, for the Bengali population it was as high as 24%. Most Bengali residents seem to be excluded from education and employment opportunities and to live with high unemployment rates and unstable jobs.

Next, we specifically analyze the poverty problem in the Bangladeshi population based on the report *Bangladeshis in London*, which sheds light on the actual situation of the Bangladeshi residents in London based on the 2001 Census (Piggott 2004). The London Bangladeshi population increased by 79% in a single decade after 1991. It has become the third largest of the non-British-born ethnic groups. It has been pointed out that the poverty problem in the Bangladeshi population is particularly notable in the aspects of employment, housing and health status.

With respect to employment, the unemployment rate for the Bangladeshi population is 20%, a rate high above the national average of 7% and highest among all ethnic minority groups (Figure 10.1). This figure has been calculated based on the age group of between sixteen and seventy-four, which is defined as the labour force (economically active).[3] Only 44% of the total Bangladeshi population is available for labour force activities. This is the lowest of the sixteen ethnic groups. Of the Bangladeshi labour force, 17% and 10% have full-time and part-time jobs, respectively. In addition to the low wages of Bangladeshi full-time workers shown in the aforementioned national data, this shows the extremely disadvantaged position of Bangladeshi workers in employment. Further, employed Bangladeshi workers are unevenly distributed among industries, with approximately 50% working in restaurants and retail businesses. This is a characteristic not found in any other ethnic group.

Figure 10.2 shows the qualification status of different ethnic groups, which makes a difference in obtaining employment opportunities. Approximately 45% of the Bangladeshi workforce has no qualification. Bangladeshi workers with high-level qualifications account for only 15% of their ethnic group. The proportion of the Bangladeshi workforce with no qualifications is particularly high in the age groups between twenty-five and thirty-four (76%) and between thirty-four and fifty-four (67%). This situation is a cause of the unstable employment and low income of the Bangladeshi workforce. The causes of this situation listed in the *Bangladeshis in London* report include (i) the short time since most of these Bangladeshi residents immigrated to London, (ii) their inability to speak English and (iii) the pressure of taking care of

Figure 10.1: Comparison of unemployment rate by ethnic group

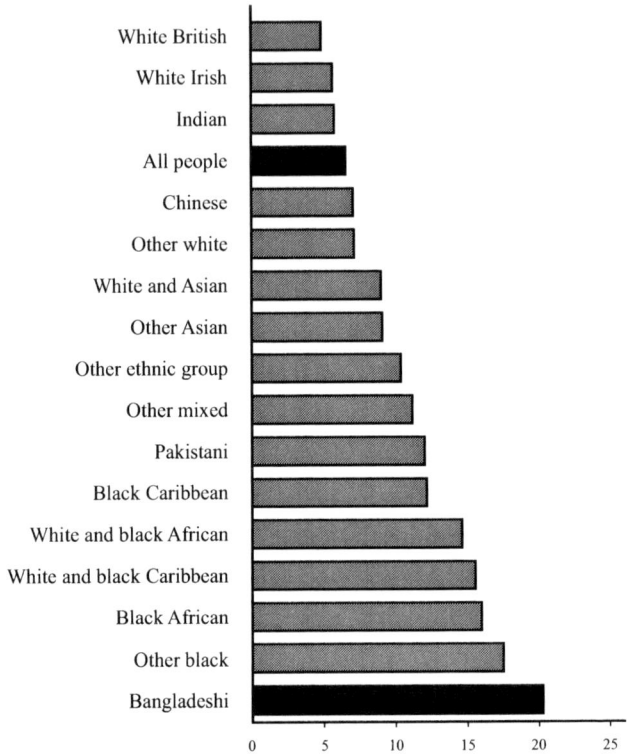

Source: Piggott (2004 : 36) 2001 Census. Commissioned table M248.

their families. However, British-born younger Bangladeshi residents have high enrolment rates and the report concludes that the situation will change with the growth of this generation.

Overcrowding accounts for most of the poverty problems in housing arrangements. The home ownership rate in the London Bangladeshi population is low, with 63% living in public housing and other social housing estates. Fifty-five per cent of Bangladeshi households live in 'housing deprivation' as defined in the report.[4] As 93% of the Bangladeshi residents are Islamic, traditional value systems such as extended family systems and patriarchy are strongly seen in the Bangladeshi population. This is undeniably associated with large family sizes in Bangladeshi households, with 30% of the households having six or more members.

Figure 10.2: Comparison of qualification by ethnic group

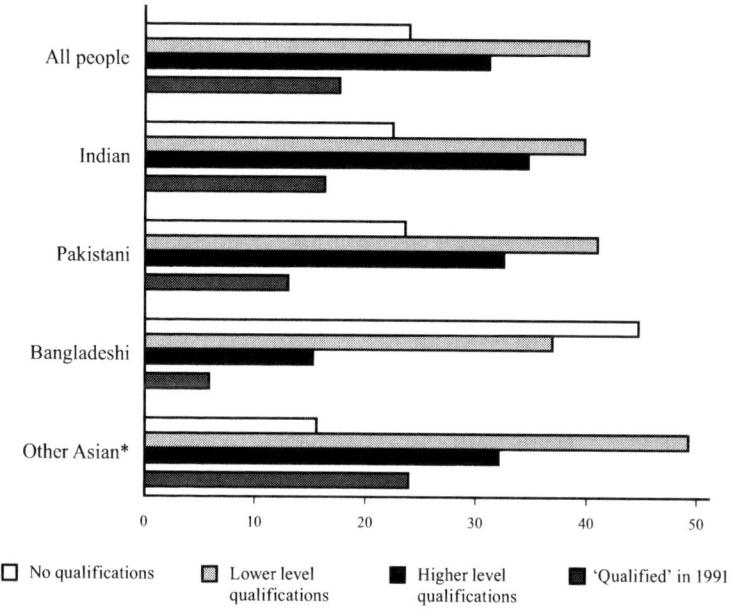

Source: Piggott (2004:43) 1991 Census LBS Table L85 and 2001 Census. Theme Table TT013.

Other Asian in 1991 may have included the mixed white and Asian ethnic group in 2001.

The third indicator of poverty is health status. Poor health status is particularly salient in the age group between thirty-five and seventy-four, with the morbidity rate being twice the average. Of all sixteen ethnic groups, the proportion of people with long-term disease is highest in Bangladeshis.

As described above, the 2001 Census shows quantitatively the poverty status of the London Bangladeshi population and gives us an understanding of the seriousness of the problems facing these Bangladeshi residents. In terms of future prospects, the report points out that, although they still maintain extended family systems, the number of family members in Bangladeshi households has been decreasing, showing a weakening of traditional Bangladeshi values. The report also expects that once the British-born fourth generation of Bangladeshi residents receives education and learns to speak English, Bangladeshis will have more opportunities for employment and social participation, which will improve the situation. However, it is not easy to solve the poverty problem in an immigrant community, which encompasses the involvement of the historical relationship between the home country and Britain, the unique religious and cultural values maintained by the immigrants, and personal relations between the immigrants and their home country. These problems cannot be solved simply by waiting for generational changes. Various measures have been taken to solve poverty in Spitalfields/Banglatown by investing large sums of public funds. However, these measures have failed to produce successful results commensurate with the amounts of funds invested. In fact, the poverty problem has become more serious. This prompted, at the beginning of the 1990s, the start of partnership projects to search for improvement plans with the cooperation of Bangladeshi communities. In the background of these projects, there had been a shift of focus of the poverty problems in ethnic minority groups from economic poverty to social exclusion. This shift had resulted in an emphasis on the history, culture and values in life of each ethnic minority community.

Social exclusion

The concept of social exclusion was theoretically deepened by Townsend (1979), who connected poverty with social participation. Poverty came to be understood not only from economic aspects but also from cultural aspects, in which the 'expansion of inequality' occurs in such forms as loss of social participation, unstable jobs, long-term unemployment and the weakening of family/community networks, and results in 'loss of social bonds' (Townsend 1979). Social exclusion is not simply a matter of poverty. It is understood as a correlation between the 'distribution issues (economic aspects),' such as poverty, destitution and inequality, and the 'relation issues (social and political aspects),' such as social exclusion, apathy, crime and violence (Bhalla and Lapeyre 2004). The various problems prevailing in advanced countries since the 1980s, including social disparity, long-term unemployment and unstable employment, can be more persuasively explained by social exclusion.

In the 1980s, with the rapid transformation of London as a global city, the City, the center of financial and real estate business activities, expanded, resulting in a rapid increase in home and land prices in the surrounding areas. The rise in land prices was unbearable for small businesses in Spitalfields/Banglatown and made it difficult for them to continue business in these areas located near the City. In Chicksand Estate, where approximately 5,000 Bengalis lived and suffered unemployment and unstable employment, there reportedly was a further increase in the number of poor households that could no longer pay rent and a rapid increase in the number of households evicted from the housing estate. There was also an increase in drug abuse and crime among unemployed young people. The Bangladeshi community became rougher and rougher. With economic globalization, wealth was accumulated in the City from which Banglatown was separated both functionally and physically, causing the destruction of the tradition and culture of Banglatown.

Alarmed by these trends, residents in and around Spitalfields organized community building organizations and began to launch various campaigns against the government's urban development projects, which were failing to benefit their communities. These campaigns demonstrated their awareness of and protest against their social exclusion. In the mid-1970s this area had already experienced a series of racial discrimination acts committed by extremist right-wingers. This had produced unions of Bengalis who criticised these acts. These unions had given this area a potential to develop political activities, including campaigns to demand rights and the campaign against the Docklands development project. These small, community-level resistance movements ultimately produced active movements for community regeneration, with the help of London-based voluntary organizations.

In particular, the Chicksand Estate provided a stage for activities to resist social exclusion and to invigorate the community. These activities aimed to reconstruct relations within the community and to reorganize jobs and distribution systems by establishing social enterprises to utilize various latent resources existing in the community. These new attempts adopted methods that would respect and make best use of the personal connections, culture and values maintained by the Bangladeshi community.

The battle against social exclusion attracted attention at the European Union level and became one of the important issues in social policy at the European Commission at the end of the 1980s and in France and other European Union countries during the 1990s.[5] In Britain solving social exclusion gradually became a policy task for the Blair administration. The task included emphasizing the spirit of self-help and nurturing social enterprises that would empower individual working abilities. The British approach is characterized by the fact that both the voluntary sector and the government sector made efforts to deal with social exclusion and that both sectors focused on social enterprises as a means to deal with the problem. The British voluntary sector was ahead of the government sector in starting pioneering work to solve the problem, with successful results. Voluntary sector activities had started in the 1980s, before the concepts of social exclusion and social enterprise became common. After all, understanding the history, culture and life of poor communities was given the first priority.

At this point, we need to understand historical characteristics of the immigrant communities in order to further analyze, and attempt to find solutions to, social exclusion facing the Bangladeshi community.

The duality of transnational poverty: the relation with the Sylhet Division of Bangladesh

In order to understand the poverty problem facing Bengali residents in London, we need to understand the fact that nearly 90% of them come from the Sylhet Division of Bangladesh.

The Sylhet Division is located approximately 200 kilometers northeast of the capital Dhaka. It is a farming area producing mainly tea and rice (Map 10.2). Most of the residents in Sylhet speak the Sylheti dialect, which is hard for Bengalis from other areas to understand. These Sylhet residents are farmers with poor education who are most likely to have no choice but to work throughout their lives for wages that barely keep them alive. Historically, the poverty in Sylhet has been a cause of discrimination against this area of the country, Sylhet being looked down upon as underdeveloped. The Sylhet Division as an administrative district has a population of approximately 7.9 million people, and nearly 60% of them are farmers. Sylhet has a strong tradition of orthodox Islam, under which women are supposed to become housewives and are in very low social positions. The literacy rate is as low as 28%, due to limited educational opportunities for women. These values can be seen in the London Bangladeshi community as well, in which the female employment rate is extremely low and opportunities for women's social participation are extremely scarce, as compared to other ethnic groups.

The poverty in Sylhet has been caused by tea plantations, which are a product of the colonial policy during the times of the British Empire. In other words, the poverty problem facing the London Bangladeshi population is associated with dual historical factors: the British

Map 10.2: Location of the city of Sylhet

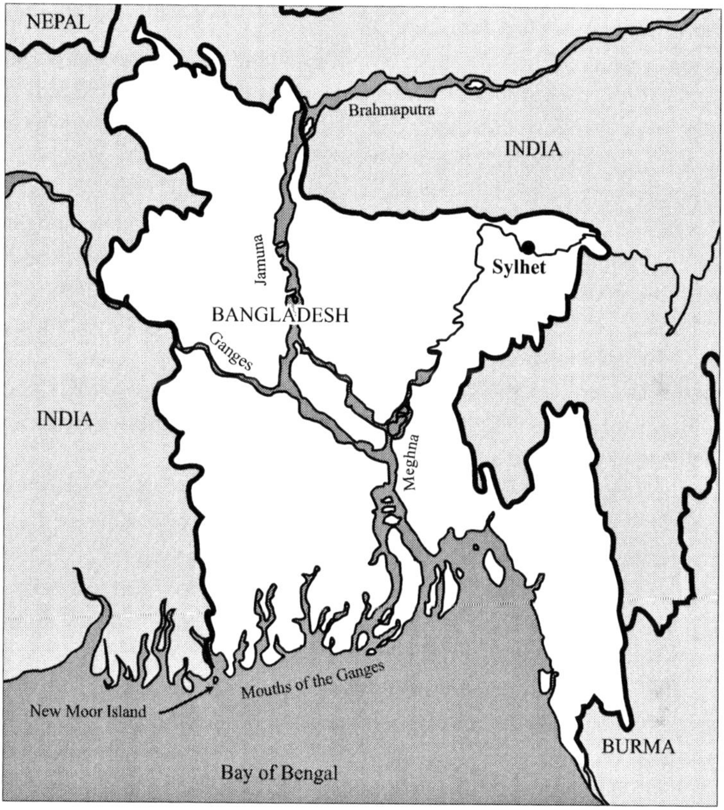

Source: Wikipedia

colonial policy and the postwar labour procurement policy to support Britain's rapid economic growth.

The relationship between Britain and Bangladesh dates back to the eighteenth century when the East India Company controlled Bengal. The Sylhet Division was part of Assam State of India under the British rule. The labour imposed on Sylhet residents was particularly hard, as tea plantations were developed in the division. High-quality tea produced in Sylhet brought immense wealth to London, and spread the tea culture in Britain. However, even now local day labourers working at British-capitalized tea farms are apparently paid a daily wage equivalent to thirty pence. Negative legacies of the Imperialist era seem to remain.

After the separation and independence of India and Pakistan in 1947, Sylhet became part of East Pakistan. Britain experienced an era of economic growth during the 1950s and 1960s and was troubled by shortages of unskilled workers. It was Bangladeshis who satisfied this demand. A great number of young Sylhetis immigrated to Britain and away from their families and supported the British economy as dock labourers, as well as unskilled workers in the manufacturing industry and other heavy and chemical industries.

In 1971 East Pakistan became independent and emerged as Bangladesh. With internal disputes, floods and the use of aircraft as a common mode of transport as great turning points, a large number of Sylhetis headed for London with their families and neighbours. These people worked at such places as Indian restaurants and formed in East London the largest immigrant community in Europe. In particular, the communities around Brick Lane are home to over 50,000 Bengalis. They have built large mosques and formed Banglatown.

Of the Bangladeshi immigrants in London, who rapidly increased in number during the 1970s, those who remain in London are in their late forties to fifties and represent the poverty problem currently facing Bangladeshi residents. Specifically, the conversion of the industrial structure and the economic globalization that has occurred in Britain since the 1980s has brought long-term unemployment to these Bangladeshis, who are unskilled workers. Although surveys have been conducted to investigate their poverty status, no effective policy has been found to help them out of the situation. Some analysts have argued that the cause of the poverty is Sylheti cultural values, which do not emphasize education and vocational training. Specifically, according to Sylheti values, they seek an escape from poverty in hands-on businesses such as restaurants or retail businesses. The aforementioned analysts assert that such values are to blame.[6]

To further understand the Bangladeshi community, it is important to know that the social and political structures of the region of their origin are reflected in the Bangladeshi community in Tower Hamlets. Bengali members of Parliament living in London have repeatedly visited the city of Sylhet and promised support. Problems facing Sylhet are shared by the London Sylheti community, which provides financial aid and various other forms of support to its homeland. Bangladeshis living in London attempt to apply their means of poverty relief available in London to Sylhet at the same time. One successful result of their attempts is the business partnership with the Tower Hamlets borough conducted in the 1990s, which is described in a later section. These Bangladeshi residents belong to the two poor Sylheti communities, both in Bangladesh and in London, and are striving to escape poverty.

Community regeneration by Social Enterprise (Chicksand Citizens Forum)

Until the 1980s various approaches had been made by the British government and private charitable organizations to provide poverty relief to the London Bangladeshi community. However, these activities had their limits because, as the term 'relief' suggests, unilateral support was always provided from one side to the other. These activities only provided standardized measures to improve the environment and uniform social services, instead of attempting to understand different needs of different ethnic groups and to find solutions to suit the reality.

Under these circumstances, Development Trusts pointed out the limits of the methods employed by the above activities, developed community residents' capabilities, and proposed ways to regenerate the community by the residents' own efforts. Development Trusts are non-profit organizations of citizens and had produced some successful results in several previous problems in London. A Development Trust is a private enterprise with a social mission recognized by the British government as charity in the form of a 'company limited by guarantee.' Activities that are characteristic of Development Trusts include establishing social enterprises to make best use of material and human resources existing in the community, and constructing a partnership system involving the government, private businesses and the community in order to regenerate the socially excluded poor community.

In the East End a Development Trust known as Chicksand Citizens Forum (hereafter the Forum) was organized in 1994 and has brought new momentum to the community. Factors in the background of the establishment of the Forum include the increasing sense of crisis in the community that the trend towards globalization might change the community and widen social disparities; the increasing solidarity against such potential harm to the community; and the demand for opportunities to receive basic education and vocational training to eliminate poverty. Below we conduct a chronological analysis of the Forum's social enterprise activities in terms of solutions provided by them to deal with the issue of social exclusion (see Table 10.2).

Table 10.2: Development of the Forum's activities

Activities	Major goals
I. First stage (1994–98)	
1994: established as a voluntary organization operating supplementary English schools.	• coping with the poverty problem • creating employment • acquiring assets.
Negotiated to acquire a plot of borough land.	
II. Development stage (1999–2004)	
2002: employed the first consultant.	• constructing buildings
2003: recognized as a charity in the form of a company limited by guarantee & constructed a business park.	• operating the business park.
2004: employed the second consultant.	
III. Expansion stage (2005–)	
2005: expanded the business park.	• supporting starters of new businesses • expanding the business park.

Educational support activities and focus on asset management: the first stage

The Forum was established in 1994 as a local voluntary organization to run supplementary schools for non-English-speaking Bangladeshi women and for children between the ages of four and twelve. The Forum made a meagre start and felt its way through the initial start-up stage, as seen from the fact that its activities were funded by parents' donations of one pound per week and took place at existing community centers. This was the Forum's run-up period, or first stage, which ran from 1994 to 1998.

In order to achieve the purpose of the Forum's establishment, it became necessary for the Forum to grasp local needs and to secure independent revenue sources, as well as receiving government subsidies. This prompted residents of the Chicksand Estate to consult with the Environment Trust,[7] a Development Trust that had an office in the neighbourhood. The director of the Environment Trust (another social enterprise in Tower Hamlets) had been acquainted with estate residents and had worried about economic and social problems facing the residents, including drug abuse among young people and unemployment. The residents proposed the construction of a community center of their own. However, the director presented a plan to build multipurpose offices and workshops that could be used as workplaces and meeting rooms, and proposed the management of these offices and workshops as community assets and the investment of proceeds in the management of the Forum. His advice was based on his experience and belief that the point in reconstructing a community is to establish mechanisms and secure a place for residents to become economically independent. This later led to the Forum's 'asset management.'

After the Environment Trust's hearty recommendation of asset management, the Forum turned its attention to lands in the estate's neighbourhood. The General Secretary of the Forum states:

> That we foster independence and self-reliance rather than existing on the whims of grant giving bodies; that we are inclusive and draw on the strengths of our communities, our traditions, cultures and businesses... we believe that communities, particularly the Black and Minority Ethnic Community, need to own and control assets for themselves in order to empower local people and contribute to the regeneration and renewal of the area (Chicksand Citizens Forum 2002).

In addition to the operation of supplementary schools, the Forum now began to plan another important project. It was to conduct a capacity building survey of 158 households in the Chicksand Estate and to construct a 'micro business park.'

The objectives of the project were (i) to create opportunities for community residents to start small businesses; (ii) to provide spaces at rents 10% to 15% lower than the market rate (at an average rent of £100 unit/week); (iii) to create employment; and (iv) to provide social and cultural services, such as supplementary schools and meal services for the elderly. The operation of this business park went into full swing in the Forum's second stage (1999–2004). This provided a turning point for the Forum, which became more and more like a social enterprise.

First, the Forum decided to acquire a piece of land (900 square meters in ground area) that had been owned by the Tower Hamlets borough and used as a car park. The plot had been incorporated in the government's City Challenge program.[8] Under the program, a branch office and other offices for the borough had already been built on the plot. In addition, the post office adjacent to these offices had been planning to build a condominium on the same plot. The Forum requested a change of plan to build offices and workshops instead, and conducted a residents' campaign.

With the help of the Environment Trust, the Forum began to negotiate with the Tower Hamlets borough to obtain the plot of land. However, as a voluntary organization, the Forum was not eligible to rent the borough land directly from the borough. To resolve the situation, Cityside Regeneration Ltd,[9] which managed Single Regeneration Budget programs for the Tower Hamlets borough, rented the land and subleased it to the Forum. Subsequently, with the strategic abilities of the Forum's chairperson and the political influence of the director, as well as the Environment Trust's achievements, the Forum successfully obtained, after short negotiations, a ninety-nine-year leasehold of the borough land for only one pound—a so-called peppercorn rent.[10]

There are nearly 200 Bengali voluntary organizations in Tower Hamlets. The reason why the Forum was selected as the lessee is said to be that the Tower Hamlets borough and Cityside Regeneration Ltd recognised the Forum's experience in the operation of supplementary schools and its proposal to construct a business park, which would empower the community (Director of Cityside Regeneration Ltd 2004).

The Forum is currently managed by a management committee comprising three officers (chairperson, secretary and treasurer) and fourteen committee members, who are elected by community residents, plus three paid staff members (one consultant director and two supplementary school teachers).[11] With the committee functioning as the hub, the Forum offers voluntary programs, including the management of a micro business park, supplementary schools, business support and lunch meetings. Staff members are paid workers, while officers and committee members serve on a voluntary basis. Most of the officers and committee members are from the city of Sylhet. The fourteen committee members are elected each year. Of the fourteen members, five are the trustee's relatives or brothers and six have the same family name, which shows that the political and social structure of Sylhet city is strongly reflected in the Forum.

As for finances, in fiscal 1999 the Forum's total revenue and total expenditure were £32,000 and £32,800, respectively. At that time, the Forum's main activity was to operate supplementary schools. In fiscal 2003 the total revenue increased to £80,000, with a surplus (after subtracting office expenses and so on) reaching as much as £30,000 pounds. It seems that proceeds from the micro business park have supported the operation of the Forum since 2003.

Building construction and management of micro business park: the second stage

After the acquisition of the land, the Forum started the construction of buildings, including the business park. The initial estimate of the total project cost was £1.3 million, which eventually increased to £2 million. Needless to say, it was impossible for the Forum alone to carry out such a large project. The Forum says that it owes its success largely to the fact that the Tower Hamlets borough was within a disadvantaged area supported by the European Union and that the Forum had had many achievements and, above all, Cityside Regeneration Ltd and the Environment Trust used their influence to help the Forum to raise funds. Eventually, the Forum received funds from seven different sources,[12] including urban regeneration subsidies from the European Union and the central government and donations from community residents. The buildings were completed in 2002.

Similarly to the land, the ownership of the buildings remained with the Tower Hamlets borough and the right to use the buildings was held by Cityside Regeneration Ltd. The buildings were subleased and handed over to the Forum in 2002 under a ninety-nine-year leasehold. As it was difficult for a voluntary organization to rent land and buildings for a nominal rent, the Forum had to be incorporated and recognized as a charity. In 2003 the Forum was recognized as a charity in the form of a company limited by guarantee. The Forum was not granted the ownership of the land and buildings because several voluntary organizations in the community had collapsed economically and because the peppercorn rent would allow the administration to intervene in the project if the property was used for illicit purposes. In other words, peppercorn rent was used here, again, in order to ensure the publicness of the land and buildings.

Currently, the micro business park has thirteen business units.[13] In order to support young Bengalis living in the Tower Hamlets borough and starting up their businesses, the Forum leases these business units at rents 10% to 15% lower than the market rates (at an average rent of £100 unit/week) and provides information and management advice. All thirteen units are occupied, with 80% of the tenants being Bengali. The maximum term of occupation of a unit is limited to three years, in order to provide more people with opportunities to start businesses by increasing turnover and promoting early success of the businesses.

Providing community residents with the opportunity to start up a business at one of these business units or to hold a sociocultural program at the hall is also a chance for the Forum to empower young people, women and the elderly who are, or are likely to be, excluded from the community. The Forum also reinvests its proceeds, including the rent from the business units, back into the community and social activities. The Forum says this economic circulation represents the Forum's goal, which is empowerment of the entire community, or 'sustainable asset management.'

Utilization of community networks by professional consultants

In the background of the Forum's successful asset management is the existence of professional consultants who utilize community networks and support business start-ups. The Forum's professional consultants are required to provide more than just expertise—uniquely, they are required to provide indirect support to residents by utilizing social relations within the Bangladeshi community and also to motivate residents.

In June 2002 the Forum employed its first consultant. The Forum's current professional consultant is David Richardson, a Caucasian man in his mid-forties. As a staff member of the Tower Hamlets borough in charge of city regeneration, he had been involved in the management of the Forum since its initial stage. Later he retired from the ward office and in 2004 was employed by the Forum. When he was employed, he was not well thought of in the Forum and had to give his first priority to gaining members' trust in him. To this end, he did not attempt to personally intervene in the community but, instead, hired a young Bengali man, who had good knowledge of the community networks, as a business consultant. This young man was a third-generation Bengali born in London and had participated in an ethnic minority enterprise project for minorities living in the borough. His parents have run a curry restaurant in the community and he had thorough knowledge of the personal relations in the community. This allowed the professional consultant to obtain information through his business consultant. Richardson himself often went to a mosque attended by Bengalis and attempted to become acquainted with community members through volunteer activities. Gradually, his method to indirectly support the Bangladeshi community through its social networks began to produce successful results in the business park project.

The specific factors that led to the success in setting the micro business park project on the right track are as follows. First, the Forum chose not to provide direct support but to always make good use of local networks and to select tenants based on their trustworthiness and motivation by referring to personal connections in the local networks. Particularly effective was the utilization of the young Bengali network through key people. Second, the professional consultant played a central role in carrying out the project. It is significant that the consultant, who switched from a position to decide whether to 'accept applications' for the ward office to a position to 'make applications,' has acquired full knowledge of techniques to win subsidies and has networked successfully.

Community empowerment developing transnationally

As seen in the case study described above, activities of the Chicksand Citizens Forum have empowered individuals who are susceptible to social exclusion, in that these activities have given individuals self-confidence to live and have encouraged them to connect with the community. The empowerment of individuals has been achieved by utilizing personal networks in the immigrant community, which has enhanced the community's problem-solving abilities and is deeply linked with the process of community empowerment.

The Forum started with various voluntary activities, including vocational training and English education for minority people who were prone to be excluded from educational opportunities. The Forum then aimed to establish a social enterprise. By possessing and managing land and buildings (that is, assets) existing in the community and owned by the local government, the Forum now helps minority people become socially independent.

In the Forum community facilities function not simply as a place for residents to gather. By providing opportunities to start up businesses or by providing education and supplementary education, these facilities also function as a place to enhance the potential capacities of residents. They provide Bengali youths and women with business opportunities, opportunities for social participation, and a place to start up businesses and seek information. In addition, operating revenue from the asset management has enabled the provision to residents of services unique to the community, including education and health services. And this asset management has been conducted by the Development Trust as a social enterprise.

The social enterprise has enabled the acquisition of land and the construction of buildings by obtaining support from the local government and quasi-government organizations. It has also organized residents by utilizing social relations networks in the Bengali community that are unique to the area. Furthermore, the Forum has carried out its projects in a smooth manner by obtaining professional support from experts and consultants. Specifically, the Forum's projects for community regeneration have been managed by a cooperative framework consisting of the management committee (representing residents, and consisting of staff and experts). Thus, the Forum has not only secured information channels for starting up its projects but has also expanded, through its projects, social capital, which may be deemed as a new form of mutual confidence. This has brought about, directly or indirectly, the restructuring of resource distribution in Bengali communities, including opportunities to start up businesses, increased income and education, and improved health. In other words, a social enterprise has the function of creating a system that links distribution issues and relation issues.

In the London Bangladeshi community there have been additional moves to deal with the issue of social exclusion by utilizing global networks formed transnationally. These moves have attempted to develop projects of social enterprises in the global city of London by utilizing Bengali networks formed in their homeland of Sylhet and by obtaining financial support from the European Union and the British central and local governments.

In 1996 the Tower Hamlets borough and the Sylhet City Corporation entered into an affiliation concerning economic development, trade investment, and cultural and social exchanges. This has promoted exchanges of information, including technical knowledge and management models, in order to provide community services more effectively in Sylhet city by taking residents' needs into account. In addition, the Sylhet Partnership Project was initiated in 2001. This project was sponsored mainly by the European Union Asia Urbs Programme. In this project the partners cooperated with each other for two years in helping Sylhet city improve its public services and create employment; in solving poverty and environmental problems; and in improving education for children. Representatives from the three cities interacted with each other to plan the partnership project, with the Danish city of Horsens, the European partner, providing support. This represents a typical example of cooperation between advanced countries and developing countries in the empowerment of communities.

Under the existing circumstances with global competition, the many ethnic minority communities in European Union countries must compete with each other in obtaining support to solve poverty and social exclusion. Areas that have obtained support from the voluntary sector in organizing their ethnic minority communities (resulting in the communities showing motivation for regeneration) are in a better position. However, a large number of other areas have been left in poverty. The example of Chicksand Citizens Forum, which started in one of the poorest areas in London, offers many suggestions as to the empowerment of such an area. For an ethnic minority group whose members strive to barely survive, it shows the great significance of the voluntary sector sharing the effort to find the way to live independently and to reconstruct the community. From the 1990s the British government switched its policy to support the voluntary sector and promoted a partnership policy that actively supported activities of voluntary organizations, including Development Trusts. Part of the above-described success may be attributable to these movements.

   It has been nearly thirteen years since the Chicksand Citizens Forum started its operations. The Forum is now expected to further stabilize its operation as a social enterprise, while maintaining a Development Trust philosophy of fighting against social exclusion. In other words, the Forum's ability is being tested as to what it can do as part of the voluntary sector to potentially empower the two transnationally linked ethnic communities by taking into account global trends that have material effects on the social enterprise's activities. These trends include political pressure from the Bangladeshi transnational communities, the anti-poverty policy in London, and the European Union's supportive measures.

Notes

Chapter 2

1 This paper overlaps with my previous work (Tarumoto 2000) in topic and some descriptions, but the topics dealt with by the two papers are different in the following aspects. First, while the previous work deals with the present situation and tasks in the study on comparative migration policies, which is a relatively small field, the present paper intends to present tasks in transnational sociology and ethnic minority research, which are broader fields of study. Second, while the previous work intends to present tasks to 'explain' the similarities and differences among the immigrant policies of advanced countries, the present paper presents a discussion to 'propose' a citizenship model that would replace the 'nation-state' model.
2 This chapter does not intend to adopt a stage theory of development by which Marshall's work is characterized.
3 Tom Bottomore has pointed out that during the four decades after the Second World War, the issue presented by Marshall has extended to include ethnicity, as well as gender, environment and so on (Bottomore 1992).
4 Ruri Itō has described Brubaker's principles of the nation-state using the same categorization (Itō 1991: 88–9).
5 There is also a view that the 'challenge to the nation-state' can be divided into the 'challenge to national sovereignty' and the 'challenge to citizenship' (Joppke 1998). According to this view, the attempted mass smuggling of Chinese immigrants and the Elian Gonzalez incident could be categorized as the 'challenge to national sovereignty' and not the 'challenge to citizenship.' However, based on the aforementioned definition of citizenship, the 'right of entry and residence' seems to constitute part of the civil rights—then, the 'challenge to national sovereignty' is understood as part of the 'challenge to citizenship.'
6 An immigrant policy that controls flows of immigrants at international borders is known as 'immigration flow policy' as opposed to 'immigration stock policy' (Tarumoto 2000: 1–2).
7 Some researchers have proposed views that emphasize factors other than the three factors described above. See, for example, papers in Joppke (1998). Needless to say, a country's internal political process and national heritage are involved in the challenge to the nation-state. Other actors involved in the challenge would include the judicial system and immigrant groups. However, whether or not to emphasize these factors is likely to depend on the difference in the level of explanation. Specifically, the factors emphasized in the alternative proposals determine how the factors inherent in the principles surrounding citizenship (i.e. the increase and diversification of international migration, the emergence of universal human rights and the pursuit of social

integration) act in each country; they do not nullify or reverse the effects of those factors inherent in the citizenship principles. In this sense, those other factors cannot 'replace' the three factors described in this paper.
8 Excellent analyses of the creation of publicness based on residence are seen in the studies on Japanese neighbourhood associations. See, as a recent work, Yoshihara (2000).
9 Some may doubt if an 'imagination' can create publicness. It is true that an imagination can only produce a pipe dream unless public systems and practice is produced out of it. However, without an imagination, no citizenship model can be created nor can any public system or practice be produced that would fit the model.

Chapter 3

1 According to a survey by Ipsos MORI (2005), 'the most important issue facing Britain today' is 'race relations and immigration' (16%), followed by 'national health service' (15%), 'crime and violence' (11%) and 'defense and international terrorism' (10%). Levels of concern about race relations (33%) and defense/terrorism (29%) are high also in the combined answer format.
2 The police had been exempt until then because the Race Relations Act prohibited discrimination in service provision by government agencies but police officers' actions toward suspects were not considered to be service (British Home Office 2001: 11).
3 References are indicated by page numbers in principle but references in reports are indicated by 'chapter (or section) paragraph number' for ease of reference.
4 New racism itself is a controversial concept. See Miles (1993) and Leach (2005) for the argument that new racism is fundamentally no different from old racism. However, it is possible to interpret that outlawing of blatant discrimination upon the passing of the Race Relations Act has thrust new racism to the fore for greater scrutiny.
5 The 2001 national census also shows a strong sense of commitment to the concept of Britishness as an identity among ethnic minorities (Office for National Statistics 2003).
6 Under the *Nationality, Immigration and Asylum Act 2002*, immigrants who wish to obtain citizenship are tested for their English language ability and knowledge of life in the United Kingdom, and a citizenship oath and pledge to the United Kingdom and the Queen is administered at a public ceremony rather than a private one. It is a reflection of New Labour's determination to integrate immigrants and ethnic minorities into Britain. Some people on the left and in minority groups have criticized the move as 'new racism' or 'assimilationism' (Burnett and Whyte 2004; Kundnani 2005). However, the year 2002 saw the rise of far-right political parties on the back of the politics of insecurity, such as the entry of National Front leader Le Pen in the French presidential election runoff. Therefore, its commitment to integration under the banner of Britishness can be considered a strategic and realistic move to achieve a compromise between the right and the left by spelling out that 'the far right is the enemy' (Blunkett 2002).

Chapter 4

1. Refer to Maki, Kitano and Berthold (1999) for the reasons underlying the choice of the word 'redress' for the movement.
2. In this chapter, 'Japanese Americans' refers mainly to Japanese immigrants (and their descendants) who immigrated to the United States in the latter half of the nineteenth century.
3. However, the applicable conditions stipulated by this Act meant that some victims received an apology and compensation, while others did not. For example, there is the issue of Japanese immigrants who were taken from Central and South America to the United States during the war, which will be dealt with in detail in another paper.
4. The examples raised by Yamamoto in relation to the redresses that occurred in the 1990s are the announcement made by the Canadian government on its apology and compensation towards its indigenous people; the apology and compensation made by the New Zealand government to the Maoris in New Zealand; and how President Chirac of France acknowledged France's responsibility towards the Jews during the war (Yamamoto 1999).
5. The Japanese American redress movement had a great impact on movements led by other groups (such as African Americans and native Hawaiians) that were demanding redress. The impact was felt in particular in terms of its movement strategy, and also in terms of its morality, or the way it appealed to the wider community about the injustice in the policies taken against particular races or ethnic groups (Yamamoto 1999). The compensation made to the victims of the Rosewood massacre in Florida is an example of compensation demands that were made using the Japanese American movement as a model (Maki, Kitano and Berthold 1999). Meanwhile, the possible application by other groups of the movement strategy and resources used by the Japanese Americans still needs more discussion (Brew 1989; Yamamoto 1999; Howard-Hassmann 2004). This point will be studied in greater detail in another paper.
6. Refer to Yoneyama (2005) with regard to this point.
7. Approximately 110,000 Japanese Americans living in the United States became the target of the forced relocation policy.
8. By the time the internment policy ended, most of the first-generation Japanese Americans were middle aged or older, making it extremely difficult for them to rebuild their lives (CWRIC 1997: 295–6). This chapter uses *Personal Justice Denied* (CWRIC 1997), the report made by the study commission on the internment policy.
9. Refer to Tsuchida (2006), which gives a full account of the issues relating to the Japanese American community in the 1960s and 1970s and the movement's formation, for the formative process of the redress movement discussed in this section.
10. A detailed explanation of JACL is provided in the next section. The overview of the redress movement covered in this section is based on Maki, Kitano and Berthold (1999).
11. For example, the political and social climate at the time was dictated by the fact that the United States was suffering from an unusually severe financial

deficit under the Republican administration. In addition, an atmosphere of 'Japan bashing' was sweeping across the country due to the trade imbalance with Japan. Therefore, while the Japanese Americans were actually 'Americans,' they were prone to be seen as one and the same as the Japanese. Hence, the Japanese Americans anticipated strong opposition towards their demands (Maki, Kitano and Berthold 1999: 3).

12 Although CWRIC also purposed to investigate the eviction policy carried out against the Aleuts in Alaska during the war, in addition to the internment policy carried out against the Japanese Americans, this is not covered by this chapter (CWRIC 1997: 1).

13 Constituency here includes those who were claiming redress, whether they were direct victims or not.

14 NCRR's predecessor included a small-scale redress movement organization. Multiple Japanese American support organizations also participated in NCRR (Tsuchida 2006).

15 At the time, JACL membership was limited to those who had American citizenship. Those of the first generation who, up until the *Immigration and Nationality Act 1952*, were 'aliens ineligible to citizenship' were not allowed to join as members (Hosokawa 1984).

16 Refer to 'Testimony of James Tsujimura,' National Archives Microfilm Publications M1293, CWRIC, Washington DC, July 16, 1981.

17 NCJAR's class action lawsuit was dismissed in 1987.

18 Words within the square brackets indicate the writer's addition. This applies throughout the chapter.

19 Taken from 'Testimony of William Hohri,' National Archives Microfilm Publications M1293, CWRIC, Washington DC, July 16, 1981.

20 Taken from 'Testimony of William Hohri,' National Archives Microfilm Publications M1293, CWRIC, Washington DC, July 16, 1981.

21 NCRR's activities were based on a loosely binding network of organizations. This chapter refers to the activities of NCRR Los Angeles, which played a central role in these activities.

22 Based on the writer's interview with K., an NCRR member (April 8, 2004).

23 Taken from 'Testimony of Bert Nakano,' National Archives Microfilm Publications M1293, CWRIC, Washington DC, July 16, 1981.

24 Based on the writer's interview with M., an NCRR member (August 11, 2004).

25 Based on the writer's interview with M., an NCRR member (August 11, 2004).

26 Based on the writer's interview with N., an NCRR member (August 17, 2004).

27 Taken from 'Testimony of Mike Masaoka,' National Archives Microfilm Publications M1293, CWRIC, Washington DC, July 16, 1981.

28 The 442nd Regiment Combat Team, composed exclusively of Japanese Americans, became the most highly decorated unit (of the same scale) for its accomplishments on the European front. However, it suffered nearly 10,000 casualties (Murray 2001).

29 Taken from 'Testimony of Mike Masaoka,' National Archives Microfilm Publications M1293, CWRIC, Washington DC, July 16, 1981.

30 Taken from 'Testimony of William Hohri,' National Archives Microfilm Publications M1293, CWRIC, Washington DC, July 16, 1981.
31 While second-generation Japanese Americans were American citizens by birth, up until 1952 those who were of the first generation were 'aliens ineligible to citizenship.' Even then, they were legal immigrants and entitled to constitutional protection.
32 Taken from 'Testimony of June Kizu,' National Archives Microfilm Publications M1293, CWRIC, Los Angeles, August 5, 1981.
33 Refer to 'Testimony of Bert Nakano,' National Archives Microfilm Publications M1293, CWRIC, Washington DC, July 16, 1981.
34 Examples of 'others' include native Americans, native Hawaiians and African Americans (NCRR 1980: 3).
35 Taken from 'Testimony of Alan Nishio,' National Archives Microfilm Publications M1293, CWRIC, Los Angeles, August 4, 1981.
36 CWRIC concluded that the internment policy was determined based on 'racial prejudice, mass wartime hysteria, and the absence of political leadership' (CWRIC 1997: 18).
37 On the political nature of memory, Kiichi Fujiwara points out that a war museum can play the role of 'an institution of enlightenment for increasing the number of people who "remember" as if they had experienced it themselves' for those who do not have firsthand experience (Fujiwara 2001: 38). The public hearings discussed in this paper can also be seen as having functioned to reproduce 'people who remember.'

Chapter 5

1 Japanese researchers have been slow to take on the subject of globalization and social movements and only a small number of empirical studies and introductory papers have been published so far (Higuchi and Inaba 2004; Inaba 2005). In international relations, the study of international NGOs has been conducted mainly by younger researchers over the past decade (e.g. Mekata 2003; Nishitani 2007). In sociology this area of study has only just started, since the local residents' movement has been the main theme for social movement study to date. Many transnational social movement organizations, including Greenpeace and Médecins Sans Frontières, have been struggling to establish themselves in Japan, and even the most successful of them, Amnesty International Japan, is only about the fifteenth largest branch in its global network in terms of budget and membership. It is fair to say that the reality that many movements have not been transnationalized is the biggest reason for Japan's slow start in this area of research.
2 GCS theory itself is not necessarily a systematic discussion of the way global governance should be. Still, it is possible to define it as a discourse on participation 'from below' based on a system of governance such as cosmopolitan democracy (Baker 2002: 933).
3 This concept of 'horizontal society' concerns 'social exclusion' or 'exclusion,' which has been frequently mentioned in French politics, mass media and academia since the 1990s. This term is not an analytical concept but it epitomizes one interpretation of today's poverty issue, which has surfaced

since the late 1980s. 'Exclusion' means 'dropping out of society' or 'dropping out of competition' and being driven 'out' of society (Paugam 1991).
4 This is almost synonymous with Touraine's concept of communes but, unlike him, Castells highly recognizes the potential of social movements by communal groups.
5 Such a polarized view of society was not expressly presented in new social movement theory in the 1980s. Offe's discussion included the unemployed and the retired as decommodified groups, but Melucci and those who came after him appeared to discuss exclusively the new middle class with higher cognitive abilities. Castells's discussion takes into consideration the cases of excluded groups in the global north and developing countries by assuming this polarization.
6 We have been involved in advocacy for the rights of migrant workers led by the Migrant Forum in Asia since 1999. In addition, Inaba has participated in WSF three times as a member of either migrant support groups or NoVox. The following accounts are based on our experiences, and the accounts of social movements by NoVox and the have-nots, in particular, are based on the participatory fieldwork and interviews we have been conducting, mainly in France, since December 1994. See Fillieule and Péchu (1993) and Péchu (2006) about DAL.
7 Interview by the author at the third WSF.
8 It continued to negotiate with the city authority after the conclusion of the forum and succeeded in securing housing for the squatting families.

Chapter 6

1 Balinese society was originally characterized by a two-dimensional construction consisting of the *adat* and *dinas* (local government). It began when Bali Hindu was placed outside the system under the Dutch colonial system, and was consolidated when it was incorporated into the system in the post-colonial era. However, as the overwhelming wave of urbanization that goes hand in hand with the advance of global tourism hits the community, it also creates a situation where the *adat* is being encroached upon by the *dinas* (refer to Yoshihara (2006) regarding this point).
2 Incidentally, Geriya (2002) posits that tourism in Bali prior to this was in a sporadic introductory stage. He argues that the roads were built with the opening of the Ngurah Rai Airport, thus spurring on the development of tourism both in quantity and quality. It was then that Bali entered into its so-called concentrated period (Geriya 2002: 15–7).
3 Tourists were later required to obtain visas in the midst of a sharp decline in the number of tourists due to the impact of the terrorist bombings. Some voiced opposition to this, saying that the number of tourists would fall even further, but so far it has contributed to increased revenue.
4 In 2000 the Bali provincial government began to take measures against *batik* factory waste fluids. Specifically, starting in 2002 a reservoir was built in each factory under the instruction of the provincial government. Furthermore, factories were required to use chemicals to dilute the wastewater colour. However, none of this succeeded in reducing the damage

done to the surrounding areas, and the factories suffered even greater criticism. Incidentally, volume 29 of the 'Purnama' newsletter published by the PPB (Persatuan Purnama Batik) association set up by *batik* factory managers described the decisions it made on 14 August 2003 as follows:
1. Regulations which the members must comply with
   a) Do not rinse *batik* in the rivers
   b) Do not dump *batik* waste fluid without filtering it first within the factory
   c) Do not dry *batik* in public areas
2. Penalties for violators
   a) Members who do not comply by the regulations will be expelled from the association
   b) Members who violate the regulations will be penalized by the *desa* (administrative village).

5 Presently, the number of *batik* factories is on a downward trend due to a lack of vacant land as a result of the rising population, steep rises in land prices and the intensifying competition with China. As for the employees, they return to Java. However, because they cannot find employment in Java, they end up coming back to Bali, after which many move to other *batik* factories. Therefore, they effectively settle in Balinese society.

Incidentally, some of the owners of the *batik* factories are starting to devise new business strategies, such as manufacturing a wide variety of products in small quantities (for example, the manufacturing of beach sarongs and bedcovers), or focusing on the artistic aspect of *batik* and the value in handicrafts. There are also owners who are attempting to work out new management strategies by moving the factories to Java, while maintaining a distributing agent in Bali.

6 Although, as mentioned in endnote 1, Balinese society is formed from a two-dimensional construction consisting of the *adat* and *dinas*, this framework applies even in the *banjar*, the lowest level of administration. Balinese community is then constructed from a combination of the *banjar adat* and *banjar dinas*. Moreover, this community is characterized by a pluralistic group composition consisting of various *sekas* (prescriptive group or voluntary association). Up until now, there was a clear cut raison d'etre in which the *banjar adat* was responsible for traditional festivities and events, while the *banjar dinas* was responsible for secular administrative duties. Today, however, we can see cases where the former is becoming formalized, particularly in areas where urbanization is progressing, and being incorporated into the latter (refer to Yoshihara 2006 for details). Even if it does not go this far, we cannot deny the fact that on the whole both parties are mutually penetrating each other. It is amidst this trend that the division of roles between the *banjar adat* and *banjar dinas* is starting to blur (in fact, in some cases the same person may have a position in both the *banjar adat* and *banjar dinas*).

Incidentally, although new movements, which are riding on the back of the decentralization policy in their pursuit to increase autonomy for the *banjar adat* in the name of the protection of Bali's traditional society, are appearing, in general they are not changing the abovementioned trend.

7 At this *banjar* the following measures are taken in response to KIPEM who are unable to pay the administrative fees. First, they are allowed to pay in three installments. Furthermore, if, for example, both husband and wife are KIPEM, the administrative fees would total 200,000 rupiah. In such a case, they are allowed to first register the husband, and then register the wife three months later. Also, the responsibility for registration is placed in the hands of the employers in the case of KIPEM employed by *batik* factories, and so the employers are required to carry out the registration collectively. Additionally, if someone registered as a KIPEM returns to Java before the three-month validity period expires, the manager is given unspoken permission to use that name for a KIPEM who has yet to be registered.

8 The loud call made by *ajeg Bali* to promote local culture was already incorporated into the government policies under colonial rule and was also an indispensable part of the post-colonial strategy of global tourism. Undoubtedly, the local culture that *ajeg Bali* is trying to revive is deeply rooted in Bali Hindu. However, its difference to the local culture that appeared in relation to globalization is not always clear. Indeed, it even appears as if it has been completely drawn into the flow of globalization.

9 While this may sound like a repeat of endnote 8, it can be noted that *ajeg Bali* may perhaps be posited as one of the new types of anti-globalization movements seen in various places today. Furthermore, it can perhaps be considered in an analogical light with the neonationalistic movement spreading across Europe, which rejects immigrant labour and has, in a way, hijacked the notion of cultural relativism. What is important here is how the *ajeg Bali* movement perceives the progress of global tourism to be undermining the social order created on the basis of 'race.' In relation to this, it is perhaps also necessary to point out that *ajeg Bali* is, on the one hand, trying to faithfully restore the doctrines of Bali Hindu. Refer to the *Bali Post* (2004) for the time being regarding this point.

10 The 'emergent' referred to here is not something that spreads without limit, or that arises from some sort of bottomless source. The debate regarding self-organization and spontaneity that is presently spreading has a tendency to take on such characteristics. The 'emergent' that I am suggesting is that which arises from the multilayered network created through relationships that real life people living in the day-to-day world make with the 'other,' and not that which exists in and of itself. Refer to Yoshihara (2005) for details.

Chapter 7

1 According to an article in the *Kompas* daily electronic edition of August 10, 2007, during the year 2001–03 there were at least seventy-four cases of the 'clearance policy' in Jakarta.

2 According to an article in the *Kompas* daily edition of May 2, 2001 and the *Suara Pembaruan* daily edition of April 7, 1998, those who are seen as a societal problem by the government of Jakarta include people who work or do business such as *kakilima* (food stalls on street sidewalks), *asongan* (selling various things at street junctions when the traffic lights turn red), *becak* (pedicabs) and *joki* 3-in-1 (substitutes in private cars whenever

the number of people in the car is insufficient to be able to pass through main streets). These workers are subject to the clearance policy of the city government. Informal sector workers who are not seen as a problem of society and who are thought of more as micro-level businesses are mainly the *pedagang keliling* (hawkers), since their decorated push-carts are thought to be unique and can be a kind of attraction for tourist.

3 According to Schaefer (2006), a minority group is (1) a subordinate group whose members have significantly less control or power over their lives than members of a dominant or majority group, (2) not limited to minority of number, (3) interchangeable with subordinate groups, (4) a group that experiences a narrowing of opportunities to success, education, wealth etc.; accordingly, the number of members of this minority group who obtain success, high educational attainment and wealth are disproportionately low compared to their numbers in society.

4 'Crisis' in this chapter points to the 1997 financial crisis that swept most of the Asian developing countries. The crisis in Indonesia then became a multi-dimensional crisis, which also led to political crisis.

5 According to Bian Poen (1983: 46), the word *kampung* has been used since 1844, during the Dutch era of colonization in Indonesia, to refer to an area inhabited by Indonesian people and to differ the area from the 'city,' where the Dutchmen lived. Urban-*kampung* in this case refers to a densely populated residential area within present-day Jakarta. Urban-*kampung* is different from a slum area, since in urban-*kampung* there is basic infrastructure, usually as a result of the implementation of the Kampung Improvement Program (known in Jakarta as Proyek Mohamad Husni Thamrin), which started in 1969.

6 Based on BPS data in Jakarta Dalam Angka 1996.

7 *Betawi* is the name of old Jakarta, and it is also the name for native people of Jakarta.

Chapter 8

1 The figure shows a typology based on my observation of the new homeless in the world. It is made based on the *main* two characteristics of the homeless, that is, single homeless/homeless living with family and socially visible homeless/socially invisible homeless. See Figure 8.1.

2 Interview with Professor Maria Cecilia Loschiard Dos Santos, August 15, 2001.

3 Administrative officers and researchers told me that they did not have any reports and papers about the street homeless. They comforted me by saying, 'it might be difficult for you to get information about the street homeless.' I could only read newspaper articles with descriptions such as, 'The inhabitants who were fire victims became homeless,' or about street children. This is the case in the Philippines.

4 The following gives a total picture of people on the streets based on the information from people I interviewed—staff of NGO1 and NGO2 addressing the squatter problems, staff of NGO3 and NGO4 addressing

Figure 8.1: A typology of the new homeless in the world

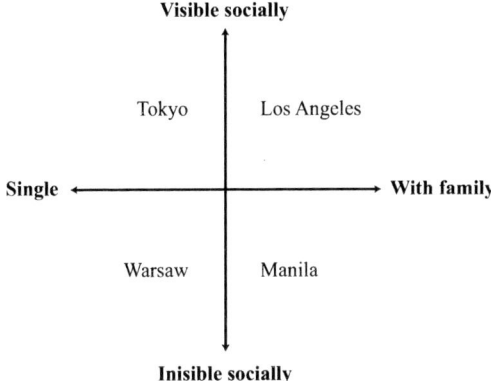

ethnic minority group problems, staff of an accommodation facility for street children, staff of a public facility for the street homeless, and others.
5 According to a survey in four relocation sites, the occupational composition of 600 inhabitants was as follows (ICSI 2000): 26.5% unemployed, 12.8% unskilled labourers, 13.8% drivers, 15.5% vendors, 8.7% construction workers, 2.3% agriculturists/gardeners, 1.5% housemaids, 8.8% technicians, 5.3% service jobs, 2.0% craftsmen and 2.7% as others. The unemployment rate was high and all jobs, except the technician jobs, were informal kinds of occupation in the relocation sites in general. Moreover, the kinds of occupation of the inhabitants in the relocation sites are fewer than those of the squatter inhabitants. In particular, the rates of vendor, housemaid and service jobs are lower in the relocation sites (UPA 2004: 17). I questioned the inhabitants of a relocation site in the mountain of San Mateo City. They worked as 'livestock raisers' and as vendors and scavengers (November 20, 2006), which were very few kinds of occupation.
6 Squatter inhabitants are defined as the 'underprivileged and *homeless* citizens' in the Urban Development and Housing Law (enacted in 1992), which designates the basis of the government's squatter policy. But there are non-poor squatters, too. The squatter class difference is ongoing. The Urban Research Consortium estimated that 20% to 25% of squatter inhabitants in Manila have a stable income and that the average income of the squatter inhabitants was higher than the poverty threshold set by the government (URC 1997: 5). Even so, most squatter inhabitants suffer from poverty. The Department of Arts and Sciences of St Joseph's College undertook a survey of 887 households that suffered poverty in seven squatter areas in Quezon City in 1995. According to the survey, the poverty incidence among all squatter families was 80.4%; the non-poor households were less than 20% of the total number of squatter families (SJC 1995). The poorest families often suffered from hunger and were almost no different from the street homeless.

7 With the industrialization of provinces, the population inflow to Manila has been reducing. And many people have moved out of Manila. Between 1985 and 1990, 456,597 people moved to Manila, and 331,389 people moved out of Manila, so the net inflow was 125,208 people (Pernia 1994: 33). The rate of newcomers among the population of Manila was reduced from 37.0% in 1970–80 to 16.3% in 1980–90 (Pernia 1994: 40). Incidentally, the population of Manila was 9,932,560 in 2000. The reduction in the rate of newcomers is also due to the fact that the number of people born in Manila has been increasing. According to a survey of District II in Quezon City, half of its inhabitants were born in Manila and 80% of inhabitants had lived in Manila for more than ten years (Endeiga 1999: 319). When I visited on November 5, 2006, the inhabitants of the squatter area along the railway said that most of them had already been there for more than twenty years and that 60–70% of the inhabitants were born there.

8 Arnold Padilla points out that the newcomers from the provinces are the biggest source of the street homeless (Padilla 2000: 6). But it may not be the real situation. The numbers of newcomers in Manila are reducing from year to year. They are the chain migrants who rely on their relatives. On the other side, there may be very few people who can migrate to Manila among the poorest people in the provinces. But there may be different circumstances in the cases of refugees of calamities and political persecution. They have the emergent reasons to flee from the hometowns.

9 The Department of Social Welfare and Development—National Capital Region (DSWD-NCR) gave special relief to 584 underprivileged people between January and March 2004. There were 405 street children, 109 adult homeless and 70 ethnic minority people (DSWD-NCR 2004a). We may regard these ethnic minority people as homeless.

10 According to a staff member of NGO3, people who come from Cordillera have four big communities in Manila (interview with Richard, December 6, 2006). Their population is unknown. According to a staff member of NGO4, the Islamic people have five big communities in Manila (interview with Alfie, December 12, 2006). The population is estimated at more than 200,000.

11 I asked officers of government agencies such as the National Housing Authority and the Department of Social Welfare and Development about the population of the street homeless. But they all answered that it is impossible to know the real number and the spatial distribution of the street homeless because the street homeless always move from one street to another. Researchers sometimes write the same thing, too (Padilla 2000: 6). However, it is possible to count the number of the street homeless, at least in round numbers, because most street homeless move in a constant spatial range, as cases in the United States and Japan show. In the Philippines there are other problems that make it difficult to count the street homeless as such; how can the street homeless be discriminated from other people who work on the streets? And how can a border be drawn between the street homeless and the squatter homeless? At any rate the truth may be that these government officers did not know the policy issue about the street homeless

and that they did not make any effort to survey the street homeless because their hands are full of the large-scale of the squatter problem.
12 The DSWD-NCR conducted outreach activities 121 times between January and June 2006 and gave relief to 2,100 street homeless (DSWD-NCR 2006c). The composition of recipients was as follows: 52% street homeless, 40% street children and 8% street families.
13 Although not sufficiently confirmed, it may be considered that people coming from North/Central Luzon stay around Monument and Cubao, the long-distance bus terminals in the northern part of Manila, and people coming from South Luzon stay around Baclaran, the long-distance bus terminal in the southern part of Manila. Some people get jobs, other people enter the squatter areas and other people become the street homeless. And they spread over the city of Manila.
14 The construction of the houses by the government is delayed because it lacks the funds to buy land and to improve residential conditions, and because it is difficult for the government to come to an agreement with the squatter inhabitants about the purchase of land and the improvement of residential conditions (Karaos and Payot 2006: 67–8). Moreover, it appears that the bureaucratic administrative organizations are not efficient in putting into practice the policies for the squatter inhabitants and that coordination between the central government and the local one is insufficient.
15 The government says that it is the basic policy to relocate evicted people within the city in order to avoid these inconveniences. It transferred the residents along the railways of the PNR-North and PNR-South to the relocation sites. The government only adopts the option to transfer people to the suburbs if it cannot secure relocation sites. In the PNR eviction cases in the City of Manila and Makati City, Laguna, Cavite and Bulacan were chosen as the relocation sites (Karaos and Payot 2006: 72).
16 Strictly, I can suggest that 'living collectively' is not the crucial criteria to discriminate the squatter homeless from the street homeless. A squatter along the waterway that I visited (on November 8, 2006) had been evicted (in April 2006) and only three of the dispersed families remained there. This cannot be considered as 'living collectively.' But they have their fixed shelters fully furnished, household effects and normal home living conditions.
17 There are various definitions of the new homeless in the United States and Japan, too. I discussed the definitions of the *nozyukusya*, the new homeless, in Japan (Aoki 2006, chapter 5).
18 A representative of NGO2 says that it is not a rare case that some families of squatters live together in one house. In such a case, the landowner should be regarded as the squatter inhabitant and other families should be regarded as the street homeless (interview with Garcia, November 20, 2006). However, in this chapter, other families also were regarded as squatter inhabitants. An NGO2 representative also says that even when a family lives with another family, they have to pay about 1,000 pesos (at the least, 700–800 pesos) per month. It may be not easy for the poorest people with no fixed income to pay even this amount of money every month.

19 Interview with Manuela M. Loza, December 4, 2006.
20 We can see a classification of beggar in a government document as follows: the 'mendicant' refers to any person who is not visible and has no legal means of support or lawful employment, who is physically able to work by calling, instead of begging, as a means of living; the 'exploited infant or child' refers to an infant or child of eight years old and below who is used in begging or one who accompanies habitual vagrants or beggars; and the 'habitual mendicant' refers to those who have been convicted of mendicancy two or more times under Presidential Decree No. 1563 (Establishing an Integrated System for the Control and Eradication of Mendicancy, Providing Penalties and Appropriating Funds, or for Other Purposes) (DSWD-NCR 2006b).
21 It is my interest to analyze the processes of such globalization that produces the 'urban bottom people' and to testify the hypothesis about the 'new labour' and the 'new poverty' that I constructed as the key concepts for the study of globalization. This chapter is a part of it. I defined 'new labour' as the new miscellaneous occupations with poor labour conditions, as well as cheap wages, and 'new poverty' as the depressed level of life brought by the cheap wages of 'new labour' (Aoki 2006, Ch. 1).
22 For example, the *main* processes by which globalization forms the new homeless in Japan and the Philippines are characterized comparatively in figure 8.2.
23 For example, the Philippine Seven Corporation opened the first Seven-Eleven convenience store in 1984. The number of stores reached 256 in 2005 (Philippines Seven Corporation 2007). Most of them are situated in Manila. The Jollibee Food Corporation opened the first Jollibee fast food store in 1975, and the number of stores in the Philippines reached 1,287 in 2006 (Wikipedia 2007).
24 Saskia Sassen enumerated the following occupations in New York State's service sector (Sassen 1988: 200): maid, cleaner (light and heavy), janitor, porter, baggage porter, bellhop, kitchen helper, pantry watcher, sandwich/coffee maker, food service, room service attendant, ticket taker, stock clerk (stock room, warehouse storage yard), washer, machine washer, dry cleaner (hand), spotter (dry cleaning, washable materials), laundry presser, laundry folder, rug cleaner (hand and machine), shoes repairer, delivery and route worker, parking lot attendant, exterminator and packager. It is surprising that the majority of these jobs are common to the new unskilled and low-paid jobs found in Manila. In the case of Manila, the unskilled are included in low-paid service jobs in the formal sectors and sales jobs in this list: for example, the saleswoman and the driver in the large-scale store. Under the influence of economic globalization, the new unskilled and low-paid jobs have increased simultaneously in both industrial and developing countries.
25 According to a report, the number of people engaged in informal occupations in Manila was 549,000 (Joshi 1997: 6). But this seems to be a very modest number. Among those people there were 351,000 entrepreneurs who owned small-sized businesses or were self-employed, and 188,000 employees. Businesses with no employees occupied 81% of the total businesses. Influenced by the casualization of labour, employees engaged in informal occupations have been increasing (Joshi 1997: 8).

Figure 8.2: Processes by which globalization forms the new homeless in Japan and the Philippines

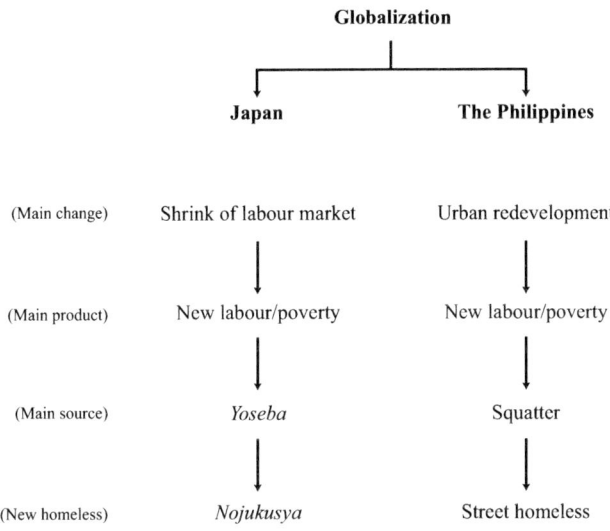

26 According to a survey by the Social Weather Station in November 2006, 17.7% of 300 respondents who were the heads of families experienced hunger at least once in the previous three months (*The Philippine Star*, December 20, 2006: 12); 5.0% of respondents answered that they were in the 'serious hunger' category every day; and 48% of respondents thought of themselves as poor. The respondents answered that they needed at least 10,000 to 12,000 pesos per month in order to remain above the poverty threshold (which means the 'subjective poverty threshold'). This level is much lower than the minimum cost of living in Manila of 17,713 pesos set by the Census 2000 (NSO 2000). We can see the respondents' strong sense of crisis in their livelihoods in such a big difference.

27 The policy of 'making beautiful towns' was spearheaded by the administration in Manila. In Quezon City, from December 1 to January 8, the city government launched regulations that excluded vendors from the sidewalks and the pedestrian bridges and permitted them to do business only in designated places; the reason given was that the vendors obstructed traffic (*The Philippine Star*, December 2, 2006: 15). It was a severe regulation, which declared that no exception was permitted, that offenders should be arrested and their goods should be confiscated. The offense of the policemen who chase the 'illegal' vendors and the defense of the vendors who escape from the policemen are repeated every day in downtown areas.

28 One facility is managed by DSWD-Central, two facilities are managed by the DSWD-NCR and three facilities are managed by the local municipalities. In addition, there are three facilities managed by NGOs (DSWD-NCR 2004b).

Chapter 10

1 Among works analyzing the mechanisms of poverty generation in the East End is: John Eade (1989), *The Politics of Community: The Bangladeshi Community in East London* (Research in Ethnic Relations Series), London: Gower Pub Co.
2 The Bengal region lies along the lower Ganges River. The eastern part belongs to Bangladesh and the western part to India. In other words, Bengal refers to a region extending over Bangladesh and India.
3 'Economically active' population includes (i) people who are employed; (ii) people who are unemployed but are seeking employment and are ready to start working within two weeks; and (iii) students working full-time, in each case in the week preceding Census Day. This definition is supposedly in conformity with the International Labour Organization's definition of 'economic status.'
4 'Housing deprivation' is measured by indicators such as overcrowding; more than one household living together; and the status of bath/toilet facilities and central heating systems.
5 For conceptual analysis of social exclusion, see Higuchi (2005) and Kashihara (2004).
6 For a newspaper article emphasizing cultural values producing poverty, see Rahman (2007).
7 The Environment Trust helped as an intermediate support organization with the birth of the Forum and, through the trust's external trading arm Environment Trust Associates, supervised as a social developer the construction of buildings by the Forum.
8 The City Challenge program was introduced in 1991. It distributes subsidies to fifty-seven designated disadvantaged areas taking into account the strategic quality of projects developed by each community.
9 Cityside Regeneration Ltd is a Quango (quasi-autonomous national government organization) operated by government, private and community sectors and was established as a community organization to manage Single Regeneration Budget (SRB) funds, which are national funds to regenerate communities.
10 'Peppercorn rent' means long-term leasehold for very cheap, nominal rent. Other forms of property conveyance from a local government include land sales for prices lower than the market value.
11 'Officer' is the Forum's designation of a director.
12 The largest fund was the European Union's community regeneration fund (URBAN), which amounted to approximately £300,000. The Forum eventually raised nearly £1 million, including SRB3 and SRB5 and skill-match subsidies from the government and subsidies from the borough. The remainder was raised from miscellaneous sources, including a charity foundation (the Bridge House Estate) and donations from residents.
13 The business park has a total floor area of 650 square meters, including a multipurpose hall (110 square meters), offices and shops. The initial plan estimated the annual rental income at £55,000.

References

Alisjahbana, Armida S. and Chris Manning (2006), 'Labour market dimensions of poverty in Indonesia', *Bulletin of Indonesian Economic Studies*, 42 (2), pp. 235–61.
Allen, Christopher (2003), *Fair Justice: The Bradford Disturbances, the Sentencing and the Impact*, London: Forum Against Islamophobia and Racism.
Allport, Gordon W. (1954), *The Nature of Prejudice*, Cambridge, Mass.: Addison-Wesley.
Anderson, Benedict (1983), *Imagined Communities: Reflections on the Origin and Spread of Nationalism*, London: Verso.
Ansell, Amy E. (1997), *New Right, New Racism*, Basingstoke: Macmillan Press.
Aoki, Hideo (2003), 'New labouring class and the new poverty class: the case of Manila,' *Yoseba*, 16, Tokyo: Renga Shobo Shinsha, pp. 110–129.
Aoki, Hideo (2006), *Japan's Underclass: Day Labourers and the Homeless*, Melbourne: Trans Pacific Press.
Appadurai, Arjun (1996), *Modernity at Large: Cultural Dimensions of Globalization*, Minneapolis: University of Minnesota Press.
Badan Pusat Statistik Propinsi Bali (1996), *Bali Dalam Angka 1996*, Denpasar: Badan Pusat Statistik.
Badan Pusat Statistik Propinsi Bali (1997), *Jakarta Dalam Angka 1996*, Denpasar: Badan Pusat Statistik.
Badan Pusat Statistik Propinsi Bali (2001), *Bali Dalam Angka 2001*, Denpasar: Badan Pusat Statistik.
Badan Pusat Statistik Propinsi Bali (2005), *Bali Dalam Angka 2005*, Denpasar: Jakarta:Badan Pusat Statistik.
Badan Pusat Statistik Propinsi Bali (2006a), *Bali Dalam Angka 2006*, Denpasar: Badan Pusat Statistik.
Badan Pusat Statistik Propinsi Bali (2006b), Indikator social ekonomi Indonesia edisi Maret 2006, Jakarta: Badan Pusat Statistik.
Baker, Gideon (2002), 'Problems in the theorisation of Global Civil Society', *Political Studies*, 50, pp. 928–43.
Balibar, Etienne (1991), 'Is there a neo-racism?', in Etienne Balibar and Immanuel Wallerstein, *Race, Nation, Class*, London: Verso.
Bali Government Tourism Office (1997), *Bali 97,Bali Tourism Statistics*, Denpasar: Bali Government Tourism Office.
Bali Post (2004), Ajeg Bali: sebuan cita-cita, Denpasar.
Bangasser, Paul (2000), 'The ILO and the informal sector: an institutional history', *ILO Employment Paper 2000/9*, Employment Paper Ref. 1020-5322, 2000/9, Geneva: ILO.
Banton, Michael (1988), *Racial Consciousness*, London and New York: Longman.

Barker, Martin (1981), *The New Racism: Conservatives and the Ideology of the Tribe*, London: Junction Books.
Bauman, Zygmunt (2000), *Globalization: The Human Consequences*, Cambridge: Polity Press.
Beck, Ulrich (1986), *Risikogesellschaft: Auf dem Weg in eine andere Moderne* (Risk Society: Towards a New Modernity), Frankfurt/Main: Suhrkamp Verlag.
Beck, Ulrich (1999), *World Risk Society*, Cambridge: Polity Press.
Beck, Ulrich (2005), 'How not to become a museum piece', *British Journal of Sociology*, 56(3), pp. 335–43.
Beck, Ulrich, Anthony Giddens and Scott Lash (1994), *Reflexive Modernization: Politics, Tradition and Aesthetics in the Modern Social Order*, Cambridge: Polity Press.
Beck, Ulrich and Johannes Willms (2004), *Conversations with Ulrich Beck*, Cambridge: Polity Press.
Beier, J. Marshall and Ann D. Crosby (1998), 'Harnessing change for continuity: the play of political and economic forces behind the Ottawa Process', in Maxwell A. Cameron, Robert J. Lawson and Brian W. Tomlin (eds.), *To Walk without Fear: The Global Movement to Ban Landmines*, Toronto: Oxford University Press, pp. 269–91.
Bhalla, A. S. and Frederic Lapeyre (2004), *Poverty and Exclusion in a Global World*, New York: Palgrave Macmillan.
Bian Poen (1983), 'Research and Development for urban management—case Jakata', Doctoral Dissertation, Rotterdam: Erasmus Universiteit.
Biro Pusat Statstik (1997), *Jakarta Balam Angka 1996*, Jakarta: Biro Pusat Statistik.
Biro Pusat Statistic (2006), *Indikator Social Ekonomi Indonesia edisi Maret 2006*, Jakarta: Biro Pusat Statistik.
Blunkett, David (2002, April 11), 'The far right is the enemy', *The Guardian*, accessed August 30, 2007 (http://society.guardian.co.uk/raceequality/comment/0.8146.682287.00.htm).
Bob, Clifford (2005), *The Marketing of Rebellion: Insurgents, Media, and International Activism*, New York: Cambridge University Press.
Boeke, Julius Herman (1942), *The Structure of Netherlands Indian Economy*, New York: IPR International Research Series Institute of Pacific Relations.
Boli, John and George M. Thomas (1997), 'World culture in the world polity: a century of international non-governmental organization,' *American Sociological Review*, 62 (2), pp. 171–9.
Bottomore, Tom (1992), 'Citizenship and social class, forty years on,' in Thomas Humphrey Marshall and Tom Bottomore (eds.), *Citizenship and Social Class*, London: Pluto Press, pp. 53–93.
Brew, Sarah L. (1989), 'Making amends for history: legislative reparations for Japanese Americans and other minority groups', *Law and Inequality*, 8, pp. 179–201.
British Home Office (2001), *Race Relations (Amendment) Act 2001: New Laws for a Successful Multi-Racial Britain*, London: Home Office.
British Home Office (2004), *Strength in Diversity: Towards a Community Cohesion and Race Equality Strategy*, London: Home Office Communication Directorate.

References

British National Party (n.d.), untitled homepage, accessed February 15, 2000 (http://www.BNP.net/).
Brubaker, William Rogers (ed.) (1989), *Immigration and the Politics of Citizenship in Europe and North America*, Lanham: University Press of America.
Bullard, Robert D. (1994), *Dumping in Dixie: Race, Class, and Environmental Quality* (2nd ed.), Boulder: Westview Press.
Burnett, Jonny and Dave Whyte (2004, October 6), 'New Labour's new racism', *IRR News*, accessed August 30, 2007 (http://www.irr.org.uk/2004/october/ak000008.html).
Cantle, Ted (2001), *Community Cohesion*, London: Home Office.
Cantle, Ted (2005), *Community Cohesion: A New Framework for Race and Diversity*, Basingstoke: Palgrave Macmillian.
Castells, Manuel (1989), *The Informational City: Information Technology, Economic Restructuring, and the Urban-Regional Process*, Oxford: Blackwell.
Castells, Manuel (1996), *The Rise of the Network Society*, Oxford: Blackwell.
Castells, Manuel (1997), *The City and the Grassroots*, Ishikawa, Atsushi, supervisor of translation, Japanese version, Tokyo: Hohsei University Press.
Castells, Manuel (1997), *The Power of Identity*, Oxford: Blackwell.
Castles, Stephen and Mark J. Miller (1993), *The Age of Migration: International Population Movements in the Modern World*, London: Macmillan Press.
Chicksand Citizens Forum (2002), *Annual Report*.
Commission of the European Communities (2001), *A White Paper on European Governance*, accessed 20 November, 2007 (http://eur-lex.europa.eu/LexUriServ/site/en/com/2001/com2001_0428en01.pdf).
Commission on Wartime Relocation and Internment of Civilians (1983), *Public Hearings on the Commission on Wartime Relocation and Internment of Civilians 1981*, Washington: National Archives Microfilm Publications M1293.
Commission on Wartime Relocation and Internment of Civilians (1997), *Personal Justice Denied*, Seattle: University of Washington Press.
Corcuff, Philippe (1995), *Les nouvelles sociologies*, Paris: Nathan.
Cornelius, Wayne A., Takeyuki Tsuda, Philip L. Martin and James F. Hollifield (eds.) (2004), *Controlling Immigration: A Global Perspective*, Stanford: Stanford University Press.
Council for the Welfare of Children (2006), CWC homepage, accessed on November 26, 2006 (*http://www.cwc.gov.ph/data-streetchildren.html*).
della Porta, Donatella and Sidney G. Tarrow (2004), *Transnational Protest and Global Activism*, Lanham: Rowman & Littlefield.
Department of Social Welfare and Development—National Capital Region (2004a), *History of SAGIP KALINGA Protect*, unpublished report, Manila: Department of Social Welfare and Development—National Capital Region.
Department of Social Welfare and Development—National Capital Region (2004b), 'Statistical data (2004.1-3)', accessed on December 3, 2006 (*http://www.ncr.dswd.gov.ph/images/articles/statdigest-1Q2004.pdf*).
Department of Social Welfare and Development—National Capital Region (2006a), 'Sagip Kalinga Community-Based Project: First Semester,

2006', unpublished report, Manila: Department of Social Welfare and Development—National Capital Region.

Department of Social Welfare and Development—National Capital Region (2006b), untitled document with the tables (acquired on November 28, 2006), Manila: Department of Social Welfare and Development—National Capital Region.

Department of Social Welfare and Development—National Capital Region (2006c), homepage, accessed on December 3, 2006 (http://www.ncr.dswd.gov.ph/images/articles/statdigest-1Q2004.pdf).

Dubet, François (1987), *La galère: jeunes en survie*, Paris: Seuil (Points Actuel).

Dubet, François (1991), *Les lycéens*, Paris: Seuil (Points Actuel).

Dubet, François (2002), *Le déclin de l'institution*, Paris: Seuil.

Dubet, François and Didier Lapeyronnie (1992), *Les quartiers d'exil*, Paris: Seuil.

Dubet, François and Danilo Martuccelli (1998), *Dans quelle société vivons-nous?*, Paris: Seuil.

Durkheim, Emile (1912), *Les Formes Élémentaires de la Vie Religieuse*, Paris: Félix Alcan.

Eder, Klaus (2000), 'Taming risks through dialogues: the rationality and functionality of discursive institutions in risk society,' in Maurie J. Cohen (ed.), *Risk in the Modern Age: Social Theory, Science and Environmental Decision-Making*, New York: Macmillan Press, pp. 225–48.

Endeiga, Dolores A. (1999), 'Who are the urban poor?' in Dolores A. Endria Rebullida and Gerakline M. Santos (eds.), *Housing of the Urban Poor: Policies, Approaches, Issues*, Manila: UP CIDS.

Erawan, I. Nyoman (1994), *Parawisata dan Pembangunan Ekonomi*, Denpasar: Upada Sastra.

ETHNOS (2005), *Citizenship and Belonging: What is Britishness?*, London: Commission for Racial Equality.

Evers, Hans Dieter and Rudiger Korff (2000), *Southeast Asia Urbanism: The Meaning and Power of Social Space*, Hamburg: LIT Verlag.

Feldblum, Miriam (1998), 'Reconfiguring citizenship in Western Europe,' in Christian Joppke (ed.), *Challenge to the Nation-State: Immigration in Western Europe and the United States*, Oxford: Oxford University Press, pp. 231–70.

Fillieule, Olivier and Cécile Péchu (1993), *Lutter ensemble: Les théories de l'action collective*, Paris: L'Harmattan.

Firman, Tommy (1999), 'Indonesian cities under the "Krismon"', *Cities*, (16) 2, pp. 69–82.

Firnandy, Lucky (2004), 'Studi profil pekerja di sektor informal dan arah kebijakan ke depan', Kajian Bappenas (unpublished), Jakarta: Direktorat Ketenagakerjaan dan Analisis Ekonomi Bappenas.

Forman, Charlie (1989), *Spitalfields: A Battle for Land*, London: Hilary Shipman Ltd.

Fujimaki, Hayao (2001), *Roji no keizai shakaigaku: Thai no informal sector ni tsuite*, Tokyo: Mekong.

Fujiwara, Kiichi (2001), *Sensō wo kiokusuru—Hiroshima, horokōsuto to*

genzai (Remembering the war: Hiroshima, the holocaust, and the present), Tokyo: Kodansha.
Gaertner, Samuel L. and John F. Dovidio (1986), *Prejudice, Discrimination, and Racism*, Orlando: Academic Press.
Gaertner, Samuel L. and John F. Dovidio (2000), *Reducing Intergroup Bias: The Common Ingroup Identity Model*, Hove: Psychology Press.
Gaertner, Samuel L., John F. Dovidio and Betty A. Bachman (1996), 'Revisiting the contact hypothesis: The Induction of a common ingroup identity', *International Journal of Intercultural Relations* (20) 3/4, pp. 271–90.
Geriya, I. Wayan (2002), *International Marriage: Tourism, Inter Marriage and Cultural Adaptation in the Family Life of Balinese–Japanese Couple in Bali*, Center for Japanese Studies, Denpasar: University of Udayana.
Giddens, Anthony (1991), *Modernity and Self-Identity: Self and Society in the Late Modern Age*, Cambridge: Polity Press.
Goodhart, David (2006), *Progressive Nationalism: Citizenship and the Left*, London: Demos.
Goodman, James (2002), 'Introduction', in James Goodman (ed.), *Protest and Globalisation: Prospects for Transnational Solidarity*, Annandale: Pluto Press, pp. viii–xxv.
Gunawan, Indrawati (1992), 'Wanita di sektor informal', *Prisma*, 5, pp. 23–37.
Habermas, Jürgen (1984), *The Theory of Communicative Action* Vol 1: Reason and the Rationalization of Society, Boston: Beacon.
Hammar, Tomas (1990), *Democracy and the Nation State: Aliens, Denizens and Citizens in a World International Migration*, Aldershot: Avebury.
Hart, Keith (1973), 'Informal income opportunities and urban employment in Ghana,' *Journal of Modern African Studies*, 11, pp. 61–89.
Harvey, David (2006), *Spaces of Neo-liberalization*, London: Verso.
Hasegawa, Koichi (2004), *Constructing Civil Society in Japan: Voices of Environmental Movements*, Melbourne: Trans Pacific Press.
Hasegawa Koichi, Chika Shinohara and Jeffrey Broadbent (2007), 'The effects of "social expectation" on the development of civil society in Japan', *Journal of Civil Society*, 3 (2), pp. 179–203.
Hatamiya, Leslie T. (1993), *Righting a Wrong: Japanese Americans and the Passage of the Civil Rights Liberties Act of 1988*, Stanford: Stanford University Press.
Held, David, Anthony McGrew, David Goldblatt and Jonathan Perraton (1999), *Global Transformations: Politics, Economics and Cultures*, Cambridge: Polity Press.
Higuchi, Akihiko (2005), 'Gendai shakai ni okeru shakai-teki haijo no mekanizumu' (The mechanisms of social exclusion in contemporary society), *Shakaigaku hyōron* (Japanese sociological review), 55 (1), pp. 2–8.
Higuchi, Naoto and Nanako Inaba (2004), 'Gurōbaru-ka to shakai undō (Globalization and social movements,' in Seiji Soranaka, Koichi Hasegawa, Takashi Machimura and Naoto Higuchi (eds), *Shakai undō toiu kōkyō kūkan* (Public spaces called social movements), Tokyo: Seibundo, pp.190–229.
Hitchcock, Michael and I. Nyoman D. Putra (2007), *Tourism, Development and Terrorism in Bali*, Aldershot: Ashgate.
Hohri, William Minoru (1984), *Repairing America: An Account of the*

Movement for Japanese-American Redress, Pullman: Washington State University Press.

Hosokawa, Bill (1984), *120% no chūsei: nikkei nisei, kono yūkiaru hitobito no kiroku* (120% loyalty—A record of the courageous nisei Japanese Americans), Tokyo: Yuhikaku.

Howard-Hassmann, Rhoda E. (2004), 'Getting to reparations: Japanese Americans and African Americans', *Social Forces*, 83(2), pp. 823–40.

Hugo, Graeme (1973), *Population Mobility in West Java*, Yogyakarta: Gajah Mada University Press.

Hussain, Yasmin and Paul Bagguley (2005), 'Citizenship, ethnicity and identity: British Pakistanis after the 2001 "riots"', *Sociology*, 39(3), pp. 407–25.

IBON Foundation Inc. (2001), *Raw Data: Forced Eviction under the Macagapal-Arroyo Government*, Manila: IBON Foundation Inc.

Imig, Doug and Sidney Tarrow (eds.) (2001), *Contentious Europeans: Protest and Politics in an Emerging Polity*, New York: Rowman and Littlefield.

Inaba, Nanaba (2005), 'Kokkyō wo koeru shakai undō' (Social movements beyond country borders), in Takamichi Kajita (ed.), *Shin Kokusai Shakaigaku* (Transnational/Global Sociology), Nagoya: University of Nagoya Press, pp. 179–98.

Institute for Employmeyment Studies (2002), *A Review of Training in Racism Awareness and Valuing Cultural Diversity*, London: British Home Office, Research, Development and Statistics Directorate.

Institute on Church and Social Issues (2000), *Socio-economic Survey of Project-Affected Persons (PAPs)—Second Monitoring Term*, Manila: Institute on Church and Social Issues.

Ipsos MORI (2005), *Poll of General Election 2005*, accessed July 15, 2007 (*http://www.ipsos-mori.com/election2005/pollsindex.shtml*).

Itō, Ruri (1991), '"Atarashii shiminken" to shimin shakai no hen'yo—imin no seiji sanka to Furansu kokumin kokka' ("New civil rights" and changes in civil society—political participation of immigrants and the French nation-state), in Takashi Miyajima and Takamichi Kajita (eds), *Tōgō to bunka no naka no Yōroppa* (Europe amid integration and division), Tokyo: Yūshindō Kōbunsha, pp. 85–103.

Jellinek, Lea (1977a), 'The life of a Jakarta street trader', in Janet Abu-Lughod and Richard Hay (eds), *Third World Urbanization*, Chicago: Maaroufa Press.

Jellinek, Lea (1977b), 'The life of a Jakarta street trader—two years later', *Working Paper No. 13*, Melbourne: Centre of Southeast Asian Studies, Monash University.

Jellinek, Lea (1988), 'The changing fortunes of Jakarta street trader', in J. Gugler (ed.), *The Urbanization of the Third World*, New York: Oxford University Press.

Jellinek, Lea (1991), *The Wheel of Fortune: the History of a Poor Community in Jakarta*, London: Allen & Unwin.

Jose Fabella Center (2006), an internal untitled report about the center's residents, Manila: Jose Fabella Center.

Joshi, Gopal (1997), *Urban Informal Sector in Manila: A Problem or Solution?*, Manila: ILO (International Labour Organization), Philippines.

Joppke, Christian (ed.) (1998), *Challenge to the Nation-State: Immigration in Western Europe and the United States*, Oxford: Oxford University Press.
Kajita, Takamichi (ed.) ([1992] 1996), *Kokusai shakaigaku* (Transnational sociology), Nagoya: The University of Nagoya Press.
Kajita, Takamichi (2001a), 'Kokusaika kara gurōbaruka he: shakaigaku wa dō taiō subekika (From internationalization to globalization: how should sociology respond?),' in Takamichi Kajita (ed.), *Kokusaika to aidentitī* (Internationalization and identity), Kōza: shakai hendō 7 (Social change 7), Kyoto: Minerva Publishing, pp. 1–30.
Kajita, Takamichi (2001b), 'Gendai nihon no gaikokujin rōdōsha seisaku saikō: seiōshokoku to no hikaku wo tōshite' (Rethinking the policies on immigrant workers in contemporary Japan: through comparison with Western countries), in Takamichi Kajita (ed.), *Kokusaika to aidentitī* (Internationalization and identity), Kōza: shakai hendō 7 (Social change 7), Kyoto: Minerva Publishing, pp. 184–219.
Karaos, Anna Marie (1996), 'An assessment of the government's Social Housing Program', *ICSI Occasional Paper No. 1*, Manila: Ateneo de Manila University.
Karaos, Anna Marie and Junefe G. Payot (2006), 'The homes promises couldn't build', in *Civil Society Monitoring of the Medium Term Philippine Development Plan (MTPDP): Assessment of the Two Years (2004–06)*, Manila: The Caucus of Development NGO Networks, pp. 67–87.
Kashihara, Akira (2004), 'Igirisu ni okeru shakai-teki haijo no torikumi (Approaches against social exclusion in Britain)', *Kōbe Gakuin keizaigaku ronshū* (Kōbe Gakuin economic papers), 35 (4), pp. 105–147.
Kaufmann, Jean-Claude (2000), *La Trame conjugal: analyse du couple par son linge*, Paris: Nathan.
Keck, Margaret E. and Katheryn Sikkink (1998), *Activists beyond Borders: Advocacy Networks in International Politics*, Ithaca: Cornell University Press.
Khagram, Sanjeev (2002), 'Restructuring the global politics of development: the case of India's Narmada Valley Dams', in Sanjeev Khagram, James V. Riker and Kathryn Sikkink (eds.), *Restructuring World Politics: Transnational Social Movements, Networks, and Norms*, Minneapolis: University of Minnesota Press, pp. 3–23.
Kitayama, Glen Ikuo (1993), *Japanese Americans and the movement for redress: a case study of grassroots activism in the Los Angeles chapter of the National Coalition for Redress/Reparations*, MA Thesis, University of California, Los Angeles.
Koido, Akihiro (2002), 'NAFTA ken to kokumin kokka no baundarī—keizai tōgō no naka deno kyōkai no saihensei (The NAFTA zone and boundaries among nation-states—reorganization of boundaries in the economic integration)', in Takamichi Kajita and Mitsuo Ogura (eds.), *Kokusai shakai 3: kokumin kokka wa dou kawaruka* (International Society, vol. 3: How will nation-states change?), Tokyo: The University of Tokyo Press, pp. 167–94.
Komai, Hiroshi, Ichirō Watado and Keizō Yamawaki (eds.) (2000), *Chōka taizai gaikokujin to zairyū tokubetsu kyoka—kiro ni tatsu Nihon no shutsunyūkoku kanri seisaku* (Overstaying foreigners and special residence

permission—Japanese immigration control policy at the crossroads), Tokyo: Akashi Shoten.

Kondō, Atsushi (1996), *'Gaikokujin' no sanseiken—denizunshippu no hikaku kenkyū* ('Voting rights' of foreigners—a comparative study of denizenship), Tokyo: Akashi Shoten.

Kuboyama, Ryō (2003), 'Doitsu no imin seisaku—imin kokka e no shifuto? (German immigration policy—a shift to an immigrant nation?,' in Akihiro Koido (ed.), *Imin seisaku no kokusai hikaku* (International comparison of immigration policy), Tokyo: Akashi Shoten, pp. 117–78.

Kundnani, Arun (2001), 'From Oldham to Bradford: the violence of the violated', *Race and Class*, 43(2), pp. 105–10.

Kundnani, Arun (2002), 'The death of multiculturalism', *Race and Class*, 43 (4), pp. 67–72.

Kundnani, Arun (2003), 'The hate industry', *IRR News*, accessed August 30, 2007 (http://www.irr.org.uk/2003/march/ak000003.html).

Kundnani, Arun (2005), 'The politics of a phoney Britishness', *IRR News*, accessed August 30, 2007 (http://www.irr.org.uk/2005/january/ak000013.html).

Kymlicka, Will (2001), *Politics in the Vernacular: Nationalism, Multiculturalism, and Citizenship*, Oxford: Oxford University Press.

Leach, Colin W. (2005), 'Against the notion of a "new racism"', *Journal of Community and Applied Social Psychology*, 15, pp. 432–45.

Levinson, David (ed.) (2004), *Encyclopedia of Homelessness*, Thousand Oaks, California: Sage.

Lipschutz, Ronnie D. (1992), 'Restructuring world politics: the emergence of global civil society', *Millennium*, 24 (3), pp. 389–420.

Local Government Association (2002), *Guidance on Community Cohesion*, London: Local Government Association.

MacDonald, Laura (1994), 'Globalising civil society: interpreting international NGOs in Central America', *Millennium,* 23 (2), pp. 267–85.

Machimura, Takashi (2007), 'Kokka to gurōbarizeishon (State and globalization),' in Koichi Hasegawa, Hideo Hama, Masayuki Fujimura and Takashi Machimura, *Shakaigaku* (Sociology: Modernity, self and reflexivity), Tokyo: Yūhikaku.

Macpherson, William. (1999), *The Stephen Lawrence Inquiry: Report of an Inquiry by Sir William Macpherson of Cluny*, London: Stationery Office.

Maki, Mitchell T., Harry H. L. Kitano and S. Meagan Berthold (1999), *Achieving the Impossible Dream: How Japanese Americans Obtained Redress*, Illinois: University of Illinois Press.

Malik, Kenan (2002), 'Against multiculturalism', *New Humanist*, accessed August 30, 2007 (*http://newhumanist.org.uk/523*).

Marinetto, Michael (2003), 'Who wants to be active citizen?: the politics and practice of community involvement', *Sociology*, 37 (1), pp. 103–20.

Marshall, Thomas Humphrey (1992), 'Citizenship and social class', Thomas Humphrey Marshall and Tom Bottomore (eds), *Citizenship and Social Class*, London: Pluto Press, pp. 1–51.

McConahay, John B. (1986), 'Modern racism, ambivalence, and the modern racism scale', in John F. Dovidio and Samuel L. Gaertner (eds.), *Prejudice, Discrimination, and Racism*, Orlando: Academic Press.

McGhee, Derek (2003), 'Moving to "our" common ground: a critical examination of community cohesion discourse in twenty-first century Britain', *The Sociological Review*, 51(3), pp. 376–404.

Mekata, Motoko (2003), *Kokkyō wo koeru shimin nettowāku: Toransunashonaru shibiru sosaetī* (Citizens' networks beyond borders: transnational civil society), Tokyo: Toyo Keizai Shinposha.

Memmi, Albert ([1982] 1994), *Le Racisme: description, définitions, traitement, Nouvelle Éditions revue*, Paris: Gallimard. (Japanese version translated by Kikuchi, Masami and Shirai, Shigeo (1996), *Jinshusabetsu*, Tokyo: Hosei University Press.)

Metro Manila Housing Plan (1996), *Update on the Manila Housing Plan*, Manila: Metro Manila Housing Plan.

Miles, Robert (1993), *Racism after "Race Relations"*, London: Routledge.

Miller, David (1995), *On Nationality*, Oxford: Clarendon Press.

Miyajima, Takashi (2004), *Yōroppa shimin no tanjyō: hirakareta shitizunshippu he* (The birth of the European citizen: towards an open citizenship), Tokyo: Iwanami Shoten.

Miyajima, Takashi (2006), *Imin shakai furansu no kiki* (The crisis of French immigrant society), Tokyo: Iwanami Shoten.

Murray, Alice Yang (1995), *'Silence, no more': the Japanese American redress movement, 1942–1992*, PhD dissertation, Stanford University Department of History.

Murray, Alice Yang (2001), 'Redress hangouts,' Santa Cruz: University of California, Santa Cruz.

Nagano, Yukiko (2007), 'The increase of immigrants and disorganization of the traditional way of life in the period of global tourism in Bali, Indonesia', *Bulletin of Yamagata University (social science)*, 37 (2), pp. 161–208.

National Coalition for Redress/Reparations (1980), *Recommended Platform, Proposal for Action and Structure*, Los Angeles.

National Coalition for Redress/Reparations (1981),'Organizing for the Commission Hearings!', *Banner*, June/July, p. 2.

National Front (2007), 'The man himself, Enoch Powell,' accessed June 15, 2007 (*http://www.natfront.com/powell.html*).

National Housing Authority (1993), *Fast Facts on Philippine Housing and Population*, Manila: National Housing Authority.

National Housing Authority (2001), *Medium-Rise Housing Program*, Manila: National Housing Authority.

National Housing Authority (2004), *Fast Facts on Philippine Housing and Population*, Manila: National Housing Authority.

National Statistics Office (2000), 'Table 2a. Poverty incidences of population by region, urban-rural: 1997 & 2000', accessed on December 19, 2006 (*http://www.census.gov.ph/data/sectordata/2000/ie00p02af.htm*).

National Youth Commission (1998), *Situation of the Youth in the Philippines*, Manila: National Youth Commission.

Neal, Sarah (2003), 'The Scarman Report, the Macpherson Report and the media: how newspapers respond to racial-centred social policy interventions', *Journal of Social Policy*, 32 (1), pp. 55–74.

Ngadisah (1987), 'Hubungan Patron Klien dalam Sektor Informal' (unpublished final report), Depok: University of Indonesia.

Nishitani, Noriko (2007), 'Takokukan jōyaku keisei ni okeru toransunashonaru shakai undō no dōteki kyōshin moderu' (The dynamic resonance model of transnational social movements in the formation of multilateral treaties), *Kokusai Seiji*, 147, pp. 95–115.

O'Brien, Robert, Ann Marie Goetz, Jan Aart Scholte and Marc Williams (2000), *Contesting Global Governance: Multilateral Economic Institutions and Global Social Movements*, New York: Cambridge University Press.

Office for National Statistics (2003), *Census 2001*, London: Office for National Statistics.

Okuda, Yasuhiro and Akiko Tateda (2000), '1997-nen no Yōroppa kokuseki jōyaku (The 1997 European Convention on Nationality)', *Hokudai hōgaku ronshū* (The Hokkaido law review), 50 (5), pp. 93–131.

Organisation for Economic Co-operation and Development SOPEMI (1995), *Trends in International Migration: Annual Report 1994*, Paris: Organisation for Economic Co-operation and Development.

Organisation for Economic Co-operation and Development SOPEMI (1997), *Trends in International Migration: Annual Report 1996*, Paris: Organisation for Economic Co-operation and Development.

Organisation for Economic Co-operation and Development SOPEMI (2001), *Trends in International Migration: Annual Report 2001*, Paris: Organisation for Economic Co-operation and Development.

Padilla, Arnold J. (2000), 'The housing crisis', *Facts and Findings*, No. 53, Manila: IBON Foundation Inc., pp. 1–20.

Padilla, Arnold J. (2002), 'The economy in midyear 2002: macro growth and people's woes', *IBON Facts and Figures*, 25 (13), Manila: IBON Foundation Inc.

Pan, Hongli (2002), 'Fukken-shō nanbu noson no dōsei ketsugō to kakyō—Sai-sei no sōzoku oyobi sōshin dantai wo chūshin ni' (Same-surname organizations and overseas Chinese from farming villages in Southern Fujian Province: a look at Cai surname lineagesand zongqinhui), in Kazuo Yoshihara and Masataka Suzuki (eds.), *Kakudai suru Chūgoku sekai to bunka sōzō—Ajia Taiheiyō no teiryū* (Expansion of the Chinese World, and the Creation of Cultures: Basic Trends in Asia and the Pacific), Tokyo: Koubundou, pp. 117–44.

Parekh, Bhikhu ([2000] 2002), *The Future of Multi-Ethnic Britain* (revised edn), London: Profile Books.

Paugam, Serge (1991), *La disqualification sociale: Essai sur la nouvelle pauvereté*, Paris: PUF.

Péchu, Cécile (2006), *Droit au Logement, genèse et sociologie d'une mobilisation*, Paris: Dalloz.

Pernia, M. Ernest (1994), 'Spatial distribution, urbanization and migration patterns in the Philippines', in Arsenio M. Balisacan, Felipe M. Medella and Ernest M. Pernia (eds.), *Spatial Development, Land Use and Urban–Rural Growth Linkages in the Philippines*, Manila: National Economic and Development Authority, Ch. 2, pp.13–105.

Philippine Seven Corporation Inc. (2007), Philippine Seven Corporation Inc. homepage, accessed on January 30, 2007 (*http://www.7-eleven.com.ph*).

Picard, Michel (1996), *Cultural Tourism and Touristic Culture*, Singapore: Archipelago Press.

Pieterse, Jan N. (2001), 'Globalization and collective action', in Pierre Hamel, Henri Lustiger-Thaler, Jan N. Pieterse and Sasha Roseneil (eds.), *Globalization and Social Movements,* Hampshire: Palgrave, pp. 21–40.
Piggott, Gareth (2004), *2001 Census Profiles: Bangladeshis in London,* London: Greater London Authority Data Management and Analysis Group.
Platt, Lucinda (2007), *Poverty and Ethnicity in the UK,* Bristol: The Policy Press (for the Joseph Rowntree Foundation).
Poole, Ross (1999), *Nation and Identity,* London and New York: Routledge.
Porio, Emma, Leopoldo Moselina and Anthony Swift (1994), 'Philippines: urban communities and their fight for survival', in Cristina Szanton Blanc (ed.), *Urban Children in Distress: Global Predicaments and Innovation Strategies,* UNICEF, Florence, Italy, pp. 101–59.
Pringle, Robert (2004), *A Short History of Bali: Indonesia's Hindu Realm,* Crows Nest, NSW: Allen & Unwn.
Putnam, Robert D. (2000), *Bowling Alone: The Collapse and Revival of American Community,* New York: Simon and Schuster.
Rahman, Zia H. (2007), 'Community without aspirations', *Guardian,* May 2.
Risse, Thomas, Stephen C. Ropp and Kathryn Sikkink (eds.) (1999), *The Power of Human Rights: International Norms and Domestic Change,* New York: Cambridge University Press.
Rothman, Franklin D. and Pamela M. Oliver (2002), 'From local to global: the anti-dam movements in southern Brazil, 1979–1992', in Jackie C. Smith and Hank Johnston (eds.), *Globalization and Resistance: Transnational Dimensions of Social Movements,* Lahnam: Rowman & Littlefield, pp. 115–32.
Ruiz, Henry (2005), 'A study of policies and programs in the Philippines addressing the right of street children to education', Child Protection in the Philippines Monthly Feature March 2005, accessed on November 11, 2006 (*http://www.childprotection.org.ph/monthlyfeatures/apr2k5b.doc*).
St Josepf's College, Department of Arts and Sciences (1995), *An Updated Community Profile of the ESC's Adopted Urban Poor Communities,* Manila: St Josef's College, Department of Arts and Sciences.
Sakernas (Departemen Ketenagakerjaan dan Transmigrasi) (1998), *Survei tenaga kerja nasional,* Jakarta: Depnakertrans.
Sakernas (Departemen Ketenagakerjaan dan Transmigrasi) (2002), *Survei tenaga kerja nasional,* Jakarta: Depnakertrans.
Sakuma, Kōsei (1998), *Henbōsuru taminzokukokka igirisu—"tabunka" to "tabunka" ni yureru kyōiku* (The changing face of multiracial Britain— Education in multiculturalism and diversity), Tokyo: Akashi Shoten.
Santos, Boaventura. S. (2004), 'The World Social Forum: toward a counter-hegemonic globalization', in Jai Sen, Anita Anand, Arturo Escobar and Peter Waterman (eds), *World Social Forum: Challenging Empires,* New Delhi: Viveka, pp. 336–43.
Sassen, Saskia (1988), *The Mobility of Labour and Capital: A Study in International Investment and Labour Flow,* New York: Cambridge University Press.
Sassen, Saskia (1996), *Losing Control: Sovereignty in an Age of Globalization,* New York: Colombia University Press.
Scarman, Lord (1981), *Scarman Report: Report of an Inquiry,* Harmondsworth: Penguin.

Schaefer, Richard T (2006), *Racial and Ethnic Groups* (10th edn), Upper Saddle River, NJ: Pearson/Prentice Hall.

Schoch, Lili N. (1985), *Kaki lima and street hawkers in Indonesia*, Jakarta: PT Indira.

Sears, David O. (1988), 'Symbolic racism', in Phyllis A. Katz and Dalmas A. Taylor (eds.), *Eliminating Racism: Profiles in Controversy*, New York: Plenum Press.

Sen, Jai (2004), 'The long march to another world: reflections of the World Social Forum process in India and internationally', in Jai Sen, Anita Anand, Arturo Escobar and Peter Waterman (eds.), *World Social Forum: Challenging Empires*, New Delhi: Viveka, pp. 293–311.

Shinohara, Hajime (2004), *Shimin no seijigaku: tōgi demokurashī to wa nanika* (Citizen politics: what is deliberative democracy?), Tokyo: Iwanami Shoten.

Sholte, J. A. (1997), 'Identifying Indonesia', in M. Hitchcock and V. T. King (eds.), *Images of Malay-Indonesian Identity*, Kuala Lumpur: Oxford University Press, pp. 21-44.

Sikkink, Kathryn and Jackie Smith (2002), 'Infrastructures for change: transnational organizations, 1953–93', in Sanjeev Khagram, Kathryn Sikkink and James V. Riker (eds.), *Restructuring World Politics: Transnational Social Movements, Networks, and Norms*, Ann Arbor: University of Minnesota Press, pp. 24–44.

Singh, Ramindar (2002), *The Struggle for Racial Justice: From Community Relations to Community Cohesion*: Bradford: Bradford Arts, Museums & Libraries Service.

Skinner, William G. (1957), *Chinese Society in Thailand*, New York: Cornel University Press.

Smith, Jackie (1997), 'Characteristics of modern transnational social movement sector', in Jackie C. Smith, Charles Chatfield and Ron Pagnucco (eds.), *Transnational Social Movements and Global Politics: Solidarity beyond the State*, New York: Syracuse University Press, pp. 42–58.

Somantri, Gumilar R. (1990), 'Hubungan patron klien dalam struktur kegiatan ekonomi sektor informal di pasar ciputat' (unpublished final report), Depok: University of Indonesia.

Soysal, Yasemin Nuhoglu (1994), *Limits of Citizenship: Migrants and Postnational Membership in Europe*, Chicago: University of Chicago Press.

Subramaniam, Mangala, Manjusha Gupte and Debarashmi Mitra (2003), 'Local to global: transnational networks and Indian women's grassroots organizing', *Mobilization*, 8 (3), pp. 335–52.

Takezawa, Yasuko I. (1994), *The Transformation of Japanese American Ethnicity: The Effects of Internment and Redress*, Tokyo: University of Tokyo Press.

Tamir, Yael (1993), *Liberal Nationalism*, Princeton: Princeton University Press.

Tanaka, Hiroshi (1995), *Zainichi gaikokujin (shinban)* (Foreign residents in Japan) (new edn), Tokyo: Iwanami Shoten.

Taqiyyah, Barratut (2002), 'Hubungan sosial dalam sektor informal di pasar tanah abang' (unpublished final report), Depok: University of Indonesia.

Tarrow, Sidney (1989), *Democracy and Disorder: Protest and Politics in Italy, 1965–1975*, Oxford: Clarendon Press.

Tarumoto, Hideki (1997), 'Eikoku ni okeru esunikku duarizumu to shiminken (Ethnic dualism and citizenship in Britain)', *Hokkaidō Daigaku Bungakubu kiyō* (The annual report on cultural science, The Faculty of Letters, Hokkaidō University), 45(3), pp. 273–96.

Tarumoto, Hideki (2000), 'Shakaigaku-teki shiminken ron no seinō to kadai— hikaku imin seisaku ron to sengo eikoku no keiken kara (An exploration of citizenship perspective from the viewpoint of postwar Britain: toward an international comparison of immigration policies)' *Nenpō shakaigaku ronshū* (The annual review of Sociology), 13, pp. 1–13.

Tarumoto, Hideki (2002), '"Jinshu bōdō" no kokusai shakaigaku: josetsu (A preface on transnational sociology of "race riots")', *Gendai shakaigaku kenkyū* (Contemporary Sociological Studies), 15, pp. 83–96.

Thranhardt, Dietrich (1992), *Europe—a New Immigration Continent: Policies and Politics in Comparative Perspective*, Munster: Lit Verlag.

Tipple, Graham (2005), 'The place of home based enterprises in the informal sector: evidence from Cochabamba, New Delhi, Surabaya and Pretoria', *Urban Studies*, 42(4), pp. 611–32.

Tomagola, Thamrin Amal (2002), 'Bara SARA kelas bawah', *Kompas*, March 11, pp. 39.

Touraine, Alain (1969), *La société post-industrielle*, Paris: Denoël.

Touraine, Alain (1991), 'Face à l'exclusion,' in Jacques Donzelot (ed.), *Citoyenneté et urbanité*, Paris: Editions Esprit, pp. 165–73.

Touraine, Alain (1994), *Qu'est-ce que la démocratie?*, Paris: Fayard.

Touraine, Alain (1997), *Pourrons-nous vivre ensemble? Egaux et differents*, Paris: Fayard.

Townsend, Peter (1979), *Poverty in the United Kingdom: A Survey of Household Resources and Standards of Living*, Harmondsworth: Penguin.

Tsuchida, Kumiko (2006), 'From community services to redress movement: forming a grassroots organization NCRR', *Shakaigaku Kenkyu* (The Study of Sociology), no. 80, pp. 193–218.

Urban Poor Association (2004), *Community and Household Profile of the Pook Daang-Tubo*, Manila: Urban Poor Association.

Urban Research Consortium (1997), *Manila Urban Housing Study, Draft Report*, Manila: Urban Research Consortium.

Urban Research Consortium (1998), *A Study of Land Values in Metropolitan Manila and Their Impact of Housing Programs: Preliminary Final Report*, Manila: Urban Research Consortium.

Wallerstein, Immanuel (1983), *Historical Capitalism*, London: Verso.

Walwipha Burusuratanaphand (1995), 'Chinese identity in Thailand', in *Southeast Asian Journal of Social Science*, 23(1).

Wapner, Paul (1996), *Environmental Activism and World Civic Politics*, New York: State University of New York Press.

Watado, Ichirō, Eriko Suzuki and APSF (eds.) (2007), *Zairyū tokubetsu kyoka to Nihon no imin seisaku—'imin senbetsu' jidai no tōrai* (Special residence permission and Japanese immigration policy—advent of an age of 'filtering of immigrants'), Tokyo: Akashi Shoten.

Wieviorka, Michel (1992), *La France raciste*, Paris: Seuil (Points Actuel).

Wieviorka, Michel (1993), *La démocratie à l'épreuve: Nationalisme, populisme, ethnicité*, Paris: La Découverte.

Wieviorka, Michel (1997), *Une société fragmentée? Le multiculturalisme en débat*, Paris: Découverte.
Wieviorka, Michel (2003), 'Un autre monde est possible', in Michel Wieviorka (ed.), *Un autre monde...: Contestations, dèrives et surprises dans l'anti-mondialisation*, Paris: Balland, pp. 15–54.
Wikipedia (2007), 'Jollibee', accessed on January 30, 2007, (*http://en.wikipedia.org/wiki/Jollibee*).
Wilkins, Roger (1984), 'Smiling racism: Ronald Reagan's race policies', *The Nation*, 239, p. 14.
Wilson , M. Constance (1983), *Thailand: A Handbook of Historical Statistics*, Boston: G. K. Hall.
Yamagishi, Toshio, Kikuchi Masako and Kosugi Motoko (1999), 'Trust, gullibility and social intelligence', *Asian Journal of Social Psychology*, 2(1), pp. 145–61.
Yamamoto, Eric K. (1999), 'What's next?: Japanese American redress and African American reparations,' *Amerasia Journal*, 25(2), pp. 1–17.
Yoshihira, Kazuo (1998), 'Soushinsoukai to daisoushi ga tsunagu' (Clansmen General Associations and Great Ancestral Halls connect peoples of the same Chinese surname), in Hiroaki Kani, Ryosei Kokubun, Masataka Suzuki and Masami Sekine (eds), *Minzoku de yomu chugoku* (China Understood from the Standpoint of Ethnic Studies), Asahi Shinbunsha (Asahi Newspaper Press), pp. 268–9.
Yoshihara, Naoki (2000), 'Chiiki jūmin soshiki ni okeru kyōdōsei to kōkyōsei—chōnaikai wo chūshin to shite' (Communality and publicness in local resident organizations—focusing on neighbourhood associations), *Shakaigaku hyōron* (Japanese sociological review), 50 (4), pp. 572–85.
Yoshihara, Naoki (2002), *Toshi to modanitī no riron* (The city and modernity), Tokyo: University of Tokyo Press.
Yoshihara, Naoki (2005), 'Conclusion', in Naoki Yoshihara (ed.), *An Asian Mega-city and the Dynamics of Local Community: Around RT/RW in DKI Jakarta*, Tokyo: Ochanomizu shobo, pp.327-341.
Yoshihara, Naoki (2006), 'An existent form of urban *banjar* : a case study of neighbourhood association in *Kota Denpasar*', *Hestia & Clio*, 3, pp. 52–75.
Yuval-Davis, Nira (2002), 'Multiculturalism, multi-layered citizenship and the politics of "social cohesion"', accessed July 15, 2007 (http:// *www.norrnod.se/temaetni/Pages/konferens/pdf/* yuval._davis.pdf).

Index

alter-globalization 76–77, 88, 91
anti-anti-racism 44, 46, 48
asset management 204–205, 208, 209
assimilation 31, 33, 53, 57, 59, 74, 173, 189

Bali Hindu 98, 106, 112, 113, 217, 219
Bali Post group 111
Banglatown 193–194, 198, 202
banjar (hamlet) 108
banjar adat (hamlets under local customary law) 110, 218–219
banjar dinas (hamlets under local government) 110, 218
Batik 102, 104, 107, 116, 217, 218–219
British National Party, the 32, 42
Britishness 42, 55–57, 213
buruh Lombok (Lombok tile factories) 106

Cantle Report, the 50–54
chain migration 151
Chernobyl nuclear power plant accident 5, 7
Chicksand Citizens Forum 203, 205, 209, 211
Chinese-Thais
  Chinese-Thai ancestral halls 176–178, 180–183, 186

ethnic Chinese in Thailand 173–177, 179, 181, 189
  Lin same-surname groups 180
  same-surname groups 176–179, 186, 188
Citizenship ix, x, xi, 12, 13, 23–27, 30, 32, 33–39, 42, 52, 54, 55, 57, 212, 213, 215, 216
city of conventions 100
Civil Liberties Act of 1988, the xi, 58
civil rights movement, the xi, 43, 61, 66
civil society x, xii, 3, 6, 9, 10, 11, 17, 19, 20, 77–79, 84–85, 91–92
common in-group identity model 42, 49
Commission on wartime Relocation and Internment of Civilians (CWRIC) public hearings, the 59, 60, 61, 62, 64, 68, 73, 75
communal groups 84–88, 91–92, 217
Communality 38
Communitarianism 85
community cohesion 42, 51, 54, 55, 57
community network 198, 208
community of communities 54
community regeneration 192, 199, 210, 226

Constitution of the United States, the 58, 75
contractualization 171

Denpasar 97, 98, 100, 102, 104, 107–109
Desa Pemogan 102, 110
Development Trust, the 192, 203–204, 209, 211
diversity within unity 54–55
dual economy 121
dual identity 49

empowerment 52, 192, 208–211
environmental harms 15–16
environmental justice 15
ethnic group 41, 42, 45, 49, 52–54, 59, 174, 175, 192, 195, 197, 200, 203, 214
ethnic identity 71, 75
ETHNOS 56
European Union, the 4, 12, 13, 18, 19, 22, 36, 199, 207, 210, 211, 226
eviction of squatters 158, 164

French scarf ban issue 4

gerobak (cart) 116
global city 191, 198, 210
global civil society xii, 11, 76–77, 92
globalization ix, x, xi, xii, xiii, 3–6, 8, 9, 11–13, 16, 17, 19, 57, 76–77, 79–86, 90, 97, 100, 113, 151, 154, 156, 163, 170–172, 191–192, 199, 202–203, 216, 219, 224
global risk society 6, 10
global tourism xii, 97–98, 100, 101, 106, 111–113, 217, 219

governance xi, 14, 17–19, 25, 216

have-nots 88–90, 217
historicity 80–82
Homeless, the
  squatter area 154–159, 162–169, 221–223
  squatter homeless 154, 156, 158, 160, 163, 166, 167, 169, 222, 223
  street children 154, 156, 159, 160–162, 166, 168, 220–223
  street dweller 159, 166, 169
  street homeless 154–161, 163, 166–170, 172, 220–223
household 9, 98, 151, 194, 223, 226
human rights model, the 36, 37

identity xii, 34, 38, 41, 42, 48, 49, 55–57, 75, 79–81, 83–86, 91, 108, 111, 213
income opportunities 121
indigenous Balinese 101
individualization 8–10
informalization 170
Informal sector 122, 124, 220
institutional racism 47–48
international brand 100
internationalization 6
Islamization ix, xii, 97, 98, 101, 113, 114

Japanese American Citizens League (JACL) 62
Japanese American community 61–64, 66–68, 71–75, 214
Japanese American redress movement ix, xi, 58–60, 214

KIPEM (Kartu Penduduk Musiman / seasonal residents identity card) xii, 108–111, 219

legitimacy 18, 25, 30, 36–38, 39, 59, 60, 73, 77
legitimizing identity 85
liberal nationalism 57

Macpherson Report (1999), the 47
minorities ix, x, xi, 3, 6, 12, 13, 15, 19, 41–44, 46, 52, 55, 56, 75, 79, 158, 208, 213

nation-state xi, 4, 13, 23–27, 29, 30–34, 36, 37, 39, 77, 86, 114, 212
National Council for Japanese American Redress (NCJAR) 63
network of relatives 122
new homeless 155, 170, 172, 220, 223, 224
new poverty 169, 224
new racism 42–48, 55, 213
new social movement 79, 80, 84, 85, 91, 217

Orde Baru (New Order) 99
oriental economy 121

parallel lives 52
Parekh Report, the 53–54
partnership xiv, 198, 202–203, 210–211
patron–client relationship 123, 124
politics of identity and insecurity xi, 42, 57

post-national membership 30
post-*Orde Baru* 100, 111
postwar reparations 58
poverty xiii, 14, 17, 70, 79, 87, 89, 92, 107, 123, 159, 163, 170, 172, 191–198, 200, 202, 203, 210, 211, 217, 221, 224–226
principles of capitalism 121
project identity 85, 86, 91
publicness xi, 38, 39, 207, 213
pull-factor 154, 170–172
push-factor 154, 171–172

quasi-government 210

Race Relations Act (1976), the 32, 45, 54, 213
reconstruction of memories 74
redress x, xi, 58–73, 75, 214–215
reference community 23–27, 29, 31, 32, 37–39
relocation 61, 62, 72, 157, 162, 165, 171, 172, 214, 221, 223
resistance identity 85–87, 91
rights-based politics 29
risk society x, 7–9

seasonal immigrants 132, 135
shadow economy 121
sidak (spot check) 110
Single Regeneration Budget, the 206, 226
Slow Food movement, the 5
social capital 9–10, 11, 42, 210
social enterprise 192, 199, 203–205, 209–211
social exclusion 17, 79, 88, 191, 192, 198–200, 203, 209–211, 216, 226

space of flows 82–85, 88
space of places 82, 84, 85, 88, 90
subak (irrigation association) 105
Sukarno 99
Sylhet xiii, 200–202, 206, 210

taming risks 20
terrorist bombings xii, 100, 108, 111, 217
Tower Hamlets 193, 195, 202, 204–208, 210
transnational social movement organizations xii, 76, 216
transnational sociological imagination, the 39

United States of America Executive Order 9066 (1942), the 61
universal human rights 29, 30, 212
unskilled labour 135
urban-*kampung* 118, 119, 131, 132, 135, 139, 142, 143, 151, 220
urban minority 154–155

Vietnam anti-war movement 61, 66
voluntary organization xiv, 192, 199, 204, 206, 207, 211

wartime internment policy 59
World Social Forum, the 76, 88